Sociolinguistics

Sociolinguistics

Goals, Approaches and Problems

Roger T. Bell

B.T.BATSFORD LTD
London

First published 1976
© Roger T. Bell 1976

Made and printed in Great Britain by
Billing & Sons Ltd. London, Guildford & Worcester
for the Publishers B.T. Batsford Ltd,
4 Fitzhardinge Street London W1H OAH

ISBN 0 7134 3218 7 (clothbound edition)
ISBN 0 7134 3219 5 (paperbound edition)

Dedicated to the memory of
Jephthah the Gileadite —
the first descriptive and
applied sociolinguist.
(*Judges* 12: 4 - 6)

Contents

The Figures

Acknowledgment

No writer is likely to be entirely free of some debt to those with whom he has worked in the creation of a book, particularly where the topic involved is a new interdisciplinary field of academic endeavour. Hence, a number of individuals and institutions should be acknowledged here.

Professor W.A. Murray, who as Chairman of the School of English at the University of Lancaster had the foresight to include the study of linguistic variation in the present-day varieties of English from the very inception of the University.

C.N. Candlin, who has shared the teaching and development of the original 'Varieties of Modern English' course with the writer and has been instrumental in the creation of the present course on Sociolinguistics reflected in this book.

My wife and son, who have been constant sources of bilingual behaviour and stern critics of my normally rather creative spelling and punctuation.

Finally, I wish to thank my students, the participants at the Advanced Summer Course at Diepenbeek, Belgium, in 1974 and the staff of the libraries of the University of Lancaster and the ETIC/CILT organizations in London who have been ever-willing to respond cheerfully and patiently to what must at times have appeared quite incomprehensible requests for very odd books and articles.

Introduction

This book has arisen out of ten years of teaching sociolinguistics at undergraduate and postgraduate level in the department of linguistics at the University of Lancaster. It represents most of the topics dealt with in courses on sociolinguistics with students whose major or minor discipline was either linguistics or English, carrying, normally, in addition, another arts subject: a foreign language, history, philosophy and so forth; or one of the 'human sciences': psychology, sociology, etc.

The topics included here have been found to be consistently of interest to such students, especially since the interdisciplinary nature of sociolinguistics makes a natural bridge between the humanities on the one hand and the sciences on the other. The reader should however be warned that this book is by no means an introductory textbook. It is assumed that the reader will have already been introduced to the techniques and principles of modern descriptive linguistics and will therefore be well able to cope with phonemic transcriptions of data and with the major assumptions and methods of grammatical and semantic analysis.

The general principle underlying this book is to begin with the fundamentals of model construction, applying models to the analysis of data in micro- and macro- situations and to stress the ways in which these activities relate the interests of the linguist concerned with the social functions of language to those of scholars in other social sciences. The approach is, then, a cumulative one which probably does not recommend itself to a teacher in search of a textbook. We believe very strongly that at this stage in the development of sociolinguistics the individual teacher will achieve the most satisfying results by constructing his own course around his personal experiences and the easily available books of readings (see below), rather than by falling back on any existing textbook. Indeed, this book most probably recommends itself as a revision text which provides an integrated picture of the whole field; a general view which can often be lost in the course of the study of detailed discussions of the goals, methods and issues of sociolinguistics.

To be explicit, the book's layout follows a development from issues at the micro- level of sociolinguistic explanation, the function of language in the individual, in dyadic and small group interaction, to the macro- level of language choice amongst larger groups and aggregates up to those of the nation or state. In terms of the correlations between these topics and the human sciences, it will have been recognized that the earlier parts of the book will be of greater interest to the student of psychology and of social psychology, the central sections to the sociologist and anthropologist and the later parts to workers in the planning and organizational sciences and politics.

In view of the aim of the book to act as a means of integrating materials and approaches from diverse sources, each chapter is divided into sections, each of which ends with a summary, and each chapter contains a conclusion in which the major points of the chapter are presented. It is hoped that such an approach will facilitate its use both as a revision text and as a means of creating new course outlines for the individual teacher.

We referred above to readings in, and introductions to sociolinguistics, and it therefore appears useful at this point to outline what is already available and so indicate in what ways this book supplements and complements them.

Five introductions to sociolinguistics written during the past five years are easily available: Fishman (1970) which 'attempts to conceptually integrate the sociolinguistic literature. . . so that micro-sociolinguistics, and macro-sociolinguistics and applied sociolinguistics can be understood in relation to each other, rather than as disparate levels or topics of analysis' (*ibid.*, p.xi). Burling (1970) approaches the subject as an anthropologist interested in 'language and culture' (*ibid.*, p.v) but attempts to conduct '. . . an investigation into the nonlinguistic factors that affect our use of language'. Pride (1971) writes from the viewpoint of a linguist seeking a '. . . more directly . . . human orientation towards social and cultural environment' (p. 106) than was normal at the time in linguistics. Robinson (1972) writes as a social psychologist attempting '. . . to achieve a perspective that might prove to be a useful framework for the study of the relationships between language and social behaviour . . . (*ibid.*, p.15). And, finally, Trudgill (1974), like Pride, comes to the subject as a linguist but one with substantial experience in dialectology, distinguishing in his book 'sociolinguistics proper' which emphasizes '. . . studies of language in its social context which . . . are mainly concerned with answering questions of interest to linguists, such as how can we improve our theories about the nature of language, and how and why does language change', from 'the sociology of language' which is more concerned with '... how people in different communities actually use language, and with social, political and educational aspects of the relationship between language and society' (*ibid.*, p.33).

The present book probably falls, in its orientation, between those of Fishman and Trudgill, since it attempts to cover both the sociology of language and sociolinguistics. It differs from them most of all in stressing, particularly in its earlier chapters, the need for adequate *models* for the explanation of the social uses of language and the importance of creating overt links between the theories, models and descriptive techniques of the human sciences on the one hand and those of linguistics on the other.

In addition to general introductions, there are also available collections of papers, normally in origin the proceedings of conferences, Sebeok (1960), Brazzaville (1964), Shuy (1964), Bright (1966), Fishman *et al.* (1968), Whiteley (1971) and Hymes (1971), covering a range of topics extending from stylistics to bilingualism and the educational implications of the use of non-standard dialects.

Some scholars — Greenberg (1971) and Ervin-Tripp (1973) for example — have recently published collections of their most important papers or have edited, in a single volume, original essays by others (e.g. Dance, 1967); but by far the most frequent form of publication in sociolinguistics is the 'readings in', beginning with Hymes (1967) and Fishman (1968), and more recently Fishman (1971), Bailey and Shuy (1973), Giglioli, Gumperz and Hymes, Laver and Hutcheson, Pride and Holmes, and Turner (all 1972).

In view of this situation, we can but reiterate the suggestion made above — the individual teacher has available to him a very wide range of easily accessible texts from which he should select in order to exemplify the points which he wishes to emphasize in his course. This book presents one way of doing this, and it is as just this, as one of many alternative skeletons on which to hang topics in the social use of language, that we hope it will be found useful.

1
Problems and Principles
of Variety Study

Since this book is an attempt to outline the relatively new approach within linguistics to the description of variation in language known as 'socio-linguistics' a necessary starting point must be some statement of what we consider 'language' to be and how 'linguistics' relates to it. We may therefore take as a definition of linguistics something like 'the scientific study of language' (Lyons, 1968, p.1) and consider what the goals of such a study might be and how both 'scientific' and 'language' may be differently viewed and hence alter the aims of the particular linguist or school of linguists attempting to create a general theory which will account for the knowledge discovered about language.

Language has been studied by various disciplines and in widely contrasting ways over many centuries: in the ancient orient – China and India – in classical Europe – Greece and Rome – and in medieval and modern Europe (Robins, 1967) but underlying the variations of approach two radically different assumptions about the nature of language can be discerned. In essence, language can be viewed either as (1) 'a system of signals conforming to the rules which constitute its grammar' (Greenberg, 1957, p.1), i.e. a pure code or communication system, or as (2) 'a set of culturally transmitted behaviour patterns shared by a group of individuals' (*idem*), i.e. code as part of 'culture'.

Clearly, the linguist who accepts the first definition or some variant of it will see as his task the specification of the component parts of the code and the description of the processes whereby appropriate sets of symbols may be combined to create 'messages'. He will see in his work close parallels with that done in communications theory and symbolic logic and will stress the system *per se* and avoid considering the use of the system by human beings, arguing that this is the domain of the social or behavioural scientist.

The student of language who finds the second definition more to his taste will seek to correlate the forms of the code with the social functions to which the code is put and will find parallels in the work of social psychologists, sociologists and indeed, where his interests lead him to attempt to relate language choice to the developmental status of a nation or society as a whole, in the studies of political scientists.

This chapter will outline some of the assumptions of the 'pure' linguist, show how the sociolinguist has challenged these and expand a little on the major divisions within sociolinguistics suggested above.

The term 'scientific' too has been interpreted differently over a long period and the contrasting orientations produced have necessarily had their impact on linguistics as a discipline. Suffice it to say by way of introduction that, while the nineteenth century was essentially preoccupied with historical studies of language development through time, which attempted to create laws of linguistic evolution similar in form to the theories of Darwin in the biological sciences, the twentieth has, by and large, rejected a dynamic evolutionary approach and concentrated on the description of specific language systems at an arbitrarily chosen point in time, often the present, a static *état de langue* − a timeless 'state of language' in which time is excluded as a significant variable.

Below we shall consider some types of scientific description which, though common to the sciences as a whole, will be shown to have clear relevance not only to the development of linguistics as a discipline but also to the present disagreements between linguists over the fundamental decisions on the limits which should be set to their field of endeavour and the means appropriate for the achievement of their goals.

1.1 TYPES OF SCIENTIFIC DESCRIPTION

It has been commonplace in the philosophy of science (e.g. Nagel, 1961, pp.20 ff.) to identify and label at least four ostensibly different patterns of scientific explanation which depend on the assumed nature of what is being explained and which in their turn influence the types of theories and models considered most appropriate for that explanation. All four types can be seen to operate or to have operated in linguistic explanations of the phenomena of language.

1.1.1 *Deductive Explanations*

Probably the most easily recognized scientific explanation is that which has the formal structure of deductive argument in which the object of explanation is seen as a logically necessary consequence of the premises of the explanation. Such deductive models are typically but not exclusively found in the natural sciences, e.g. an explanation of the phenomenon that ice floats on water would contain premises which reiterated the Principle of Archimedes and would indicate that ice viewed as an instance of a 'body' and water as a 'fluid' must be subject to the laws of the Principle. Linguistics in this century has moved steadily towards the acceptance of the principles of deduction in its attempts to explain language and has therefore drawn nearer both in its goals and methods to those of the natural sciences but, as we shall see below, at a cost which sociolinguists in particular regret. In essence then, a deductive approach in linguistics commits the linguist to the search for universal abstract truths about language from which he moves, via sequences of rules, towards the establishment of individual facts: a development from the general, and ideally, universal features of language *per se* to the specific facts of actual language. We shall see below that such an approach implies a strict specification of the degree of abstraction involved and a necessary distance from the observable data on which the abstractions are postulated.

1.1.2   *Probabilistic Explanations*

Many sciences, however, are involved not in the statement of logically necessary truths but in the probabilistic explanation of phenomena. Whereas a deductive argument is likely to state 'given X, Y will occur', a probabilistic explanation will be couched in terms of the likelihood of the occurrence of Y in the presence of X and will, therefore, in the search for regularity, depend heavily on statistical evidence. Much recent work in sociolinguistics has made use of probabilistic explanations. This is particularly true where the investigator has been attempting to explain the relationship of the choice of a particular language or linguistic variant to the socioeconomic class membership or the aspirations of individual users. Such an approach, it will be recognized, makes very different assumptions about the degree of abstraction necessary and contains within it, as we shall see below, an acceptance of and close involvement in, the crucial problem of variation in language.

1.1.3   *Functional Explanations*

Related to but in its major assumptions different from the probabilistic explanations above are functional or teleological explanations which suggest that features can be explained in terms of their use, e.g. the phenomenon of the giraffe's long neck can be explained in terms of the need to reach foliage high up in trees. The biological and human sciences typically make use of such explanations and, to the extent that sociolinguistics attempts to make correlations between linguistic and social structure (in the broadest sense of the term), the sociology of language must make use of a similar orientation. We shall see in chapter 3 (3.1) how crucial functional explanations are to sociolinguistics and indeed a major task of the book as a whole will be the attempt to outline such a model — rules, that is, for language use.

1.1.4   *Genetic Explanations*

The fourth type of explanation, the genetic, was much in vogue in the nineteenth century when, *post facto,* the development of languages from some hypothetical prehistoric 'ancestor' to their present-day forms was explained in terms of a set of invariant 'laws' — Grimm's and Grassmann's for example. Though limited almost exclusively to phonology, these laws were, in fact, extraordinarily plausible and led to the reconstruction of the historically antecedent 'proto' languages underlying language 'families', particularly the Indo-Aryan, which embraces most of the languages of Europe and the northern parts of the Indian subcontinent.

1.1.5   *Summary*

In summary, we may note some of the crucial differences which emerge when these four types of explanation are compared. There is a shift of emphasis discernible between them, both in terms of the static-dynamic dimension and the degree of abstraction and distance from the primary observable data they are attempting to explain. Indeed, the first approach, by postulating the existence of a mechanical system, entirely excludes time, in contrast with the other three in which time as a significant variable is included and explanations of past states or 'predictions' of future states of the system are made possible. We shall see later that these four approaches to the explanation of linguistic data have important implications for the goals which various different kinds of linguists pursue and the models which they attempt to build in the course of their explanations.

1.2   LANGUAGE

We have been stating in the section above that the four types of scientific explanation derive from assumptions about the nature of the object of description. In the case of linguistics then, the differences of approach depend on assumptions about the nature of language. The way in which the linguist sets about his description and explanation of the phenomenon known as 'language' will depend on his answer, overtly stated or covertly assumed, to the question 'what is language?' We suggested earlier two polar definitions of language which now deserve consideration in a little more detail.

The nineteenth-century answer to the question was unequivocally 'language is change', in keeping with the genetic explanations in use and the goals of linguistics at the time; the reconstruction of the 'original' form of existing languages as it was presumed to have been at some remote point in the past. During this century, for reasons which we will see below, historical linguistics has been less fashionable but has not of course ceased — few students of English at university fail to learn at least a little of the history of their mother tongue, no matter how strongly orientated the department is towards literary criticism or modern linguistics.

During this century, essentially through the influence of de Saussure (see 1.3.1 below), language has been seen as an 'object' describable by deductive methods similar to those of the natural sciences. More precisely, language has been seen as a system with its own components and relationships describable in and for itself, not in terms of the use to which it might be put. De Saussure was quite adamant in his demand for autonomy for linguistics — 'la linguistique a pour unique et véritable objet la langue envisagée en elle-même et pour elle-même' (de Saussure, 1915, p.317).

In short, during the first half of this century, most linguists turned away from the consideration of the external aspects of change and use to concentrate their attention on the internal features of language as system and structure rather than human social behaviour. This is not to say that the study of language in its social context died with the last European student of rhetoric in the nineteenth century; the attempt to correlate linguistic form with social function certainly did continue, but, by and large, as an adjunct to sociological, educational or psychological research. The only substantial group of linguists (leaving aside for the moment such 'anthropological linguists' as Firth and Malinowski in Britain and Sapir and Whorf in the U.S.A.) still concerned with the external aspects of language use were the dialectologists, about whom we shall need to speak later (see 1.4.1). However, even they tended to be limited in their goals by the strong historical tradition in which most of them had been trained and this had the result that their dialect surveys were, almost without exception, rural rather then urban, orientated towards the 'preservation' of the speech of the elderly and the discovery of the extent to which older speech forms had survived in isolated communities (see Orton, 1962).

1.3   THE PROBLEM OF VARIATION IN LANGUAGE

At the root of the problems facing the linguist in his choice of a definition of language with which to work and a methodology for making statements about his discoveries lies the strangely complex and dual nature of language itself. It is both a highly structured and abstract system shared by all the members of a speech community — yet observable only as individual behaviour — and at the same time seemingly prone to capricious idiosyncracy. The linguist is not alone in facing such a dilemma. The social psychologist sees in social interaction an equally '... fascinating and baffling object of study: on the one hand it is immediate and familiar, on the other it is mysterious and inexpressible — there do not seem to be the words to describe it, or the concepts to handle it' (Argyle, 1967, p. 85).

In view of this, most modern students of language have opted for the limited goal of attempting to explain the code alone — its syntax and latterly its semantics — in which variation which cannot be explained by reference to the structure of the code itself has, at worst, been ignored or, at best, labelled 'free variation'.

Hence, it may be of value to restate some of the major axioms on which twentieth-century descriptive linguistics have rested and to indicate why it is that the sociolinguist finds that he can no longer leave them unchallenged.

1.3.1   *Some Axioms of Descriptive Linguistics*

Despite some relatively minor adjustments, the two key assumptions on which most descriptive linguists still rely can be traced back to de Saussure (1915). These may be stated, admittedly in a somewhat extreme form, in the following way:

1. There is a dichotomy between *langue* (the code shared by the speech community) and *parole* (the actual use of language). Once this is accepted, together with the assumption that *parole* is insufficiently well-structured to permit study, *langue* comes to be seen as the only appropriate object of study for linguistics.

2. There is a dichotomy between *synchronic* or static-state description and *diachronic* or dynamic-system description. In a sense, this view follows from the *langue-parole* dichotomy but was motivated, particularly in the case of de Saussure, by the desire to throw off the historical orientation of nineteenth-century linguistics. In view of this, linguistic description comes to be defined as the *synchronic* description of 'states of language' at a specified point in time, rather than the *diachronic* description of the mechanisms of linguistic change.

An operational difficulty arose however when linguists began to describe *langue*, since it seemed clear at the time that an empirical approach was only valid as part of a description of *parole*, being available to direct observation by the senses, and inapplicable to *langue*, housed as it was in the 'collective consciousness' of the speech community. Hence, a strict application of de Saussure's dictum would have left linguists able only to describe what was uninteresting and quite unable to cope with their stated object of investigation! Two solutions to the dilemma have been tried out: (1) *induction*, generalization based on data produced by a single informant; and (2) *deduction*, the use of introspection to gain insights into the structure of the language. It will have been realised that, different though these two approaches appear to be, both make the same fundamental assumption that language is in some way an attribute of the individual user; real in the case of the first and idealized in the case of the second.

We are now in a position to restate the key axioms on which descriptive linguistics in this century has rested and present counter arguments and alternative axioms from sociolinguistics.

1.3.1.1 *Langue-Parole and Competence-Performance*

Throughout the ages linguists have been attempting to 'discover' the idealized 'pure' form of the language concealed amidst masses of real and highly variable data of language use. For the nineteenth-century linguist, no less than for Plato, the 'pure' form existed only in the past and present-day speech was seen as a 'degenerate' version of it. De Saussure too, for all his novel and pioneering ideas, was in search of the pure homogeneous system which he believed to exist, not in the past but in the 'collective mind' of the community. For Chomsky, the location of the 'pure' form is more abstract — the mind of the 'ideal speaker-hearer'.

What is most striking is the way in which all share a common belief — real speech, *parole, performance, speech, usage*, whatever the term used, is too variable to be described. The sociolinguist cannot but take issue with this. No one would deny that speech is variable but the linguist attempting to create a 'socially realistic linguistics' (Labov, 1966.b, p. 14) cannot accept that performance is no more than a pale and grossly distorted reflection of competence, so chaotic that it is not amenable to description. He would point out that part of 'knowing the language perfectly' (Chomsky, 1965, p.3) consists of knowing how and when to perform and that without these skills the 'idealised speaker-hearer' would be a 'cultural monster' (Hymes, 1967b, p.639f.).

How far the sociolinguist would wish to press his argument depends on his conception of the goals of linguistics in general and of sociolinguistics in particular. He might accept (as does Fromkin, 1968) that the major aim of sociolinguistics is to create a theory of performance. Conversely, he may make a more dramatic claim (as does Searle, 1969) that the present competence theories are inadequate and that sociolinguistics is in fact 'linguistics' which has had its place so to say 'usurped' by 'grammar'. The weak and strong claims of sociolinguistics will be considered in more detail below (1.5.1).

1.3.1.2 *Synchronic-Diachronic Descriptions*

The strict division between synchronic and diachronic demanded by de Saussure, understandable as it was as a reaction against the strong diachronic bias of nineteenth-century linguistics, is being increasingly seen as a methodological convenience which is outgrowing its usefulness. This is true not only in the case of sociologically orientated research and particularly where attempts have been made to produce satisfactory analyses of continuum situations (see 5.3.1) but even in work which falls clearly within the mainstream of the discipline. For example, some transformationalists (Chomsky and Halle, 1968) are now willing to accept within the general framework of a synchronic model, linguistic data from earlier stages of the language and to incorporate such data within the rule-system of the present-day language. In particular, the decision to make the 'underlying form' of a lexical entry its orthographic representation implies that part of the ideal speaker-hearer's 'knowledge of the language' is some notion of the late Middle and early Modern English provenance of lexical items. Moreover, though the time scale is shorter, recent work on 'presuppositions' implies a 'knowledge' of earlier uses and connotations and begins to bring into sharp relief the realization that language, even when thought of as static is, in fact, a dynamic system in which it is speech which is the mainspring of change – as de Sassure (1915) himself put it 'enfin, c'est la parole qui fait évoluer la langue' (p.37).

1.3.1.3 *The Data of Linguistics*

Linguistics, in common with the other sciences, is working towards the discovery of the structure of its data by '. . . making models, the essence of which is the construction of a certain sequence of abstract schemes which should be a more or less close approximation to the data of actual reality' (Revzin, 1966, p. 3). Just what these models might be is discussed in chapter 2 but it is our concern here to discuss the nature of linguistic data – the sources from which it may be drawn and the degree of abstraction involved in creating objective descriptions.

The traditional structuralist approach to the description of language began with the operational assumption that a single carefully chosen informant was capable of providing sufficient data for the general description of an entire language. However, it was recognized that such data could not possibly be completely regular and therefore the linguist was enjoined to exclude 'variations of . . . pattern from individual to individual, or from group to group, within a speech community' (Hockett, 1958, p. 1), and to 'eliminate certain types of variation of minor interest . . . by restricting attention . . . to utterances produced by one speaker under a single set of circumstances' (Gleason, 1955, revised edn 1961, p.391), i.e. to 'assume that all styles within a dialect may be roughly described by a single structural system' (Harris, 1951, p. 11).

It is not hard to see why such a limitation should have been accepted for the sake of operational efficiency, even though de Saussure (1915) himself made it clear that he did not conceive of *langue* as being complete in the mind of any single individual but to exist perfectly only in the aggregated minds of the entire speech community: 'un système . . . dans chaque cerveau, ou plus exactement dans les cerveaux d'un ensemble d'individus : car la langue n'est complète dans aucun, elle n'existe parfaitement que dans la masse' (p.30). Indeed, a strict adherence to the single informant dictum would, in fact, lead to the description not of a dialect or a language but an idiolect 'the speech habits of a single individual' (Robins, 1964, p. 51).

Transformational-generative linguists naturally reject the final part of de Saussure's comment on *langue*, if it is made to apply to their description of *competence*, since their informant being a perfect idealization of the native user of the language is therefore, by definition, master of the entire system.

However, just as the sociolinguist might raise sociological and statistical objections to generalizations based on the necessarily biased data provided by a single actual informant, on the grounds that it seems implausible that there exists a representative informant, so too the more abstract idealized informant of the transformationalist is vulnerable to the objection that there is little likelihood of there actually being a representative set of intuitions about the structure of a language either.

Both structuralist and transformationalist have adopted approaches to data which the sociolinguist would seek to modify. For him, part of the data of actual reality which he believes should and can be incorporated into a linguistic model of functioning language has been avoided. The very variation passed over by the mainstream of linguistic inquiry is sought out by the sociolinguist and made his chief preoccupation and interest even though his ultimate goal may well be essentially the same as those of the more 'orthodox' linguist.

One final point needs to be made, before we attempt to outline the scope of sociolinguistics, and that is the size of the individual pieces of language data, however collected, on which the linguist bases his analysis. Until very recently, linguistic description has stopped at the sentence. The typical structuralist procedure is well illustrated by the sub-title of A.A. Hill's book *Introduction to Linguistic Structures* (1958): 'From Sound to Sentence in English', while that of the transformationalists is clear in the initial symbol of their grammars – Σ : 'sentence'. Although the direction differs, the first being in essence synthetic and the second analytic, both adopt, as a terminal point, the sentence. A sociolinguistic description would wish to extend beyond this to larger structures of which sentences would be components and attention would need to be focused not merely on individual sentences produced by individual speakers (however idealized) but on speaker-hearer interaction and on the structure of larger texts: conversations, speeches, oaths, question and answer routines, etc. (We take this point up again in 4.2 and later in chapter 8.)

1.4   THE SCOPE OF SOCIOLINGUISTICS

It may appear from what has been said above that the sociolinguist rejects all that has gone before him in linguistics but this is far from the truth. The great achievements of the nineteenth century, the outcome of decades of patient work, laid the foundations of phonetics and phonology and, by their very dominance, led de Saussure to seek a new orientation for the subject, an orientation which, in itself, has borne valuable fruit. We now know today, far more about the nature of language than we did a hundred years ago; an intellectual achievement which cannot be lightly rejected in the service of some new whim. No. It is significant that the majority of sociolinguists see themselves as *linguists*, with the avowed aim of attempting to discover regular correspondence between linguistic and social structure and, moreover, see their role as calling into question some of the assumptions of linguistics in order to arrive at a fuller and more satisfactory description of language. As Labov (1966b, q.v.) puts it ' . . . to solve linguistic problems, bearing in mind that those are ultimately problems in the analysis of social behaviour' (this point is discussed in more detail below in section 1.5). Indeed the sociolinguist, in his interest in variation, can see himself as the heir to the dialectologist and, in his attempts at the extension of linguistic description beyond the sentence, as a reviver of the very ancient tradition of rhetoric which, until quite recently in terms of the history of the discipline, formed, with grammar, the two mainstays of linguistic scholarship. If this is so, then it may be useful to specify in what ways sociolinguistics differs from the work both of the dialectologist and the rhetorician.

1.4.1   Dialectology and Sociolinguistics

Probably most sociolinguists would wish today to include dialectology
within their domain, on the grounds that the study of dialect has traditionally been centred on the speech habits of social groups who differed from
the rest of the community in employing a system which was clearly
distinguishable from the 'standard', the variety normally described by the
'pure' linguist. In its two major interests, however, dialectology can be seen
to contrast with modern sociolinguistics. Its approach has been, in the
main, diachronic, seeking to answer such questions as 'how historically is
this dialect related to that?', 'what features of older forms of the standard
language have been preserved in this dialect?' and so forth – a tendency
'to focus on the forms themselves and their cognates rather than on the
verbal habits of the speakers that use them' (Gumperz, 1964, p. 127).
Sociolinguistics, in contrast, has tended to adopt a synchronic approach,
taking samples of language at some particular point in time and attempting
to correlate the choices made by speakers with extralinguistic criteria;
seeking to create a description of a language state, rather than to emphasize its dynamism as a system in change. Of course, not all dialectology
has had a historical bias. In particular, the Linguistic Atlas of the U.S.A.
and Canada, begun in 1929, mixed both approaches (Kurath, 1939).

In another respect also, dialectology and sociolinguistics diverge : on
the choice of the primary unit of analysis. The first treats languages and
dialects as though they were monolithic structures between which there
would be, ideally, clear dividing lines – the notion of the *isogloss*, a 'line
drawn on a map defining areas characterized by the occurrence of certain
linguistic features', (Wakelin, 1972, p.7f.) clearly depends on such an
assumption. Sociolinguistics, on the other hand, has tended to focus on the
social group and the linguistic variables it uses, seeking to correlate these
variables with the traditional demographic units of the social sciences:
age, sex, socioeconomic class membership, regional grouping, status and so
forth. More recently too, correlations have been attempted between
linguistic forms and social functions in intra-group interaction, on the
micro-level and between language choice and large-scale social functions in
inter-group interaction at the macro-level (see below).

1.4.2   Rhetoric and Sociolinguistics

F om classical times, Cicero and Quintilian in particular, through the
Elizabethan Age, Puttenham in his *Arte of English Poesie* among others,
until the latter part of the last century in Britain and without a break in
North America, rhetoric – the art of the persuasive use of language – has

been taught. The interest in the reasons for linguistic choices and the effects that those choices have on hearers and readers forms a common ground between rhetoric and sociolinguistics but, as with dialectology, a sharp difference in approach can be seen between the two. In the simplest terms, while rhetoric has traditionally had as its goal the specification and indeed prescription of the 'best' methods of persuasion and only secondarily the description of these methods, sociolinguistics seeks a descriptive and objective listing of language skills, in the broadest sense of the term and of the appropriate choices of these skills in communication situations. It is also possible to see in 'stylistics' — traditionally the linguistic description of literary texts — the growth of a new 'descriptive rhetoric', side by side with the traditional normative rhetoric of the manuals on literary style and composition (Leech, 1969, p. 2).

Common to both types of rhetoric and to sociolinguistics is the focusing of attention on the text but, here again, the limited field of rhetoric, essentially 'persuasive language' and often in its written form, contrasts strongly with the wide aims of sociolinguistics in which all texts, spoken or written, dealing with any topic and demonstrating any purpose fall within its domain. A major problem of sociolinguistics and one which we shall need to return to later is the limitation of the field and the inapplicability of many of the categories and much of the terminology of rhetoric, more especially in interaction situations which have been ignored by rhetoricians in the past. For example, the sociolinguist faced by the problem of the linguistic analysis of, say, a committee meeting, feels intuitively that there are units larger than the utterance but smaller than the whole of the 'speeches' of an individual participant and searches in vain for any existing classification which will help him in his task. Among the reasons for this must be the present lack of precise correlations between linguistic form and social function (Wilkins, 1972) 'speaker-hearer grammars' (Rigter and Moore, 1974) and 'text grammars', all having failed to appear as a direct result of the limitation of descriptive linguistics to the level of the sentence and to the idealized output of the idealized individual speaker. Hence, a major task of sociolinguistics, and many would now argue of linguistics itself, is to move analysis on beyond the sentence, a move which must carry in its wake profound influences on the discipline as a whole and ultimately on the educational system (we take up the topic of 'discourse' in more detail in chapter 8.).

1.4.3   Micro- and Macro- Sociolinguistics

We suggested above that one of the defining characteristics of sociolinguistics was its emphasis on the study of the use of language by social groups.

It is, however, possible to adopt two rather diverse views of the structure of the group which, when correlated with language, tend to produce strikingly different results. The opposed views may be summarized in terms of the relationship which is assumed between the individual and the group. Either the individual or the group may be taken as primary and the linguistic features of the interaction within and between groups can be described in terms of individual or group dynamics.

The first approach, which takes the individual as its focus of attention, clearly shares areas of common interest with psychology in general and with social psychology in particular. The second is more sociological in its emphasis and has clear ties with sociology itself, economics, anthropology and political science, depending on the nature, composition and size of the group.

Naturally, the division between the two approaches is far from clear-cut but it is convenient to adopt and adapt, on the analogy of sociology (Timasheff, 1957, p. 269) the terms *micro-* and *macro-*, applying the label *micro-sociolinguistic* to analyses in which the emphasis is on the individual in small informal intra-group interactions and *macro-sociolinguistic*, where the locus of investigation is interaction at the large inter-group level: to the extent of studying nations and states in contact.

1.4.3.1   *Micro-sociolinguistics*
In essence, the distinction between micro- and macro-sociolinguistics appears to be a philosophical one, hinging on the definition of *individuality*. For the microsociolinguist, the most appropriate interpretation of the term highlights the differences between individuals, e.g. 'the sum total of the characteristics of an individual which distinguish him from other individuals' (Krech *et al.*, 1962), i.e. emphasis is on the ways in which the individual does *not* fit into some arbitrarily defined sociological category. In linguistic terms, such an emphasis, in its pure form, would lead to the description of collections of autonomous and unrelated idiolects which would defy grouping into dialects and defeat the stated object of sociolinguistic description: the correlation of linguistic with social structure. In practice, of course, the dilemma is resolved by shifting the emphasis of inquiry onto linguistic *interaction* and away from the static notion of group *membership*. The kind of question that might be asked would be along the lines of 'given that groups consist of individuals, how is it that each individual draws upon the resources of the language to facilitate person to person interaction in the groups of which each is a member?'.

The linguistic feature most central to this kind of investigation will clearly be the *speech act* (Searle 1965) as it occurs within the Primary Groups of the sociologist (see 4.3.1 below) and is modified by such variables as status, intimacy, kinship, attitude and goal between the individual participants in the encounter. Most of the linguistic variables will be found to fall under the general heading of *register* (Crystal and Davy, 1969) rather than *dialect*, variations caused by the *use* to which the individual is putting the language in the particular situation being investigated, rather than those caused by the relatively permanent characteristics of the *user* such as age, education, social class membership and so forth.

In attempting to deal with the complex phenomena of the speech act in such a way as to create viable models of the micro-processes in which it functions as a unit, the linguist is forced more and more into the consideration of data previously excluded from linguistic investigation: the 'extra-linguistic' communication channels which make use of gesture, eye contact, spatial proximity and the like which, for some considerable time, have been the particular province of psychology and psychiatry (Argyle, 1969). How these ancillary communication systems can be correlated with language and the two integrated into a larger semiotic system is clearly one of the key challenges of the future for the socio-linguist. At the moment, only imprecise suggestions have been made but even they are fascinating in their implications. It might be, for example, that gestures form a highly structured system analagous to that of phonology and that an adequate description might require us to list and show the interrelationships between sets of 'gesturemes' and their 'allogestures', just as we have been traditionally accustomed to the interrelations of 'phonemes' and 'allophones' in structuralist phonology (Birdwhistell, 1952).

1.4.3.2   *Macro-sociolinguistics*

The macrosociolinguist, in contrast, appears to accept a definition of individuality of the type '. . . the unique individual is simply the point of intersection of a number of quantifiable variables' (Eysenck, 1952, p.18) and seeks to account for the distribution of language differences through a society in terms of '. . . the age, sex, education, occupation and ethnic membership of the speakers studied' (Labov, 1966 b, p. 25.). He will have, that is, a commitment to the correlation of linguistic variables with the categories of the demographer, seeking to discover, in the apparently idiosyncratic usages of the individual speaker, indications not of his individuality but of his group affiliations. He will take, as it were, the social groupings of the social scientist as primary and lay these on the individual, whom we will then evaluate for 'closeness of fit'. The linguistic features he isolates will be readily seen to fall together under the heading of *dialect*, in the rather broad sense of the term suggested above, rather than *register*, i.e. user- rather than use-based variables.

The border-line between micro- and macro- in sociolinguistics, is as has been suggested above, rather fuzzy but the macrosociolinguist will be typically found studying inter-group communication, perhaps within the context of a single society, for example the use of the mother tongue and the local language by minority linguistic groups, working together with sociologists and educationists or he might well be concerned with questions of a larger scale, such as decisions on the choice of the Official Language for a new political federation, the defence of linguistic minority rights or working in concert with political scientists and planners.

1.5   AIMS AND PROBLEMS IN SOCIOLINGUISTICS

The initial motivation for sociolinguistics was stated clearly almost a decade ago: '. . . to show the systematic covariance of linguistic and social structure — and perhaps even to show a causal relationship in one direction or the other' (Bright, 1966, p. 11). Such a goal led, as we shall see later in this book, to a correlational approach which assumed that linguistic structure and social structure were discrete and separable entities, already partially described by the 'parent' disciplines of linguistics and sociology. However, it soon became apparent that the original definition was rather more ambiguous than it at first appeared and that there were, in fact, at least two substantially different approaches to the description of socially situated language use.

The first, most properly labelled *sociolinguistic*, has as its goal the inclusion of such social data as will make the models of descriptive linguistics more powerful and general, i.e. the approach is fundamentally *linguistic* and concerned with extending the range of linguistics beyond the sentence towards grammars of 'speaker-hearer' interaction. We shall see below that a strictly sociolinguistic approach is, paradoxically, 'self-liquidating' (Fishman, 1971, p. 9), since its success will be absolute when it has been accepted as the norm by all linguists.

The second approach, that of the *sociology of language*, seeks a broader, inter-disciplinary, goal: the integration of linguistic and social structures in the form of some theory of signs which would unite linguistics with the human sciences through the study of the way in which signs are used within the context of social life. Such a view of linguistics itself is fore-shadowed in de Saussure's (1915) *sémiologie* (p. 33.) and, more recently in Pike (1967) in his attempt to create an 'integrated theory of human behaviour'. A very comprehensive definition has been proposed by Kjolseth (1972) 'The sociology of language can be viewed as an integrated, interdisciplinary, multi-method and multi-level approach to the study of natural, sequenced and socially situated language behaviour'.

1.5.1 The Relationship of Sociolinguistics to Linguistics

We have so far only touched upon the relationship between linguistics proper and sociolinguistics (1.3.1.1) and it therefore seems crucial to try here to state the two extremes of attitude it is possible for the sociolinguist to take up. There appear to be two fundamentally different orientations depending on the strength of the claims for the discipline made by the individual scholar: (1) a weak claim which sees in sociolinguistics an ancillary study dependent on and subordinate to the study of grammar – in the broadest sense of syntax, semantics and phonology – and (2) a strong claim which denies the adequacy of present linguistic descriptions and insists on the reassessment of the goals and methods of linguistics in order to include socially relevant data in a wider semiotic model of language use. The two claims will be outlined below.

1.5.1.1 The Weak Claim of Sociolinguistics

Some linguists (e.g. Fromkin, 1968) accept the limits proposed by Chomsky (1965, p.15) for the incorporation of the data of actual use within the general framework of a description of language, i.e. that some linguists should be concerned with the creation of models of performance. In order to do this – a mere 'by-product of work in generative grammar' (ibid.) – the describer must accept the dichotomy between competence and performance, must subscribe to the view that

'linguistic theory is concerned primarily with an ideal speaker-listener ... [and not with] such grammatically irrelevant conditions as memory limitations, distractions, shifts of attention and interest, and errors (random or characteristic) in applying his knowledge of the language in actual performance' (*ibid.*, p.3)

and through his researches provide feedback for the grammarian which will lead to the creation of more and more powerful models of competence.

1.5.1.2 The Strong Claim of Sociolinguistics

Some sociolinguists, however, following the work of philosophers such as Austin (1962) and Searle (1969) on 'speech functions' and 'speech acts', would reject the subordinate status proposed for them above and would deny the necessity for the dichotomy between competence and performance (and *langue* and *parole*) particularly the implication of lack of structure in actual performance, arguing that language use entails 'knowledge of the language' of which only a part is the competence of the ideal speaker-listener. The proper goal for linguistics, it would be suggested by the maker of the strong claim, is the specification of the speaker-listener's *communicative competence*, i.e. his knowledge not only of what is grammatically correct but of what is socially appropriate and acceptable. Searle, in particular, is most critical of existing competence models, attacking them as 'necessarily incomplete' and stigmatizing them for their limitation to the description of purely formal features which he compares to 'a formal study of the currency and credit systems of economies without a study of the role of currency and credit in economic transactions' (*ibid.*, p.17). His underlying assumption is clearly stated: '. . . speaking a language is performing speech acts. . . such as referring and predicating: and secondly . . . these acts are in general made possible by and are performed in accordance with certain rules for the use of linguistic elements' (*ibid.*, p.16). Hence, '. . . speech acts. . . are the basic minimal units of linguistic communication' and 'an adequate study of speech acts is a study of *langue*' (*ibid*).

1.5.1.3 *Summary*

Whether the sociolinguist wishes to make the weak or the strong claim for his work, the specification of the inherent structure present in actual language use must have, and indeed is in some ways already having, an influence on the overall goals of the discipline at large. Several recent investigations in syntax into the deepest level of structure – the deep structure or, to use a newer term, the base, on which transformations operate – propose that a substantial set of sentences have in their underlying form performative verbs which themselves describe the speech act they perform (see Leech, 1974 p.344f.), the notion going back to Austin (1962), and in all cases 'presuppositions' on the part of the speaker-listener, which together with an increasing concern over 'degrees of grammaticalness' (Chomsky, 1965 pp.148–53), all show a narrowing of the gap admittedly self-made between the 'linguist proper' and his sociolinguist colleagues. Indeed, some transformationalists are ready to concede, particularly in the context of 'low level' phonetic processes, that 'the specific competence-performance delimitation provided by a grammar represents a hypothesis that might prove to be in error when other factors that play a role in performance and the interrelation of these various factors come under investigation' (Chomsky and Halle, 1968, p.111). Clearly then, as far as linguistics is concerned, the duty of the sociolinguist is to attempt to build models which integrate code forms and processes with speech acts and the two with the social functions of language, as a step towards a new and broader-based linguistics.

1.6 CONCLUSION

The sociolinguist in his attempt to correlate linguistic and social structure questions many of the fundamental tenets of 'orthodox' linguistics. He seeks out variation (see 2.1 on this) which has traditionally been a minor concern of the linguist and attempts to demonstrate not only that there are different types of variation but that much of it is systematic rather than random. He chooses an orientation to his data which includes features normally thought of as 'extra-linguistic' and thereby is forced into the realization that the existing deductive models are often inappropriate for his purposes, particularly where their aim is to describe, sentence by individual sentence, the internalized knowledge of the code possessed by the idealized speaker-listener, i.e. to create a grammar which '. . . is not a model for a speaker or a hearer' but a characterization of '. . . in the most neutral terms possible the knowledge of the language that provides the basis for the actual use of language by the speaker-hearer' (Chomsky, 1965, pp.8–9). He will, like the sociologist, '. . . be interested in competence *and* performance or situated usage, for it is the interaction of competence and performance that is essential for the understanding of everyday activities' (Cicourel 1973, p.44).

How widely the sociolinguist will choose to define his field hinges on his notions of what kind of a 'system' he believes language to be and the size of the units he seeks out for analysis. At one extreme, his interests may be the microprocesses of interaction between the individual members of a small group. At the other, he may be concerned with the linguistic choices available to whole states as media of internal or external communication. Hence, the convenient polar division of sociolinguistics into micro- and macro- which is followed through and expanded upon, in the course of this book.

2
Models for the Description
of Variation in Language

Having rejected the concept of language as a monolithic homogeneous object and adopted in its place a view of language as a heterogeneous dynamic system, sociolinguists are forced to seek out variation and to evolve new modes of explanation and new models through which to present such explanations.

This chapter has as its aim the consideration of the implications of this changed orientation, discusses the notion of 'model' and outlines several kinds of model, drawing wherever possible from examples of the world-wide variations observable in English.

2.1 TYPES OF VARIATION

Before considering possible models for the description of variation in language, it is of some importance to look in a little more detail at what we mean by the term 'variation'.

We shall make use of several distinctions proposed by Labov (1966b and 1963): *variables* and *variants* and three types of linguistic variable — *indicators, markers* and *stereotypes*.

First, in formal terms, *variables* may be distinguished from *variants*. A variable is 'an inconsistency or disagreement that a particular form of language may exhibit from an abstract standard', while a variant is 'a specific value of a variable'. For example, in his work on New York speech, Labov isolated, among others, the variable (r) : the occurrence or non-occurrence of word final or preconsonantal /r/ in such words as *car, card, fire, fired*, etc. He discovered two important variants: a constricted 'r-like' sound and an unconstricted 'r-less' glide, [ə] or merely a lengthening of the vowel. Hence, a word like *car* might be realized as [kɑr], [kɑ^ə] or [kɑː] . We shall see later (2.4.1.4) how this clarifies two aspects of the 'diaphone': a concept much used in earlier work on 'co-existent' phonemic systems.

In addition to having formal values, variables can have different social values associated with them. A variable may act as an *indicator* which has an indexical value correlating with the socioeconomic class membership or some other demographic characteristic of the user. Such indicators are recognized by the community at large but are not subject to stylistic variation, i.e. they are relatively permanent characteristics of the speech of certain individuals and groups, which do not change from one situation to another, e.g. the use of centralized /aɪ/and/ a / dipthongs by some groups on Martha's Vineyard (Labov, 1963).

Markers, in contrast, have indexical value just as indicators have but are, unlike them, subject to stylistic variation. In the New York study (Labov, 1966b), the (r) variable was shown to be a particularly good example of a marker, indicating social stratification but being subject to use or non-use as the same informant shifted between his 'casual' and 'careful' styles.

Stereotypes, are the mirror image of indicators, since they do not relate to social factors, in the sense we have been using the term above, but are subject to stylistic shifting. An example of this might be the use of the uvular 'r' in the North-East of England. Most native speakers of English in the U.K., when asked to mimic a 'Geordie' will make use of such 'r' sounds and so will those who live in the area when called upon to tell traditional stories or sing local songs, in spite of the fact that the [ʁ] is, except amongst the elderly in isolated rural areas, extinct. Stereotypes are of considerable interest, since they demonstrate views about the norms of speech which may be quite at variance with the actual facts and based on recollections of speech habits which were, in fact, common several generations earlier.

Figure 2.1 below may be of assistance in clarifying the differences between these three types of variable.

FIGURE 2.1   *Sociolinguistic Variables*

TYPE	SOCIAL STRATIFICATION	STYLE SHIFTING
Indicator	+	−
Marker	+	+
Stereotype	−	+

It will have been recognized that some of the sources of variation have been traditional topics of interest in linguistics, at least where the causes have been seen as 'internal' to the linguistic code itself. We refer here to the commonly noted 'allophonic' variations of traditional phonemic theory.

But, there are, equally, external motivations for linguistic variation which derive, crudely, either from characteristics of the user or else from the use to which the language is being put. Again, such informal terms as 'dialect', 'register' and 'style' are familiar.

A further concern of the describer of linguistic variation who aims not merely at the listing of contrasting forms but at their integration within some schematic model must necessarily be to specify at what level within the linguistic system each variation occurs. In addition, if his model has the capacity, he will try to indicate internal and external causal relationships, between the existence of certain variables and others and the particular sets of variants typically chosen.

We shall therefore consider below first the sources of variation, both internal and external, and then move on to a placing, initially in a rather taxonomic manner, of variations within a linguistic model.

2.1.1   *Sources of Variation – Internal*

Even if we were to limit our attention to differences of form within the language which exist within the code purely by virtue of processes within the code itself, we should still be faced by the existence of variation and the necessity to explain it. It was indeed just such internal variation and change that was the concern of nineteenth-century linguists whose 'laws' demonstrated how one sound or group of sounds influenced others or were influenced so that change took place. The Great Vowel Shift in fifteenth-century English, in which 'long vowels' became progressively raised and, where such raising would have led to the loss of vowel quality entirely, diphthongized, is a well-known example (Baugh, 1951, p.187ff).

Given this limitation and the concentration on the language of the single informant using one style, linguistics, for a considerable period, avoided variation and its external causes as far as possible. As Martinet put it 'seule la causalité interne intéresse le linguiste' (1961, p.81). Items which resisted inclusion in their systems were therefore termed 'irregularities' or 'loans' and, should the code being described contain too large a number of these, the whole system would be dubbed a 'mixed dialect'. This procedure, unfortunate enough in the case of dialectal and stylistic description where it tended to conceal much interesting information had, in the long term, the result, little short of disastrous, of making bilingual description all but impossible.

However, there are internal variations, most noticeable in phonology, which are worthy of comment and which indeed form part of the essential data of the sociolinguist. For example, conditioned allophonic variation has been included in the phonemic descriptions of languages as a matter of course. RP has, for example, two phonetically distinct realizations of the phoneme /1/ − a 'clear' [1] and a 'dark' [ɫ], occurring in contrasting phonetic environments; [1] initially and medially before vowels in a word although not finally and [ɫ] in the remaining positions; never initially but medially before consonants and in word-final position. Phonology is well able, within the assumptions of its deterministic principles, to cope with this kind of variation; after all, the two forms are entirely predictable from their environment. Given a particular configuration of phonemes one of the two realizations will occur but not the other.

But there are other kinds of variation, even in phonology, which linguistics has found difficult to include in its models, for the reason that their causation has been seen to be external to the code in which they occur. Such variations are considered below.

2.1.2   *Sources of Variation − External*

There remain three more types of variation to be considered − inter-personal, intra-personal and inherent variation − all of which derive from sources outside the code.

2.1.2.1   *Inter-personal Variation*

Among the types of variation traditionally considered to be 'free variation' are those which have been consistently described by dialectologists, since they represent choices from the code of items which correlate with certain characteristics of the individual user. Hence, it is possible, to some degree, to predict that a particular specified user will choose particular variants and conversely, given data in which a user consistently makes particular choices, fairly strong predictions can be made as to the age, sex, geographical or social provenance of the user. Clearly, any model which attempts to specify such relationships must be probabilistic rather than deterministic in its approach. Ideally, a precise specification of the characteristics of a user would correlate perfectly with the choices he makes but, in practice, the sociolinguist is often more concerned to generalize about the common usage of a group as a collection of individuals showing similar norms rather than to aggregate the usages of its individual members. He therefore will make statements, not about the 'dialect of social class X' or of 'Y county', as though these were monolithic and homogeneous but will state 'given a user with the following characteristics, it is probable (maybe even x% probable) that he will use a variant *a, b* and *c* but not *x, y* and *z*'.

2.1.2.2 *Intra-personal Variation*

There are, however, even within the 'same dialect', variations which cannot be predicted, either from the internal structure of the code, like the allophones of /1/ in RP, or from the individual characteristics of the user, like the /æ/ of most American and Northern British English, in contrast with the RP /ɑ:/ in *bath* etc. These seemingly less predictable variations are conditioned, not by linguistic factors nor by the static categories of the demographer but by the dynamic aspects of situated language use. For example, as far as internal and interpersonal criteria are concerned, there is no way of predicting in my speech whether I will realize pre-consonantal /t/ as [t] or [ʔ]: whether that is, I will pronounce *fortnight* as ['fɔtnait], ['fɔ:ʔnait], ['fɔ:tnaiʔ]. But this is not to say that my choice of [t] or [ʔ] is random. Far from it. The conditioning factor depends on the degree of 'formality' or 'informality' of the situation in which the utterance occurs: [t] tending to co-occur with the more formal and [ʔ] with the less. Such variations are clearly *stylistic* rather than *dialectal* and form part of some kind of system which it is the task of the sociolinguist to describe.

2.1.2.3 *Inherent Variation*

Even assuming that all possible linguistic choices available to users of the language and all conceivable internal and external correlations with those choices had been made — an enormous and maybe, in practice, impossible task in itself — there would still remain variations which were unpredictable and appeared to mark nothing but the inherent variability of language. Such variations would constitute true 'free variation', e.g. the choice of /i:/ or /e/ as the initial vowel of *economics* in RP which seems for some to be entirely unpredictable, even in the speech of the same user in the same situation. That such inherent variations exist should not be a matter for concern, indeed they are one of the features which make language the amazingly powerful and flexible tool it is. Inherent variability has too a crucial role in linguistic change, since without it individual freedom of choice would be lacking; each form irrevocably tied to some internal or external conditioning factor, making change impossible.

2.2 LEVELS OF VARIATION

So far, we have been discussing variation in language solely in terms of its internal or external causes but any description of variation needs not merely to attempt to correlate variant forms of the language with their motivations but to differentiate the levels within the structure at which variations occur. At this stage, we shall suggest a taxonomy for ranking variations, accepting that there are alternative models which will be reviewed later (2.4.2).

A further limitation, for the sake of clarity, will be accepted here – variation in phonology only will be considered, firstly because it is in phonology that varieties of the same language differ most noticeably from one another and secondly because, as will be suggested later, both they and variations in grammar and in lexis can be more economically described in terms of a quite different kind of model.

The taxonomy outlined below is based on those proposed by Kurath (1939) and Wells (1970) for the description of phonological variation in English dialects. In essence, four levels are suggested – systematic, distributional, incidential and realizational – extending from the most general and 'deepest' differences, to the most specific and 'surface' realizations. We shall attempt to assign variations to one level or another, recognizing that the essentially non-discrete nature of dialect data makes the unambiguous placing of such features extraordinarily difficult – a point to which we shall need to return later (5.3.1).

2.2.1 *Systematic Variations*

Within the context of the traditional phoneme theory, the most significant and deepest contrast between two codes – styles, dialects or languages – would be at the phonemic level. The world's languages show wide contrasts in the total number of phonemes in their individual phonemic inventories and in the distribution within their inventories between vowels and consonants, e.g. Hawaiian has only five vowels and six consonants, while at the other extreme, Abkhaz (a language of the Caucasus) has only two vowels but no less than sixty-eight consonants (Lotz, 1956). Hence, a comparison of varieties of the 'same' language may demonstrate the existence of different total inventories or the same total but different items within it. Where there are different phonemes, we use the term 'systematic variations' (Wells, 1970), in essentially the same sense as the 'phonemic hetrogloss' of American dialectology (Kurath, 1939, p.2). For example, several varieties of English differ in possessing or not possessing a /hw/ – /w/ contrast in such words as *which* and *witch*. Such a variation would be labelled 'systematic' here, since, for the variety in which the distinction is made use of, it creates a difference of meaning between the two lexical items, in contrast with the variety which has only /w/ in both cases and makes the two items homophonous.

2.2.2 *Distributional Variations*

Distributional variations occur when there is a difference in the phono-

tactic privileges of occurrence of phonemes in the systems of the varieties
being compared. For example, a major distinguishing feature, which of
itself acts as a fairly clear indicator of regional provenance amongst mother
tongue speakers of English, is the occurrence or non-occurrence of the
pre-consonantal and word-final /r/, a useful variable which suggests
a crude division of English into 'r-full' and 'r-less' dialects.

At this level, the describer would attempt to discover which phonemes
were involved, what rules could be deduced to explain the variations and
whether one variety was more restrictive in the combinations it permitted
than another.

2.2.3   Incidential Variations

The choice of a different phoneme for the 'same' lexical item between
varieties can in some cases be explained, in part at least, in distributional
terms – though of a probabilistic kind – and such partially but not
wholly internally predictable variations have been termed 'incidential' (or
in Kurath's (1939) usage 'incidental'). An example from English is the
variable (a); the use by some varieties of the variant /æ/ rather than /ɑ:/ in
such lexical items as *dance*. Many varieties of American, Northern British
and Australian English consistently choose /æ/ in contrast with the /ɑ:/
of RP, Southern African and some Eastern American dialects. This choice
can be partly explained in distributional terms, since the /æ/ appears
before a nasal plus another consonant. However, the occurrence of one
variant rather than the other is by no means 100 per cent predictable. RP
for example has *romance, random* and several others, with /æ/ rather than
the expected /ɑ:/. Perhaps, yet again, we are seeing evidence of the continuum nature of linguistic data on which the imposition of absolute
rules tends to conceal rather than clarify the structure.

2.2.4   Realizational Variations

Realizational variations ('phonetic hetroglosses' in Kurath, 1939) are
caused by the differences in phonetic realization of individual phonemes.
Inevitably, at this level of delicacy of analysis, even individual idiolects
will vary from each other, and to some extent differ within themselves
over time, and the describer must beware of becoming bogged down in a
mass of phonetic detail, from which would emerge, in the long term, the
staggeringly trivial fact that every mother tongue user of English in the
world pronounces words differently from every other! We have to keep
a sense of proportion here and accept that we must limit our descriptions
of realizational variations to the most distinctive and·phonetically gross

distinctions. Although tiny differences of articulation are probably what the speaker of English most notices in the 'accent' of others, they are of least interest to the linguist in his search for system amongst the heterogeneous data at his disposal, except perhaps in so far as they are clues to the reasons for the adoption of attitudes to linguistic variation within a community.

2.2.5   Summary

We have been considering, so far in this chapter, the notion of variation and have outlined, mainly with phonological examples drawn from English, the major types of variation which will occur in language and the sources of these variations, and have made a suggestion of an initial hierarchical approach to the inclusion of variation within a model of language. It is this point which we need to take up next. What kinds of model are available to the linguist who feels obliged to handle variation and how is he to choose between them?

2.3   MODELS AND VARIATION

Once the step is taken to attempt descriptions of language by drawing upon data derived from more than one idiolect, however idealized, further problems present themselves: chief among them the need to create models which can handle variation between idiolects in an adequate way. We shall therefore discuss two aspects of this problem below. What kind of *system* is language? What *models* are most appropriate for the description and explanation of such a system?

2.3.1   Language as a System

We have been using the terms 'system' and 'model' in relation to language so far in an improperly vague and undefined way. In this section, we shall suggest how language should be viewed as a particular kind of system and how such an approach will lead us towards hints about the kinds of model which will be most useful to us (see Bell, 1975c).

Let us begin by defining the term 'system'. Considerable thought has been given to 'systems' in the sciences and so, inevitably, a wide range of possible definitions are available (Emery, 1969, gives a selection of readings which are valuable). However, almost all agree on seeing a system as an independent framework in which independent but related parts are placed, i.e. the organization or arrangement of variables which, when organized, constitute a *whole:* a conceptual or physical entity (see Ackoff, 1960).

A basic distinction between two fundamentally different types of system can be seen when the relationship of the system to its environment is considered: *closed systems* which are, or are considered to be, independent of the environment in which they exist and *open systems* which are in some way connected with their environment so that their structures are influenced by it (von Bertalanffy, 1950).

2.3.1.1   *Language as a Closed System*

Until very recently, language has been studied as though it were a closed system consisting of relationships between elements expressed in terms of their influence on each other, rather than their influence on the society which uses the language and the influences that society has on the code itself. Linguistics has, by opting for this view of language, concentrated on description of static *états de langue*, as though language were a wholly predictable mechanical system, insulated from internal change and external influence, like the systems of the physical sciences. Language has been treated as a mechanical system, in much the same way as the solar system, for example, has been treated by astronomy. One interesting result of this has been that such a synchronic description implies the exclusion of time as a significant variable, i.e. the system has no past or future, only a series of 'present' states.

Following from this assumption has been the emphasis on 'grammaticality' which, unlike 'acceptability', is defined purely in terms of the internal structure of the system: 'a sentence is grammatical or not without any reference to the situation of speaking. All that is needed to judge it is within it, in its structure and in the language under whose rules it is formed' (Gleason, 1965, p.111f.).

If we limit our description of language to the code alone, considerable success can be expected by treating it as a closed system, but as soon as we attempt to relate the code to its uses, we are forced to reassess the object of our investigation, to take into account external influences and to approach language as an open, rather than a closed, system.

2.3.1.2   *Language as an Open System*

From what has been said earlier, it must be clear that the sociolinguist will wish to emphasize the 'openness' of language as a system. He will accept that '... living systems, whether biological organisms or social organizations, are acutely dependent upon their external environment and so must be conceived of as open systems' (Katz and Kahn, 1966).

There are, no doubt, many types of open system and, indeed, substantial numbers which, like language, contain sub-systems which are more or less 'closed', but two major kinds of open system have been suggested:

pattern and *evolutionary* (Boulding, 1967, pp.199-203), both of which have relevance to the description and explanation of language and relate to our earlier comments of varieties of scientific description (see 1.1).

Pattern systems derive from attempts to produce probabilistic explanations of phenomena, which necessarily fall short of the 100 per cent predictability possible with closed mechanical systems. Models based on them will therefore contain, not absolute statements, but suggestions of the likelihood of the occurrence of particular events or states, hedged about with provisos, frequently expressed in statistical terms. The human sciences, dealing as they are with continua rather than the discrete units of the natural sciences, make considerable use of pattern systems. The sociolinguist shares the same view. He assumes that, in addition to the highly predictable system of the linguistic code itself, language and especially language use, can be seen as an open, pattern system, in which there is constant interplay between elements of the system and the context of its use.

It should not be thought that such a view of language is new to linguistics. Work in phonology, and more particularly in phonetics, has always had to come to terms with the non-discrete nature of its data and has been obliged to seek out patterns within it. Recent research has shown interesting patterning of co-occurrence between syntactic structures and pause phenomena in speech (Goldman-Eisler, 1968), has recognized the notion, albeit in 'performance', of 'characteristic error' (Chomsky, 1965, p.3) and, most importantly, the need for *discourse* – language use above the level of the sentence – to be seen in pattern rather than mechanical terms (Sinclair and Coulthard, 1975).

Evolutionary systems, as the term implies, relate to genetic explanations of phenomena and differ from pattern systems most clearly in their relationship to time as a variable. Time is included within the system but is not reversible, i.e. *post facto* insights into the functioning of the system can be made and often with considerable accuracy, but, in contrast, prediction of future states is virtually impossible, except that 'trends', which are assumptions of patterning, can be isolated and tentative predictions based upon them. Evolution itself constitutes the most obvious example of such a system and it was the acceptance of a degree of isomorphism between biological and linguistic evolution which led, as we have seen earlier (1.3.1.2), to the preoccupation of nineteenth-century linguistics with diachronic studies of linguistic change over time.

2.3.1.3   *Summary*

Language has been viewed mainly as a closed system during this century, but this is at variance with the earlier assumptions of nineteenth-century historical linguists who saw it as an open evolutionary system, and is equally at variance with the needs of the present-day sociolinguist, who is reasserting the open pattern system nature of language use and thereby blurring both the distinction between the systematic code of *langue* and the seemingly unsystematic *parole* and the dichotomy between synchronic and diachronic description. The sociolinguist wishes to reaffirm the non-discrete nature of the linguistic system *in use* and the necessary corollary that the system is in constant change.

Language, then, is viewed by the sociolinguist as a highly complex system, essentially open and changing but with a central sub-system which is virtually closed in which change only takes place very gradually. The task, for sociolinguistics, is to create a model of language which reflects both the closed mechanical aspect of the code and the pattern and evolutionary aspects of its use and which links, through a systematic set of statements, both the inner form and the external functions of the system.

2.3.2   Models of Language

The term 'model' has become very popular recently. It is therefore worth spending a little time on defining how we intend to make use of the term.

We began this book by asking the question 'what is language?' It is now clear that the question was not well formulated, since the only really acceptable answer would be 'language is language'. A more appropriate form of the question would have been 'what is language *like*?' To this question we might respond by suggesting 'evolution', 'a code' and so on. In effect, we should be assuming certain characteristics of language to be 'typical' and then seeking out an analogous system. The comparison of the two would lead us to the creation of a *model:* a simplified representation of the system we are trying to describe.

In common usage, the word 'model' has at least three different meanings. As a noun, model means representation, perhaps in three dimensions, of a projected structure, e.g. a scale model of a building, an aircraft or a machine. The adjective implies perfection or idealization, while the verb means to demonstrate, reveal, show what something is like. It has been suggested (Ackoff, 1972) that in the sciences *models* have all three of these connotations. They represent states, objects and events. They are simplified and idealized, since they include only what are thought to be the relevant properties of the system being modelled. They 'model' in the sense of attempting to reveal what the system is like.

Several types of model have been suggested. These range from *pictorial* or *iconic* models, in which there is an evident isomorphism between elements in the model and elements of the reality it represents, to *analogue* and symbolic models. In analogue models, the isomorphism is less, by virtue of making use of one property of the model to represent a different property of the object, while in *symbolic* models, the relationship between the 'real' object and the model cannot be immediately grasped.

An important point here is that all models are constructed on the *as if* principle, e.g. the 1.7-inch piece of plastic in my 1:444 scale model of the actual airliner acts as if it were the actual 62-foot tailplane of the aircraft. The principle applies equally to the relationship between the flying of such a model in a wind-tunnel simulating actual flight, the pumping of water through a pipe to simulate traffic flow or the use of a computer to simulate, through the manipulation of abstract symbols, either of these activities.

Linguistic models have become more and more symbolic and hence less easy to relate to our conceptions of what language 'really' is. This fact has had a twofold effect on students of language. On the one hand, many are confused and worried by the 'abstractness' of linguistics, while on the other, the adoption of symbolic models has allowed easy manipulation of the variables and hence rapid revision of the models themselves and of the theories underlying them.

2.3.2.1   *Linguistic Models and Reality*

It may seem self-indulgent in the context of a book on sociolinguistics to consider, even in outline, the epistemological issue of the 'reality' of abstract notions and constructs and this would indeed be the case but for the widespread confusion in the minds of many students of linguistics as to the existential status of 'phonemes', 'transformations' and so forth.

The question of whether electrons, for example, can be thought of as existing in the same way as rocks, trees and animals has a considerable history dating back, in Europe, to classical times, re-emerging in the Middle Ages in the dispute over 'universals' — does the attested existence of red objects imply the existence of 'red', for example? — and appearing again in this century, first in mathematics and now in linguistics (see Quine, 1953).

The medieval alternatives, *realism, conceptualism* and *nominalism* are reflected in modern philosophy by their counterparts, *logicism, intuitionism* and *formalism* and all are available to the modern linguist as possible positions which he can take up in relating his theories and models to the data of his discipline.

Realism holds that abstract entities exist independently of the mind and that, although the mind can discover them, it is incapable of creating them.

Conceptualism denies that abstract entities exist prior to their creation by the mind but accepts that, once created, they have existence.

Nominalism takes a stand in direct opposition to that of realism. It denies both that abstract entities pre-exist their 'creation' by the mind and that once 'created' they thereby come into existence, even in the mind.

We do not, in this book, wish to commit ourselves on this issue but do feel that yet another of the characteristics which may divide the mainstream of linguistic speculation in this century from sociolinguistic thought, is the strongly *realist* orientation of the former and signs, at least in some scholars, of the contrary, *nominalist* approach of the latter.

The majority of linguists have, during most of this century, assumed a realist view of their constructs, borne out by the preoccupation with 'discovery procedures', through which the underlying abstract system of the language might be discovered in the data contained in a corpus of utterances in that language (Lyons, 1968, p.157).

Even the revolution brought about by transformational-generative linguists in the 1960s does not appear to have shaken the prevailing realism (Chomsky, 1968 and 1972) and indeed the assumption of a close relationship between linguistics and psychology can lead the unwary into imagining that linguistic models are also psychological models of the processes which take place in the mind of the user as he produces and responds to language. The close connection between linguistic and psychological models of language is most clearly stated by Chomsky (op. cit. p.28) in his definition of linguistics '. . . the subfield of psychology that deals with . . . [the] cognitive system developed . . . by the normal speaker-hearer . . . that constitute (his) knowledge of a language'.

The opposite, nominalist, view is best expressed by Firth and his colleagues in the 1930s. Firth strenuously denied the reality of the abstract units of linguistics, considering them to be no more than '. . . ordered schematic constructs, frames of reference, a sort of scaffolding for the handling of events. . . (not) having being or essence' (Firth, 1957, p.181). In addition, he insisted that linguistics itself was 'a group of related techniques for the handling of language events' (ibid.) not falling within the domain of psychology but forming a part, and a crucial part, of the social sciences in general and of anthropology in particular. (It is interesting to compare Firth's view of *linguistics* with Kjolseth's view of the *sociology of language* quoted earlier − 1.5).

2.3.2.2   *Summary*

Models of language, in common with models of other systems, tend to be symbolic, rather than iconic or analogue. Such models have the advantage of easy manipulation but the disadvantage, for the student at least, of being much more abstract than the 'reality' they are designed to describe and explain. Whether or not models of language are themselves 'real' is an essentially philosophical issue, on which the individual describer must decide for himself but there appears to be, in linguistics as a whole, a strongly realist orientation, which suggests belief in some degree of isomorphism between linguistic and psychological models of language. The sociolinguist, in particular, needs to reconsider his position where his models of language in use are concerned and decide whether he can incorporate his models within some kind of cognitive sociology (Cicourel, 1973) or cognitive anthropology (Tyler, 1969) or else side with Firth and deny existential status to them altogether.

2.4   ALTERNATIVE MODELS

Three types of model − structuralist, transformational and implicational − are considered below, often with several examples of alternative formulations.

2.4.1   *Structuralist Models*

In its pure form, a structuralist theory of language postulates that language activity is wholly physical and explicable in terms of cause and effect. Hence the facts of language are assumed to be the physical manifestations of speech and writing and are to be treated as though they are the facts of a natural science.

The process of description is, therefore, the construction of a symbolic model of a closed mechanical system (in the sense we have been using the terms above: 2.3.1.2) by the induction of structure from attested data.

Such assumptions and procedures, it will be recognized, involve a belief in the homogenicity of language which is by no means borne out by the evidence. Even so, and in spite of the variability of speech, the high degree of mutual intelligibility between different varieties of mother tongue English, for example, certainly seems to imply the existence of some underlying shared system, of which the actual surface realizations, with all their contrasting forms, might be seen as individual manifestations. Structuralist linguists, especially those working in dialectology, have all accepted this view but proposed several alternative models in their explanations. Some of these will be reviewed below.

2.4.1.1   *Common Core and Overall Pattern*
Taking the notion of 'mutual intelligibility' between dialects as primary, Hockett (1958 pp.332-7) proposed the existence of a *common core*; 'the total set of shared features' common to all idiolects which are

mutually intelligible (ibid., p.332). This notion seems to have its roots in the facility remarked upon by de Saussure (1915) in his definition of *langue*: '. . . l'ensemble des habitudes linguistiques qui permettent à un sujet de comprendre et de se faire comprendre' (ibid., p.112), and certainly appears, *prima facie*, to support one's intuitive feeling that the mother tongue varieties of English, for example, do share a largely common syntactic, lexical, semantic and phonological system. There are however, two crucial problems which arise with such a notion and we shall consider these in a moment.

The *overall pattern*, in contrast with the common core, is thought of as the total system of the language — productive and receptive — available for inclusion within the common core. This term allows us to include within 'English' not only those elements actually in use by speakers — the common core — but also, for example, the huge potentially useable lexicon contained in dictionaries and in the neologizing processes inherent in the language as a whole. Hockett (1958) puts his position very clearly; 'the overall pattern of a language is a sort of arsenal; each idiolect represents a selection from it. . .' (p.337). Once again the influence of de Saussure (1915) is apparent, since part of his definition of *langue* as a 'storehouse' filled by the users of the language — '. . . un trésor déposé par la pratique de la parole dans les sujets appartenant à une même communauté' (p.30) — closely parallels Hockett's conception of the 'overall pattern'.

Two major objections to such a model of variation can be raised. Firstly, the dependence on the notion of 'mutual intelligibility' forces the describer into attempting to make use of an ill-understood concept and one which has proved, for extra-linguistic reasons, extraordinarily difficult to measure. As Hockett (1958) himself is forced to admit: 'In actuality. . . "mutual intelligibility" is not only a matter of degree, rather than of kind, but it is not always even mutual' (p. 327). Secondly, given a listing of the shared features contained in the 'common core', what models are there for their representation and having created a model, how can the use or non-use of sets of features be specified?

The second objection has received considerable attention, typically by linguists attempting to make of the 'common core' some kind of macro-system from which the individual micro-systems — dialects, styles, idiolects — might be derived.

2.4.1.2   *The Trager-Smith English Vowel System*
The model proposed by Trager and Smith (1951) for the description of the vowel phonemes of English represented a major advance, since it attempted, for the first time, to create a system for a major aspect of the structure of the underlying phonological make-up of English as a whole, or

rather, for the standard dialects of American English. Their proposal was, in brief, to postulate the existence of nine 'short' vowels as the stable basis of the system (see Figure 2.2 below) and to accommodate 'long' vowels and diphthongs by representing them as 'glides', i.e. 'short' vowels + one of four 'semivowels' – /r/, /w/, /y/, /h/. Thus *beet* and *bit* would be distinguished by the symbol /iy/ in the first and /i/ in the second, *card* and *cad* by /ar/ or /ah/ and /æ/ and so forth. The choice of the 'short' vowels, in their neat 3 x 3 matrix, as the key to the system was a very imaginative one, which seems to have substantial support from the diachronic fact that it is just these vowels which, over the centuries, have changed least in English, e.g. the vowel of *ship* in present-day speech differs little from the vowel of King Alfred's day (Gimson 1962, revised edn. 1970 p. 102). The model then makes available a grand total of 36 vocalic nuclei.

FIGURE 2.2   *The Trager-Smith Vowels*

i	ɨ	u
e	ə	o
æ	a	ɔ

Numbers of defects, however, also appear with this model of the English vowel system. Although the model shows that there are 36 vowels and diphthongs 'available' to the user of English, no dialect actually makes use of all 36 of them and, perhaps a more serious objection which attacks the fundamental basis of the explanation, not all even employ all nine of the short vowels. RP, for example, cannot be shown to use more than eight and Australian English only seven (Cochrane, 1959). An additional problem is raised by 'mixed' dialects, in which some linguists (e.g. Fries and Pike, 1949, see 2.4.1.4 below) would argue two or more systems coexist, perhaps in some kind of sociolinguistic equilibrium, perhaps in conflict (a point we shall return to later, when we consider models for the description of continuum and bilingual situations 5.3.1).

2.4.1.3 *The Diaphone*
During the course of his work on phonemes, Jones (1962) proposed, in addition to the terms 'phoneme' and 'phone' (speech sound), the entity

diaphone to represent 'families of sounds which could be substituted for each other without changing the meaning of the word' (Trubetzkoy, 1969 reprinted in Fudge, 1973, p. 56). One interpretation of the diaphone as '. . . a sound used by one group of speakers together with other sounds which replace it consistently in the pronunciation of other speakers' (Jones 1964, p.53f.) clearly indicates a useful way of dealing with the problem of variation in phonology, at least to the extent that it groups together, perhaps under the umbrella of some kind of 'macrophoneme', such variants as the /əu/ of RP, the /o:/ of much Northern British English and the /əʊ/ of much American English. If this was Jones' intention, the term seems in some ways to anticipate the generative phonologists (Chomsky and Halle, 1968) and to facilitate the attempts made by other linguists (e.g. Weinreich, 1952) to build models of dialects in the form of diasystems (see 2.4.1.4 below).

2.4.1.4   *Coexistent Systems and Diasystems*
Fries and Pike (1949), taking issue with the assumption that 'it is at least unlikely that a given speaker will use two or more different styles in addressing a single person' (Bloch, 1948) and recognizing that 'Socially pertinent differences of style cannot safely be ignored. . . (but) must be handled in some way in our phonemic assumptions and procedures' (Fries and Pike, 1949, p.29, note 1), were led to suggest 'that two or more phonemic systems may coexist in the speech of a monolingual, . . .' and set about attempting '. . . to outline a procedure for determining the nature of these coexistent systems' (ibid.). The notion of the coexistent systems has been a very fruitful one, since it made possible, in principle at least, the handling of such diverse problems as 'loans' from other languages or dialects, changes in form correlatable with inter- and intra-personal variables and the phenomenon of bilingualism in general and was one of the earliest challenges to the monolithic concept of language – one of the key assumptions now rejected by modern sociolinguistics.

Weinreich, first in studies of dialects (1952) and later in work on bilingualism (1953), developed the notion of coexistent systems into a model of language as a *diasystem*. A hypothetical example will be given below to illustrate how this might be applied to the description of two varieties of a language.

Where phonemes match in a one-to-one manner, the diasystem can be shown in the following way – assuming a five-vowel system and two varieties marked 1 and 2.

$$1, 2. //i \sim e \sim a \sim o \sim u //.$$

Where such an exact matching does not occur, for example where variety 1 has /a/ but variety 2 has a pair of phonemes /a/ and /ɑ/, the *compound,* one-to-many relationship can be shown by a system of bracketing:

$$1, 2. \;/\!/ \; i \sim e \sim \quad \dfrac{1. \qquad /a/}{2. \quad /a/ \sim /ɑ/} \quad \sim o \sim u \;/\!/$$

It might be, however, that the relationship between two varieties is not compound, as in the example above but *complex;* many-to-many rather than one-to-many. For example, variety 1 may have two phonemes, say /ə/ and /ɜ:/, in contrast, while variety 2 has four /ə/, /əʳ/, /ɜʳ/ and /ɨ/. Such a set of relationships might be shown in the following way:

$$1, 2. \;/\!/ \; \dfrac{1. \qquad / ə \sim 3:/}{2. / \; ə \sim ə^{ɪ} \sim 3^{ɪ} \sim \dot{+}/} \;/\!/$$

In actual fact, the contrasting relationships between the 'central vowels' of 'r-less' and 'r' dialects of English might be illustrated by just such a model.

So far we have been building diasystems — models involving only two varieties. However, our need is for models which permit the representation of the structure of several systems simultaneously, i.e. *polysystems,* as has been illustrated below by a further hypothetical example involving five varieties, numbered 1 to 5 and the letters a — f as symbols for phonemes (in a completely abstract sense, i.e. 'a' is not intended here to represent /a/).

$$1, 2, 3, 4, 5. \;/\!/ \; a \sim b \sim \quad \begin{matrix} 1. \\ 2. \\ 3. \\ 4. \\ 5. \end{matrix} \dfrac{/ c \sim d}{/ c \sim d \sim e/} \quad \sim f \ldots \;/\!/$$

This 5 variety polysystem is to be understood as follows:
Each variety (1 — 5) has the phonemes *a, b* and *f* in contrast. Varieties 1 and 2 have *c* contrasting with *d,* while 3, 4 and 5 have, in addition to the *c — d* distinction, a phoneme *c.*

We shall draw on the notion of the diasystem later, as a prior step towards the discussion of a more powerful model for the description of variation in language. There are, first of all, some problems involved in the use of this model, not least of which is its cumbersomeness. It is clear that polysystems present a substantial problem of display and further, that an acceptance of the four levels of variation in phonology suggested earlier (2.2) forces us into four separate restatements of the polysystem: one for each level.

2.4.1.5 *Summary*

In our search for a model appropriate for the explanation of linguistic variation, we have come a long way from the assumption of homogenicity initially prevalent in linguistics and now appear able, with some success, to include within our models both the internal sources and the interpersonal external sources of variation (2.1.2). We are, however, still unable to accommodate intrapersonal (stylistic) and inherent variation – true 'free' variation – in our models.

The next section (2.4.2) will suggest ways of dealing with the first through transformational models. Inherent variation, as we shall see, has to be approached in a rather different way (2.4.3).

2.4.2 *Transformational Models*

Transformational-generative models of language derive from a set of postulates concerning the nature of language and assumptions of appropriate methods for explaining its structure which are, in essence, the converse of the structuralist approaches outlined in the previous section. The structuralist sees language as an essentially physical activity to be explained by *induction* – events observed; hypothesis set up; hypothesis tested; creation of theory – which makes use of *parole* as the source data, suitably edited, through which access can be obtained to *langue*. The transformationalist assumes that language is essentially a mental rather than a physical activity, access to the structure of which is possible by introspection on the part of the describer of his own mother tongue; an adoption of the method of *deduction* frequent, as we have seen earlier, in the natural sciences – a pattern is perceived in the events observed; a model is created; the model is checked against the describer's intuitions; creation of the theory – a rejection of the empirical, data-orientated approach of the structuralists.

The process of description for the transformationalist is, therefore, the construction of symbolic models, as it was in the case of the structuralists but by means of deduction of system from the internalized knowledge of the user-describer, rather than induction from external data.

Underlying transformational-generative models is much the same assumption of homogenicity of language which we noticed above during our outline of structuralist models. The ideal speaker-hearer model of the structure of language has exactly the element of 'non-surprise' we noted above in mechanical systems; there are no surprises in a transformational model. If you have written your rules correctly, the grammar will generate the expected surface realizations. However, some linguists working within the transformational framework have attempted to include variation in their descriptions. We shall review a number of these, suggest how they might be improved and indicate what problems still remain.

2.4.2.1   *Traditional Transformational Models*

Before considering how variation might be included within a transformational model, it seems wise to outline the major components of the 'normal' model which, through several changes in form and scope since 1957, has avoided dealing at all with variation. At present, most transformational models consist of four components – base, transformational, phonological, phonetic – but there is some dispute as to the status and placing within the model of the semantic component; some preferring semantics to be integrated into the base, others seeing it as a separate level. Figure 2.3 below shows, in a schematic way, a rather conservative form of the model (essentially that of *Aspects* and the *Sound Pattern of English* and drawn from Botha, 1971, repr. in Fudge, 1973, p.230).

2.4.2.2   *The Bailey Morpheme Variants Model*

The first comprehensive polylectal rather than monolectal grammar to be attempted within the general framework of TG was one produced for Jamaican Creole (B.L. Bailey, 1966). The model was essentially that of *Syntactic Structures* (Chomsky, 1957), which therefore contained *optional* as well as *obligatory transformations* – a distinction abandoned in *Aspects* (Chomsky, 1965), in which all transformations are obligatory – but departed from the 1957 model in proposing, in order to cope with the continuum situation of the creole (a point we shall make much more of later: 5.3.1), the notion of *morpheme variants*. The prime assumption was that all varieties of the creole could be described by means of the same phrase structure (roughly analagous with the *base* of later models) and transformational rules, variation occurring in the morphophonemic structure (accommodated within later models as a part of the readjustment rules). The morpheme variants, then, were suggested in order to list 'all variants in the form of morphemes which speakers throughout the island use indiscriminately' (Bailey, 1966, p. 138). It should be noted here that, although the writer of the grammar was well aware of the fact that the term 'Jamaican Creole' actually covered a wide range of variable codes demonstrated by the 'state of flux in which the language now exists' (ibid., note 1), variants were seen as either (1) 'unmarked', indiscriminate 'free variation' or else as (2) 'dialectal' consisting of two types '. . . geographical variants //G and morphemes borrowed from English / /E' (ibid., p. 138) and no attempt was made to explain 'free variants' in terms of kinds of intrapersonal or 'stylistic' variation suggested above (2.1.2.2).

However, the model was a considerable advance, in spite of its

FIGURE 2.3   *Components of the Model*

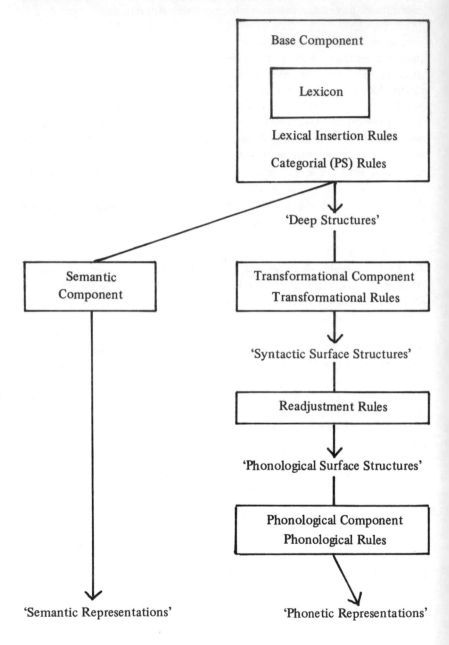

weaknesses. The existence of variation was accepted and its inclusion attempted. Some effort was indeed made, albeit in a rather crude way, to label the sources of the variants and, perhaps in the long run more importantly, the model, by its very precision, forced others to search for improvements which, in their wake, began the fundamental reassessment, first of the status of pidgin and creole languages in relation to their 'parent' languages (see 6.4 later) and secondly, gave an important impetus to the orderly investigation of variation within linguistics. Fundamentally, though, the model fails to give, as part of its listing of variants, a clear indication of the correlation between any of the variant forms and the sociological or psychological features of the users of that form. In short, the model is, in essence, static rather than dynamic and linguistic rather than sociolinguistic and has, because of the lack of specification of linguistic-social correlates, little predictive capacity, i.e. we know what forms are available but not who would choose which in what circumstances. One model for the inclusion of such correlates is outlined next.

2.4.2.3   *The Labov Variable Rules Model*
During the course of work in the latter part of the '60s on non-standard Negro English in the USA, Labov (1966 a, 1966b) became steadily more convinced of the 'logic of non-standard English' and set about constructing models of the rule systems governing what had previously tended to be dismissed as 'a series of badly connected words' (Bereiter, 1966, quoted in Labov 1969a). To accommodate such rules within a TG framework but to avoid the kinds of criticism made above of the Bailey model, Labov proposed the notion of the *variable rule*, in addition to the existing 'normal' transformational rules.

A crude illustration of what is intended may be given below, drawing upon the example we used earlier (2.1.2.2) of the variation between [t] and [ʔ] in my own speech in such words as *fortnight*.

The co-occurrence of [t] with 'formal' situations and [ʔ] with 'informal' permits us to write a rough rule of the kind:-

$$[t] \text{ }^{opt} [ʔ] \text{ } / \text{ } v \text{ } \underline{\hspace{3cm}} \begin{bmatrix} - \text{ formal} \\ + \begin{vmatrix} C \\ \# \# \end{vmatrix} \end{bmatrix}$$

The rule can be read as follows: 't may optionally become a glottal stop in the environment following a vowel and preceding a consonant or a word boundary when the social context is informal.' Where '/' is to be interpreted as 'in the environment of (a convention drawn from Chomsky and Halle, 1968) and 'C' as 'consonant'.

Our example is, in itself, a rather trivial one but the implications of the approach are far from trivial, since it begins to show, not only how variation can be included within the existing TG model, but also how the 'systematicness' of variation can be demonstrated, even in the apparently ungrammatical utterances of 'everyday speech' (Labov, 1966a). In addition, the notion of the variable rule, coupled with Labov's general sociolinguistic principle that users of a subordinate dialect will, when in contact with those of a superordinate dialect in a formal context, shift their rules in an unsystematic way towards those of the superordinate, (Labov, 1971, p. 450. Further discussion of this, and other axioms of sociolinguistics, can be found below in section 8.1) suggest new and fruitful approaches to 'hypercorrection' (Labov, 1966c) amongst 'lower class' speakers of English on the one hand and the moot problem of the 'decreolization' of much creole speech in contact with standard English (de Camp, 1971) on the other.

A problem with the model on the purely linguistic side is to decide whether or not variable rules are to be incorporated into our explanations as part of a single but variable system or as manifestations of coexistent systems – a point we have touched upon already (2.4.1.4) and shall return to later in our discussion of bilingualism (5.1). Two further problems remain, one linguistic the other sociological. The model is, it seems, able to make correlations between linguistic forms and two of the major external causes of variation – inter- and intrapersonal; dialectal and stylistic – but inherent variation still remains as true 'free variation' within the system (see 2.4.3 below for proposals on this). The sociological problem lies in the rather vague terms 'formal', 'informal' which we are forced into using as the contextual markers of stylistic choice. This too is a matter to which we shall return, when we consider the microprocesses of intra-group interaction (4.2.2).

2.4.2.4 *Summary*

We have now reached the point in our survey of models for the explanation of variation in language where, within certain limits, both internal and external sources of variation can be integrated, in principle at least, into a model of language. We are left, however, with inherent variation still outside the model and a recognition that, for all the use of such terminology as 'generate', our models are still essentially of steady states – closed mechanical rather than open pattern systems – and that they somehow fail to illustrate the dynamism of actual language use. Some suggestions for coping with this are made below and expanded upon in 5.3 later.

2.4.3   *Dynamic Models*

One weakness, which we have been continually pointing out, with linguistic models, a weakness often shared by models in sociology, is the tendency for the dynamism of the systems being described to be played down in favour of static descriptions of the systems, as though they were in equilibrium and impervious to influences which are the cause of change and disequilibrium. Many sociologists today would regard change 'as a part of the qualities of social systems rather than primarily as an alien and intrusive element' (Moore, 1963) and insist that there is system and direction in change, which can be represented by dynamic, probabilistic models. We shall see below how such an orientation, as examplified in a technique from social psychology can be brought to bear on complex sociolinguistic data in such a way as to provide ordered insights into the most unstable form of variation which we have been so far unable to handle — inherent variation.

2.4.3.1   *Guttman and Implicational Scaling*

Work on the construction of attitude scales and on the evaluation of responses to items on such scales led to a desire, on the part of the researchers, to demonstrate that answers to questions on attitude were not randomly distributed for each individual but closely and even hierachically related. For example, the responses to a Social Distance Scale (e.g. Bogardus, 1925 is one of the first) might consist of the choice of one of seven classifications within which a particular social, ethnic or other group would be placed. The classifications are likely to run from extreme closeness — 'admit to close kinship by marriage' — to extreme distance — 'would exclude from my country' — with intermediate classifications between. By presenting the respondent with several groups to classify, the researcher can build up an overall picture of the social distance an individual adopts towards others.

There is, however, another way of using the same data, i.e. by recognizing that the choice of a particular classification implies the choice of others. For this reason, cumulative scales in which the implications could be easily included were designed (Guttman, 1944). A perfect example of this would be a scale concerning height. If I state that I am over five feet eleven inches, this clearly implies that I should give positive answers to questions like 'are you over four feet six inches?', i.e. a positive response to a question implies positive answers to all questions of lower value. Such a scale is, it will have been noticed, unidirectional and, given the questions and the scale representation of the answers of a group of respondents, the answers themselves are reproduceable. Figure 2.4 below represents a hypothetical Guttman scale.

FIGURE 2.4 *A Hypothetical Guttman Scale*

	1	2	3	4	5	6	
A	+	+	+	+	+	+	+ positive
B	−	+	+	+	+	+	response
C	−	−	+	+	+	+	− negative
D	−	−	−	+	+	+	response
E	−	−	−	−	+	+	1 a question
F	−	−	−	−	−	+	A a respondent
G	−	−	−	−	−	−	

It may appear that such a scaling technique is either trivial or, if valuable for social psychology, inapplicable to linguistics but as we shall see below, this is far from the truth.

2.4.3.2 *The Bailey Wave Model*

We have, all along, been stressing the need, not merely to *list* variants in language but to *label* them in terms of their provenance and attempt to demonstrate the systematic nature of variation. One of the first to recognize the implicational relationships which exist between choices of linguistic variables and to present these in a form very similar to (though not it seems derived from) Guttman Scaling was Bailey (not the B.L. Bailey referred to above − 2.4.2.2 − but C.J. Bailey, 1969) drawing in his work on creole languages on earlier suggestions made by De Camp (1968). A further hypothetical model of linguistic variation is represented by Figure 2.4 above, if we interpret 'A' as an informant and '1' as a particular variant. It is significant that, in terms of traditional linguistics, only A, who uses all six variants and G who uses none can be successfully included in normal models. It is exactly on this point that the sociolinguist diverges most in his interests from the orthodox linguist. For the sociolinguist, A and G, because of their invariant choices, are of no particular interest except as 'boundary markers'. They are 'typical' examples of users of two specific dialects. For the sociolinguist, B to F, because of their contrasting choices are the locus of investigation.

We can now produce a very much simplified scale for part of an attested set of variants in certain common varieties of Northwestern English English (crudely, Lancashire and adjacent areas of neighbouring counties): 1, the use of *happen*, /'apn/ and the like, for the standard 'southern' *perhaps* or *maybe* and 2, the use of /v/ rather than /ʌ/ in *but* etc. The scale, considerably idealized for reasons which we shall see below, represents a model of usage for three informants A, B, C.

FIGURE 2.5   *An Example of a Bailey Wave*

	1	2
A	+	+
B	−	+
C	−	−

Yet again A and C are wholly predictable in their choice of variant. A, by using both, is clearly definable as a speaker of a 'broad' variety of the local dialect. C, in contrast, has a usage identical to that of the standard. It is probably possible too to postulate certain socioeconomic and other demographic characteristics of the two speakers on the basis of their unambiguous choices. It is B who is most interesting, since he rejects the 'broad' variant 1 but retains the 'regional' 2, making him a user of a 'modified regional' English (cf. Gimson, 1970, p.87).

The great strength of this model lies in its ability to rank variations, not within the linguistic level at which they occur, as we did earlier (2.2) but across levels – as here, where 1 is lexical and to some degree also grammatical and 2 is phonological – in a hierachical manner from most to least socially distinctive. The effect of this on the previously static conceptions of language and the clear removal, through its dynamic nature, of the distinction between diachronic and synchronic brings us simultaneously closer to our data. In addition it permits us, as it were, to describe in terms not of instantaneous snapshots of states of language but, to continue the analogy, through a kind of slow-motion film in which we see, not frozen states but waves of change passing through the speech community.

We have, this far, been dealing with very idealized data and, therefore, very hypothetical models. In actuality, the influence of the external sources of variation discussed earlier tend to produce scales far less unambiguous than those above. Figure 2.6 shows the kind of problem which tends to arise:

FIGURE 2.6   *A Linguistic Variation Scale*

	1	2	3		
A	+	+	+	1	a variant
B	±	+	+	A	an informant
C	−	±	+	+	use of variant
D	−	−	±	±	variable use of variant
E	−	−	−	−	non-use of variant

This model, unlike the perfect Guttman scale, contains cells in which ± occur. If the model is to function properly, each ± will need to be replaced by either + or –. Clearly, the ± arise in the model because of the influence of inter- or intrapersonal or inherent variation which should have been compensated for earlier in the description. Indeed, though it would be possible to subdivide each informant, labelling B as Bi – B in an informal situation – and Bii – B in a formal situation – it seems far better to adopt a model similar to that of Labov (2.4.2.3) to filter out such variables and leave the present model to cope with inherent variability. Though in the end there must still remain a small number of free variations which cannot be accounted for, either because there is a weakness in the model being used or else because a small set of variation really are in completely free variation.

2.4.3.3 *Summary*
The Bailey Wave model seems, on the face of it, to provide a means of handling the most intractable of linguistic data, i.e. that which occurs in linguistic continuum situations, where there appear to be totally erratic and unpredictable choices of linguistic form made by the same informant in the same situation. We shall see later how powerful a model this is in relation to the description of creole languages and how it illustrates, once again, the actual non-discreteness of linguistic data (5.3.1). But its limitations must be recognized: it is not, in itself, a grammar but rather a means of setting up '. . . hypotheses about hierarchies of precedence among features . . . and thus to create a provisional order among apparently conflicting data which may serve as a basis for further investigation and the eventual writing of formal rules' (Bickerton, 1972, p.7).

2.5 CONCLUSION

We began this chapter with a consideration of the nature and causes of linguistic variation and continued with a search for appropriate models for its description. In the course of this we were forced to consider what we meant by the terms 'model' and 'system' in relation to language and then to examine three approaches – structuralist, transformational and implicational – to the explanation and modelling of variation. Ultimately, we recognized that, in principle at least, all types of variation were now explicable but at the cost of abandoning two of the major tenets of descriptive linguistics in this century; the assumption of homogenicity and the dichotomy between synchronic and diachronic description.

In the next chapter, we shall examine more closely the sub-area of sociolinguistics known as microsociolinguistics; the study of the systematic co-occurrences of linguistic forms and social roles in the context of interaction within small groups.

3
Functional Models of Language
- the Components

In the previous two chapters, we have been concerned with variation in language and its explanation in terms of internal and external causation, by means of models of various kinds. We pointed out how most available models of language are of idealized static systems, where the influence of the environment in which the language is actually used is neglected and we reiterated the need for dynamic models of language in use: functional models which demonstrate the processes through which linguistic choices and social skills are related when language is used as the vehicle of communication between human beings.

In this chapter, we shall consider *how* language communicates and *what* it communicates in face-to-face interaction. The division between this chapter and the next should not be seen as absolute in any sense. The contrast between the contents of each is rather one of focus; this chapter setting out the components or parameters involved and the next showing how the mechanism is set in motion and the rules by which interaction is made possible.

We shall see, in the course of these two chapters, how our interest is largely shared by the human sciences in general and by anthropology, sociology and social psychology in particular, although many of the methods of investigation and some of the goals of these disciplines are different, in kind or in degree, from those of the sociolinguist.

3.1 FUNCTIONAL MODELS OF LANGUAGE IN USE

It should be stated at the outset, that what is intended here by the term 'functional' must not be confused with the use of the same term by linguists of the neo-Prague School, most typically Martinet, 1961, in their descriptions of language. The Prague School approach is based on the assumption that linguistic units are no more than 'values' which arise from the oppositions or distinctions between them (Martinet, 1968, repr. in

Fudge (ed.), 1973, p. 74); epigrammatically stated by de Saussure (1915, p. 166.) from whom the notion originally derives, 'dans la langue il n'y a que des différences': in *langue* there are only differences, i.e. the notion applies to the code *per se,* not to the correlation between the form of the code and its social functions. The sense in which we intend 'functional' below is, in contrast, just such relationships between code and use.

In order to construct models of language in use, we shall need to consider the kinds of definition of language typical of the human sciences and see whether some of these provide us with a convenient starting point. A crude initial definition and one which has its origin in Aristotle's *organon* or tool notion of language (Hörmann, 1971, p. 5) along the lines of 'language is an arbitrary symbol system by means of which individual members of communities exchange information' will serve our purpose for the moment.

3.1.1   *Information Theory Model*

Although originally developed by Shannon, 1948 (cited by Hörmann 1971, p.51) in the context of communications engineering, the model of information transmission represented in diagrammatic form below can be drawn upon as a model of the events that occur when one speaker communicates a single message to a single hearer, i.e. of a *speech event* containing a single *speech act* (4.1.4).

FIGURE 3.1   *An Information Theory Model*

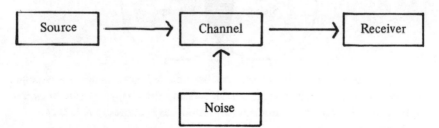

In an ideal system, with a perfect source, channel and receiver, there would be no *noise,* i.e. the message as transmitted by the source would arrive entirely unchanged at the receiver. However, all communication systems do, in fact, contain noise; disturbances which prevent the 100 per cent reception of the message. This is equally true of language, inefficiencies arising from some defect in any or all of the three component parts of the communication event and indeed, many of the kinds of variation considered in chapter 2 can be seen as 'noise' in this sense. Clearly, in order to specify the nature of the noise generated by the human participants, we need to modify the model to include the notion of *repertoire*, the entirety of the communication skills which a speaker or hearer can draw upon in an information exchange situation. Such a notion has obvious connections with competence as previously described but includes more than linguistic competence — the social skills which permit the appropriate choice of code elements and facilitate the whole process of communication — in short the communicative competence of the user.

In an ideal speech event, the speaker and hearer would share a common repertoire but, of necessity, individuals being individual implies that this cannot be so in a real situation. Hence, the efficiency of the information transfer depends on the degree to which there is overlap between individual repertoires. Hockett's concept of the common core (2.4.1.1), which we rather cavalierly dismissed earlier, begins to re-emerge in this context as a rather useful notion. The model may now be represented in its revised form in Figure 3.2 below; the shaded area representing the shared repertoires and the lower arrows, noise generated by the differences between them.

FIGURE 3.2   *A Revised Information Theory Model*

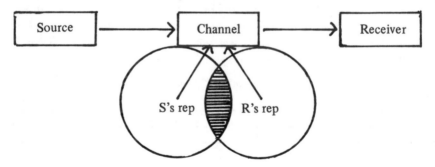

One essential element, which will be included later, when we expand the model to deal with several speech acts and the change of role between speaker and hearer, is missing from this model as it stands — *feedback.*

3.1.2   *Anthropological Models*

Anthropologists have consistently studied the relationship between language and culture, not only because command of the language of the members of the culture being studied was a *sine qua non* for the fieldworker (Boas, 1911) but also because of the recognition that 'Cultural activity, even of the simplest kind, inevitably rests on ideas or generalizations; and . . . ideas, in turn, human minds seem to be able to formulate and operate with and transmit only through speech' (Kroeber, 1963, p. 33). There has, of course, been considerable controversy in anthropology as to the relationship which exists between the two – language *and* culture or language *in* culture – to some extent resolved by a compromise of the type 'So far as the process of their transmission is concerned and the type of mechanism of their development, it is clear that language and culture are one. For practical purposes it is generally convenient to keep them distinct' (ibid.). Some anthropologists, Whorf, for example, in the famous hypothesis which bears his name, have argued the dependence of culture on language, i.e. that language determines, rather than reflects, culture (Whorf, 1962). Perhaps the clearest statement of the position is that made by Sapir (1929, repr. in Mandelbaum, 1966, p. 69) 'The fact of the matter is that the "real world" is to a large extent unconsciously built up on the language habits of the group'. The controversy still rages, not only in anthropology but also in linguistics, social psychology and, because of its application to language differences between children of different social classes (Bernstein, 1966), in education. It is not our intention here to take sides on this issue – it has been mentioned solely to show how and why there is common interest in and dispute over, the nature of language between anthropologists and linguists. Indeed, some were arguing twenty years ago that although the methods of anthropology and linguistics are to a great extent different, their data is essentially the same and that socio-linguistic research in particular offers new approaches to many of the traditional problems of anthropology (Voegelin and Harris, 1947) and it is certainly true that during the 1950s and '60s the gap in methods has narrowed considerably (Lévi-Strauss, 1972, is an important example).

Below, in schematic form, is a possible model for showing the relationships which exist between language and culture (Bright, 1968, p. 20). Some notes are required to make sense of the model. First, the observational universe, the *etic* (the term is from Pike, 1967, as is *emic*), in which linguistic behaviour is located, is distinguished from the structural universe, the *emic* of the human mind (see 3.3.2.2 for an explanation of these terms). Next, linguistic behaviour is distinguished from its content. The three relationships *a, b, c,* are of particular importance to the anthropologically orientated linguist. They are (*a*) the field of the linguist *qua* linguist – the relationship, whether arrived at by inductive or deductive methods, between performance and competence; (*b*) the parallel field and techniques of the anthropologist – relating actual objects and events to patterns of organization; (*c*) the field of the semanticist – the relationship of lexical units to each other and to the cultural matrix of the use of the item.

FIGURE 3.3   *An Anthropological Model*

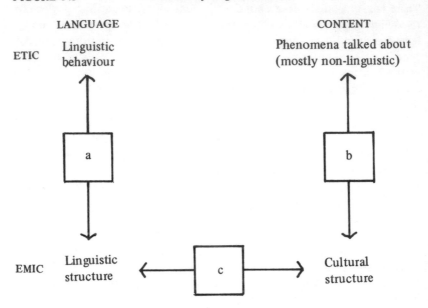

We may now return to our definition of language above and compare it with Sapir (1929, p. 8) 'Language is a purely human and non-instinctive method of communicating ideas, emotions and desires by means of a system of voluntarily produced symbols'.

Clearly, sociolinguists and anthropologists seem to see language in much the same light. Let us next consider how language is viewed by the closely related discipline of sociology.

3.1.3 *Sociological Models*

Like anthropology, sociology studies man in society but tends to focus its attention on large groups and processes within economically highly developed societies, while anthropology normally concerns itself with small relatively homogeneous and technologically less developed groups. However, though the social unit of anthropology is usually quite small, the aim of the science is extremely large — the description of the total culture. Conversely, the large populations studied by sociologists provide data and a testing ground for the development of the theories of, for example, social order — 'the underlying regularity of human social behaviour' (Inkeles, 1964, p. 27).

Hence, sociology too has an interest in language, seeing '. . . a network of transactions. . . with words and situations partially co-varying' (Gross,

1967, p. 13.) and the role of language as crucial in the process of social-ization – 'individuals learn their roles through the process of communi-cation' (Bernstein 1966, p. 255). If this is the case, the fears expressed earlier that sociolinguistics might be seen as parasitical on sociology appear groundless, since the hypothesis being proposed is not the weak one of there being correlations between language form and social class membership but that, to some degree at least, social class can be defined in linguistic terms.

The domains of sociology – the primary units of social life, basic social institutions and fundamental social processes (see Inkeles, 1964, p. 12, table 1) – are all mediated, and to a degree made possible, by language. We shall return to some of these topics later (4.2.1), in our discussion of social groups. Meanwhile, we can present, in diagrammatic form, an essentially sociological model in which psychological, sociological and linguistic structure are shown as integrating and generating speech events. (Based on Bernstein, 1965, p. 160, and Lawton, 1968, p. 100).

FIGURE 3.4   *A Sociological Model*

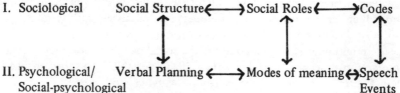

Levels of Abstraction
I. Sociological   Social Structure⟷Social Roles⟷Codes

II. Psychological/   Verbal Planning ⟷Modes of meaning⟷Speech
    Social-psychological   Events

This model suggests that social structures, the roles and the codes that typically co-occur with them, all inter-react making change possible in society, in social interaction and in language. At the psychological level, verbal planning, itself influencing and influenced by the social structure, creates and is modified by created meanings demonstrated by the role behaviour and code usage made concrete by speech events. Note how there is both horizontal and vertical influence, always reciprocal, between the six elements of the model. Clearly, though, we shall need, bearing some model of this kind in mind, to specify in much more detail what is intended by most of the terminology above and to exemplify it with evidence, at least for the interrelationships between roles and codes and codes and speech events (see 4.3.2 below).

3.1.4 *Psychological Models*

We have been moving, in our all too brief survey of the kinds of conception of language and models available for its description in the human sciences, steadily towards the smallest unit of study — the behaviour of the individual and, in social psychology, the study of the social behaviour of the individual. Typical of social psychology is the assumption that the unit of investigation should be the *interpersonal behaviour event* and that the goal of the discipline should be the creation or discovery of laws which explain the nature, development and change of such events (Krech *et al.*, 1962, pp. 3f.).

In the attempt to reach these goals, social psychology draws upon the principles of general psychology in order to understand '. . . how the individual develops his social goals, how he perceives persons and groups, how he learns social behaviours' (ibid. p. 9).

Social psychology, in part, shares the field of interest of sociology — social class, status, norms of behaviour, the nature and organization of groups, etc. — but differs from it in concentrating on the behaviour of individuals, rather than aggregates of individuals, within and between such social structures and as participants in such social processes. Here again, language can be seen as a key factor, whether within the mind of the individual 'as an instrument of conceptual analysis and synthesis' or 'socially, as a means of intercommunication' (Drever, 1952, p. 151).

We might now attempt an outline of a social-psychological model of the interaction process — speech events — made possible by a series of speech acts. Figure 3.5 below is based, partly on Argyle (1967, p.95).

This model suggests that the speaker begins to generate a message, the form and content of which is subject to modification under the influence of various situational constraints (see 3.3 below for a fuller discussion of these), including his own linguistic and social competence and feedback, non-verbal, from the hearer. The decision-making mechanism, the speaker's communicative competence, is thus seen as a kind of 'mixer' which relates linguistic to social competence and then reorganizes the intended message into a more 'appropriate' form. This modified message is then transmitted by means of the available channels and is received by the hearer. The degree to which the hearer 'understands' the message will be a reflection of his expectations and of his own communicative competence to 'make sense' of the message in terms of his own linguistic and social competences. His modified understanding of the message leads to two simultaneous outcomes: (1) he begins to plan his own response, i.e. begins to prepare himself for the role of speaker and (2) provides non-verbal feedback which itself forms part of the series of situational constraints which act as

FIGURE 3.5   *A Social-Psychological Model*

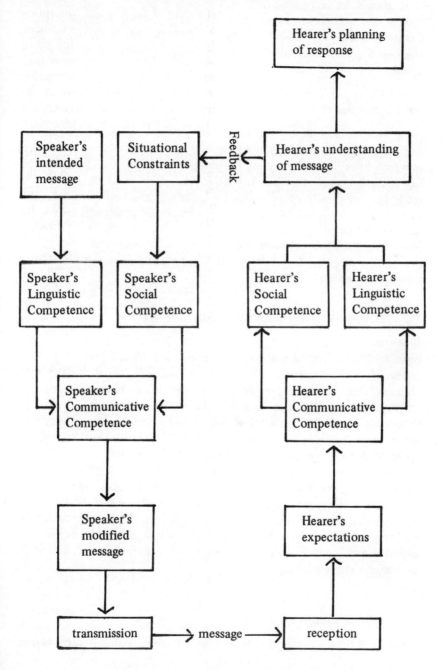

modifiers of the speaker's next intended message.

It should be recognized that this is only a partial model. Interested readers are recommended to study the proposal for a Speaker-Hearer Grammar made by Rigter and Moore (1974) and in particular their Diagram 5 which exemplifies the major elements omitted from the model above.

3.1.5 *Summary*

We have been considering the nature of a functional model of language and attempting to outline models for language use by looking at the ways in which information theory, anthropology, sociology and social psychology view language. This has led us to the point at which we need to recognize the grossly oversimplified picture we have been presenting. We must now try to specify (1) the *communication channels* available to the speaker and hearer, (2) the *kinds of information* carried by these channels, (3) the mediating *situational constraints* which influence and interact with the choice of channel and (4) type of *information content* involved in face-to-face speech events.

3.2 COMMUNICATION CHANNELS AND CONTENT

If we shift our attention from language as defined by linguistics — the code itself described in terms of the grammar, lexis and phonology or in terms of the competence of the ideal speaker-hearer — to the total communication system available to man, we recognize immediately that language use consists not only of grammatically correct but socially acceptable utterances and writing backed up by a wide range of communication skills including the choices of such diverse features as voice quality, speed of delivery, gesture, proximity and even dress, posture and so forth. Though the linguist is not primarily interested in these ancillary channels, he must recognize that a functional model of situated language use has to take them into account in some way, since they do, in fact, play a part in communication and, indeed, may be crucial to the efficiency of the exchange of information. We shall consider below, first what channels are available and secondly, what total information is transmitted during the course of a verbal exchange.

3.2.1 *Communication Channels*

It has been long recognized that though 'we speak with our vocal organs

. . . we converse with our entire bodies' (Abercrombie, 1968, p. 55), and it is not without significance that teachers of rhetoric, i.e. of effective communication, were at great pains to instil, not merely the correct choice of words but also the appropriate supporting social skills of elocution – vocal and gestural (Bell and Bell, 1878, pp. 18-28) – through exercises on articulation, accentuation and intonation.

In order to introduce some degree of system into what, at first appears to be an extraordinarily hetrogeneous mass of means of communication, it will be necessary to distinguish the various channels along three parameters: independent-dependent, static-dynamic audio-visual, drawing on work by several linguists (Crystal and Quirk, 1964; Abercrombie, 1968; and Laver and Hutcheson, 1972).

3.2.1.1   *The Independent-Dependent Parameter*
The independent channel *par excellence* is, of course, language itself but, given that nods, head shakes, interjections such as 'tut tut' can act as surrogates for words, we need to recognize a second channel which we shall term *pseudo-linguistic*.

The dependent channels supplement the independent but cannot replace them in the sense used above, though we shall see below that certain kinds of information are far better transmitted by them than by purely linguistic means. This class of channel, which includes such diverse features as posture, spatial proximity, dress, gesture, facial expression, qualities of voice, etc,. we shall term *paralinguistic*.

3.2.1.2   *Static-Dynamic Parameter*
Static channels include both writing and such paralinguistic phenomena as posture, traditionally thought of as part of the 'setting' of the speech event, while dynamic channels consist of speaking, gestures, voice qualities and the like.

The dichotomy is not an entirely happy one however, in view of the fact that a static 'deadpan face', for example, may easily change into a smiling one during the course of interaction. Nevertheless, it may stand for the moment as a useful, though arbitrary, division.

3.2.1.3   *The Audio-Visual-Tactile Parameter*
While the essential distinction between the two major media of linguistic communication –speech and writing – can be clearly seen in terms of the use by the first of the audio and the second of the visual channel, both the pseudo- and paralinguistic channels have both media available to them. We need too to take into account the tactile component of communication: the kiss, the handshake, the pat on the head all communicate and, at times,

'louder than words'.

The distinction between the pseudolinguistic nod, which is visual, and the interjection, which is audible, is clear, as is the visual element of the gesture, but a very large number of paralinguistic features are realized via the audio rather than the visual channel. These include all the prosodic and paralinguistic features (as the terms are used in Crystal and Quirk, 1964, see esp. table 5, pp. 66-8) of tone, tempo, prominence, pitch range, rhythmicity, tension, voice quality, verbal qualification and pause. We shall list these in more detail below, since many of them have a crucial role in face-to-face communication, as modifiers and even as reversers, of the linguistic meanings of utterances. We shall attempt too, to group these features in terms of the linguistic units within which they typically occur.

At the level of the *tone group* (Halliday, 1967) a choice of tone — fall, rise, fall-rise, rise-fall, etc. — has to be made, and clearly it is possible to make choices within the pitch range of the tones chosen — narrow, wide, monotonous — which will have communicative implications.

The *foot* — the unit of rhythm — can equally be modified across a range extending from staccato to legato, by the overall tempo of delivery — allegrissimo to lentissimo — and the degree to which the tempo is varied — accelerando to ralentando, giving the impression of a clipped or drawled speech.

The *syllable* can likewise be modified in its delivery by the degree of tension — slurred, lax, tense, — with which it can be pronounced, by the prominence given to it — pianissimo to fortissimo — and by the overall voice quality assigned to it — whisper, huskiness, falsetto, resonance and so forth.

Pause phenomena, though to some degree predictable (Goldman-Eisler, 1968), can occur at any point in an utterance — silent pauses or *ums* and *ers* — while the remaining qualifiers — laughs, giggles, tremulousness, sobs, cries — though often occurring on syllables or as fillers in pauses, can extend over a whole utterance or several and are, so to speak, talked *through*, rather than included in, the utterance.

We are now in a position to represent the system of channels available to the language user in a schematic form (Figure 3.6 below) but before we do, a point should be made which is of crucial importance to the argument. The available choices of channel and the need for choice to be correlated with other social skills makes the fact that we are dealing with a highly complex but necessarily rule-governed system self-evident. In view of this, it is all the more remarkable that in all the world's cultures the normal native six-year-old child has already mastered the system, at least in its essential; surely, as Pittenger and Smith declare (1957, p. 62), the greatest intellectual achievement the individual ever makes and one which forces us

FIGURE 3.6

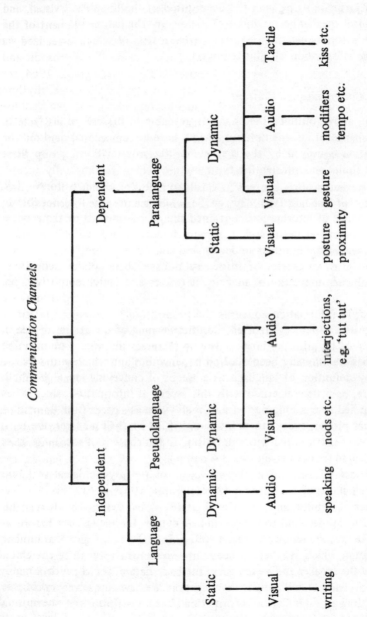

yet again to reaffirm our belief that sociolinguistics must take upon itself a task far larger in scope than the description of the linguistic competence of the ideal speaker-hearer and seek to specify the nature and function of the user's communicative competence by means of which he is able to exchange information with his fellows.

3.2.2 Communication Content

We have, above, outlined the channels available to the user in the face-to-face exchange of information but, as yet, have not considered the kinds of information conveyed by the system nor the interrelationships between channel choice and information type.

By 'communication content', we intend here not so much the 'macro-functions' of language (Halliday, 1973), which we propose to cover below, but the kinds of information contained in and transmitted by the process of communication itself, and in some instances recognized and intended by the speaker and in others under far less conscious control.

Three gross categories of information have been isolated: cognitive, indexical and interaction management (Laver and Hutcheson 1972, pp. 11f.).

Cognitive information concerns the propositional or factual content of the linguistic structures involved, i.e. the meaning of the utterance is seen in terms of its primary, idea-conveying features; the aspect of meaning which has traditionally been studied in semantics and which underlies the everyday definition of language as a means of conveying ideas. We shall, therefore, be little concerned with this aspect of information, since it has been studied over a long period and is still seen as a part of the domain of linguistics proper, except to point out that, as we shall see later, the term 'cognitive' needs a rather wider definition in the context of sociolinguistics than it has so far been given (see 3.4 below).

Indexical information conveys aspects of the psychological make-up and social status of the speaker (Abercrombie, 1967, p. 6) – his identity, attributes, attitudes and emotional state – and serves to portray his attitude to himself and to others and to define the role he sees himself as playing in the interaction (Argyle, 1969, p. 140). Now, it is just this kind of information which the hearer needs in order to interpret fully the utterances of the speaker and which form the basic data of social-psychological, sociological and sociolinguistic investigation. We have, ourselves, in chapter 2 been drawing on indexical information in our descriptions of the sources of inter- and intra-personal variation in language.

Interaction management information is exchanged as a means of initiating, continuing and terminating the interaction itself, since, for there to be successful communication, the participants must adopt positions relative to each other in space to make an exchange possible, have shared procedures for beginning, changing roles, providing feedback, marking stages in the transaction and finally bringing it to a conclusion.

It is of some interest that the first type of information, – cognitive – tends to be more or less under the conscious control of the speaker and to form the major part of the verbal planning processes which underlie his speech production, while the other two types – indexical and information management – go virtually unrecognized, at least by the speaker. The hearer, in contrast, is well aware of all three kinds of information and is dependent on the two last in his assessment of the role he is to play and the meaning he is to attach to what he hears. One has only to conduct the simple experiment on the telephone of not saying 'yes', or the like, every five seconds or so to realize, from the frantic 'hello, hello, are you there?' such an action illicits, how dependent on feedback, for example, the speaker actually is.

Equally, the 'stage marking' information involved in interaction is crucial to the structuring of discourse as a whole and indeed recent work (Schegloff, 1968; Sinclair and Coulthard, 1975) seems to be demonstrating the existence of interaction blocs with fairly clear beginnings and ends within which sentences (traditionally the largest unit handled by linguistics) form a component part.

3.2.3   *The Integration of Channel Choice and Information*

It is clear that all channels of communication are open to the participants during an interaction and equally clear that all or several tend to be activated simultaneously. Are there, then, any strong correlations between channel choice and information type? It appears that, to some extent, there are.

Cognitive information tends to be conveyed mainly by linguistic means and on occasion by pseudolinguistic replacements of linguistic items, although such substitutions are narrow in scope, little more than affirmation and negation.

Indexical information is carried by all three channels; the speaker's linguistic choices will imply a great deal about his state and status, so too will his selections from the pseudo- and paralinguistic features at his disposal.

Interaction management tends to be facilitated through the paralinguistic channel – head and eye movements particularly – although pseudolinguistic and occasionally linguistic means are adopted; rarely though, since the linguistic channel is normally already being used to full capacity in transmitting cognitive information. For example, it is normally only when speech is not face-to-face that actual verbal signals are needed for the handling of 'turn-taking' and the like. The radio operator's formulaic 'over', 'over and out' are excellent cases of this. A schematic representation of the network of relationships between channel and content is given below in Figure 3.7

FIGURE 3.7   *Relationships Between Channel and Content*

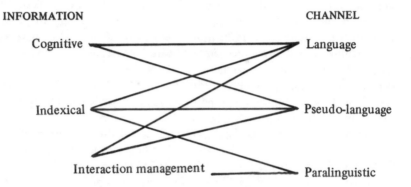

3.2.4   *Summary*

We have seen that the skills required on the part of both speaker and hearer in a speech event are of a high order of complexity and clearly represent an integrated system, in which choice of channel and information content are closely correlated. Before we can go further however, we need to look more closely at the components of the communication situation and the functions of language within it. In the course of this it will become even more apparent that communication skills are rule-governed and not haphazard and can be presented as a model of the underlying communicative competence on which the individual draws as he participates in speech events with other individuals.

3.3   THE COMPONENTS OF THE COMMUNICATION SITUATION

In 3.1.4 above, we outlined a psychological model of language use, presented in schematic form in Figure 3.1, limited to a dyadic interaction, i.e. between a single speaker and a single hearer. One major feature of this model, which now needs to be greatly amplified, is the element labelled 'situational constraints' — a crucial influence on the speaker's intended message, as he modifies it for actual transmission. In short, what is now needed is some kind of listing of the component parts of the situation in which the act of communication takes place, still limited for the moment to face-to-face interaction between only two participants. We shall return below (4.3) to the greater complexity involved in larger scale intra- and inter-group communication.

3.3.1   *Linguistic Approximations*

Traditionally, three factors have been long recognized as the prime components of the communication situation – speaker, hearer and topic – and we have been implicitly or explicitly assuming such a three-way division in the models outlined above. We shall see below that a model of this kind is too crude to handle even dyads and certainly impracticable, where the number of participants is greater than two. However, as a beginning, we shall consider some earlier approaches to the specification of the component parts of the context of human communication and then go on to suggest improvements of several kinds.

3.3.1.1   *Firth (1964)*

An early and quite elaborate model was suggested in the 1930s by Firth in his notion of the *Context of Situation*, derived from Malinowski for whom it was '. . . a bit of the social process which can be considered apart and in which a speech event is central and makes all the difference. . . ' (Firth, 1964, p. 182). For Firth, the context of situation was a '. . . schematic construct to apply to language events. . . a group of related categories at a different level from grammatical categories but rather of the same abstract nature' (ibid.), consisting of 'a convenient abstraction at the social level of analysis. . . ' and providing '. . . the basis of a hierarchy of techniques for the statement of meanings. The statement of meaning cannot be achieved by one analysis, at one level, in one fell swoop' (ibid., p. 183). Hence, the notion of Context of Situation was, for Firth, crucial in the semantic description of language and the key factor in his contextual theory of language which, together with his stated aim – 'to link language studies with social human nature' (ibid., p. 186) – certainly places him as one of the Founding Fathers of sociolinguistics.

The actual components of the context of situation were listed as follows:-

1. The relevant features of participants – persons and personalities including their verbal and nonverbal actions.
2. The relevant objects.
3. The effect of the verbal action.

Although some of these factors are rather vaguely stated, we shall see that the concept has had large repercussions on the study of situated language use, particularly in the work of 'neo-Firthian' linguists such as Halliday (1973), whose approaches to a theory of speech functions we shall consider below and Crystal and Davy (1969) *inter alia*, in research on 'register'.

Given that the categories suggested by Firth are rather imprecise and that the use of the term 'relevant' begs a very large question indeed (see Pike's *emic-etic* distinction 3.3.2.2 below), the context of situation does provide a first approximation to a specification of the components of the communication situation and hence a step towards answering both the question 'how is it that, in spite of a lack of perfect and consistent correlations between language and situation, the native speaker, given the text alone (a tape recording say) is often able, with a considerable degree of accuracy, to reconstruct the situation?' and its corollary 'given a situation, how does such a person produce language which is appropriate?' We are already, as Firth said, '. . . a long way from de Saussure's (1915) mechanistic structuralism' (p. 183) and moving towards a definite sociolinguistic orientation.

3.3.1.2 *Gregory (1967)*

An important advance on Firth's model was made by Gregory in an attempt to specify the relationships between linguistic choice and situational elements. In brief, three categories were suggested — mode, field and tenor of discourse — which correlate with three situational features — the medium, role and addressee relationship — roughly equated with the channel, topic and relationship between the participants. He also suggested an additional variable within the choice of medium — crudely speech and writing — which clarifies the nature of 'style' in a rather useful way. It is obvious, even from a cursory glance at written texts, that there is a striking difference between those written to be read silently, to be read aloud, to be read as if not read and so forth, e.g. a novel, a poem, dialogue in a play. A further substantial step forward. (see Figure 3.8 below) For example, it is by adopting a device from poetry, the rhymed couplet, that Shakespeare marks the ends of many of his scenes.

3.3.1.3 *Crystal and Davy (1969)*

As a prerequisite for a stylistic analysis of English, Crystal and Davy were led to a reassessment of the notion 'situation' and its correlation with linguistic choice and proposed, in place of the rather loose term 'situational variables', a set of 'dimensions of situational constraint' and to the attempt

FIGURE 3.8

Types of Medium

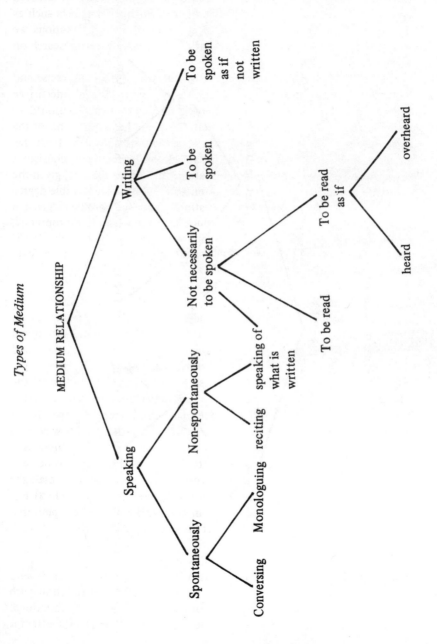

FIGURE 3.9

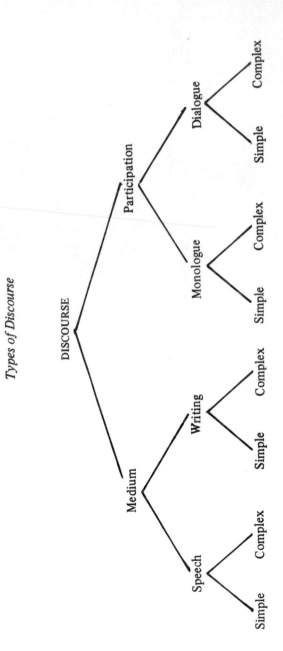

Types of Discourse

to specify 'the role every linguistic feature plays. . . in terms of one or more of these dimensions' (ibid., p. 64). Among the constraints are listed the familiar dialect and addressee relationship features suggested above and, in order to further disambiguate some of the medium relationships, the notions of simple/complex medium and participation. This permits the contrast of writing which is written to be read, with writing written to be read as if not being read: for example, a radio news broadcast as against the dialogue of a radio play. Equally, a monologue which does not contain changes in accent and so forth on the part of the speaker may be contrasted with one which does (see Figure 3.9 below). Here a clear example is the joke in which the teller adopts a single accent for a single character as against the joke in which there are several characters and the teller makes use of different accents to distinguish them.

Linking all three of the approximations outlined above – Firth, Gregory and Crystal and Davy – is an important orientation which marks them off from what is to follow. In each case, the correlation sought is between linguistic forms contained in a text and situational variables of various kinds, i.e. the approach is linguistic rather than sociolinguistic, since the language is, so to speak, 'given' and 'explained' in terms of its 'extralinguistic' context. Crystal and Davy (1969) state their objective most clearly in their hypothesis 'any use of language displays certain linguistic features which allow it to be identified with one or more extra-linguistic contexts' (p.11).

3.3.2   Sociolinguistic Approximations.

So far, we have been considering approaches to the correlation of linguistic to situational variables which have had an essentially linguistic orientation: proceeding from form to function. Below we shall look at the converse, sociolinguistic approach, taking function first and asking what forms are typically chosen, in specific situations, in the achievement of specific social goals.

3.3.2.1   *Hymes (1972)*

Work on the 'ethnography of speaking' has led to several specifications of the situational components involved during communication between individuals, the most clearly articulated of which appears to be that exemplified by Hymes in which he proposed a taxomony containing no less than 13 elements, neatly reduceable to the happy acronym SPEAKING, not all of which are ever activated simultaneously however. Each is listed below:

1. *Setting* and *Scene* — refer to the general physical circumstances in which the communication event takes place, particularly the time and place, in the case of the first term and the cultural definition of the occasion in the second. For example, a lecture might be defined within a *setting* such as, 'the lecture theatre, 11.0 a.m. Thursday 14 March 1974' and the *scene* 'relatively formal'.

2. *Participants* — speaker, sender, addresser and hearer, receiver, audience or addressee. For example, in a dyad, face-to-face communication would involve a speaker and a hearer, while a telephone conversation would require a sender and a receiver and in large interactions like a lecture an addressor and addressee(s) or audience.

3. *Ends* — divided into *outcomes* — results, intended and unintended — and *goals* — individual and general. For example, a lecture may be intended to be illuminating and entertaining but in the event turn out to be vague and boring, while the lecturer's goal may be to engender interest in an aspect of sociolinguistics but that of the audience to spend an hour in a warm comfortable atmosphere!

4. *Act sequence* — the *form* and *content* of the message: how and what is said; the 'words' and the 'topic'. To continue the example of lecture, the *form* would be fifty minutes or so of text analysable by well-tried, and some less well-tried, techniques of descriptive linguistics, while the *content* might be subjected to semantic analysis of various kinds and an integrated description of the two attempted.

5. *Key* — the manner in which the message is conveyed, e.g. the lecture might be delivered in a precise way or perhaps in a light-hearted way.

6. *Instrumentalities* — these include both the *channels* employed (in the sense used above 3.2.1) and the *forms of speech*, language, dialect, etc. To return yet again to the lecture, the *channel* would be essentially spoken language, including the ancillary pseudo- and paralinguistic resources suggested above and probably back-up use of the written channel; handouts, notes on the blackboard and so on, while the *form* be the lecturer's own brand of English, possibly with shifts into other varieties, where the topic required examples from other dialects and even into other languages, where appropriate quotations from the works of non-English speaking linguists were incorporated into his notes.

7. *Norms* — both the *interaction* itself contains norms of behaviour on the part of the participants and the *interpretation* of the communication can be similarly seen as containing norms, in the sense of expectations, particularly on the part of the receivers. In a lecture for example, the British lecturer and his audience usually expect a mono-

logue, free of interruptions, with questions left until the end, although each group has considerable latitude in this respect and often the lecturer will state, at the beginning of a course, what rules he expects the interaction to follow. Similarly, the audience will expect the cognitive meaning of the utterances they hear to be those intended by the speaker. They will not, unless they are accustomed to the lecturer's style, (i.e. key), expect remarks to be ironic for example, indeed one of a lecturer's greatest disappointments is that his most humorous remarks fall flat, simply because the audience is not expecting them to be anything other than serious.

8. *Genres* – categories which can be fairly clearly identified through the linguistic forms they typically employ; the lecture is actually a good example of a particular *genre* and, of course, the term has a considerable history in literary studies.

3.2.2.2   *Pike (1967)*

We have so far been dodging a particularly intractable philosophical issue which we cannot avoid any longer. It has been assumed all along that, in some sense, the 'same' linguistic choices tend to recur in the 'same' situations but, in an absolute sense, all situations are unique non-recurring events. This problem was faced by Pike in his attempt to create a unified theory of human behaviour which would naturally include language and we have already drawn upon his proposed solution earlier in our discussion of anthropological models of communication (3.1.2). A way out of the dilemma is to recognize that all societies treat some groups of situations as so minimally different that, for practical purposes, they are considered to be the same. Hence, there must be, in any situation, features or combinations of features which can be varied without a change of classification and others which cannot. The phonetician is actually in a very similar situation when faced by the need to describe the phonemic structure of a language he does not know, on the basis of a heterogeneous mass of varying phonetic data: which, and how many features must two items share before they can be classified as variants of the same underlying norm? In traditional phonological terms, how many of the same phonetic features must occur in two phones, before they can be classified as allophones of the same phoneme? Typically the appeal has been to meaning – does the difference produce 'different words'?

Pike's suggestion was that, on the analogy of phonology, other types of human social behaviour might be analysable in the same way by postulating features which were *etic* and did not change the 'meaning' of the event for the participants, in contrast with *emic* features which did. It might be, to push the analogy even further, that there are, as it were, 'allofeatures' –

some perhaps in complementary distribution (like the two /1/ realizations in RP) and others in 'free variation'. How far the analogy can be sustained will clearly be an issue to be resolved by future empirical research but it does seem plain that some emic-etic notion is of value and may lead to a recognition of some hierarchical ranking of the components we have been considering above.

3.3.3 *Summary*

In this section, we have been outlining, from a microsociolinguistic viewpoint, the component parts of the communication situation involving two participants, (Hymes' model can, of course, cope with more than dyadic interaction). Two types of approach have been suggested, the linguistic — attempting to correlate form with social function — and the sociolinguistic — attempting to begin with function and correlate that with linguistic form. Several problems still remain, hence the label 'approximations' attached to the suggested models and chief among these are a clearer specification of the term 'functions' of language and the expansion of the model to account for communication within and between larger social groups. The next section will attempt to clarify the meaning of function but the relationship of language choice to social group will have to be deferred until the next chapter.

3.4   LANGUAGE FUNCTIONS

Although we have considered the kind of information carried willy-nilly by the communication channels available to speakers and hearers, we have only commented very briefly on the kinds of intentional information conveyed by speakers. This is clearly an omission which should be rectified, if only for the commonsense reason that people use language in order to exchange information — that is its primary purpose. We shall, below, look at suggestions about the kinds of purposive information language exchanges and then in Section 3.5 take up again the implication, running through the whole of this chapter, that the functioning of so complex a system as language within a society cannot but be rule-governed, that the rules can be stated, that such rules form part of 'the knowledge of the language' which the speaker has and therefore their description must be included in the goals of descriptive linguistics.

3.4.1   *The Traditional Three-Function Model*

Traditionally, three supposedly separate but actually rather overlapping functions have been suggested for language, the distinction resting on the kinds of information being conveyed by each.

The prime function of language has been assumed to be the *cognitive*: the expression of ideas, concepts, thoughts. This corresponds well with the 'commonsense' view of the purpose of language as a vehicle for the expression of thought and, indeed, has, at least until recently, been the generally accepted opinion of the teaching profession for whom users of non-standard varieties of the language have been viewed as both linguistically and culturally deprived (see Robinson, 1972, esp. pp. 154-72 for a spirited defence of the Restricted-Elaborated Code theory and Baratz and Baratz, 1970, for opposing arguments).

The second function, the *evaluative*, has been thought of as conveying attitudes and values and the third, the *affective*, as transmitting emotions and feelings.

It is of some interest to realize that the same division appears to co-occur in the types of language use singled out by the different branches of the human sciences. Linguistics and philosophy have tended to focus on the cognitive, sociology and social psychology on the evaluative and psychology and literary criticism on the affective.

3.4.2   *Modifications to the Traditional Model*

Dissatisfaction with the three-function model has led, particularly since 1960, to several suggested revisions two of the most interesting of which – those proposed by Jakobson and Halliday – will be outlined below.

FIGURE 3.10   *Jakobson's Aspects and Functions*

ASPECT	FUNCTION
Addresser	Emotive, Expressive, Affective
Addressee	Conative
Context	Referential, Cognitive, Denotative
Message	Poetic
Contact	Phatic, Interaction Management
Code	Metalinguistic

3.4.2.1   *Jakobson's Language Functions*

Although primarily concerned with the nature of literary language, Jakobson's model (1960) provides a means of listing six major language functions by indicating how the shift of focus from one aspect of the speech event to another defines the function of the language used in it.

We shall give the six aspects and their associated functions in tabular form and then give examples:

Examples
1. *Emotive:* the addresser aims at the direct expression of his attitude to the topic or situation.
2. *Conative:* focus is on the person(s) addressed. Most typical of this function is the use of vocatives and imperatives – calling the attention of another or requiring them to carry out some action.
3. *Context:* probably the most common function of language: focusing on the object, topic, content of the discourse.
4. *Message:* focusing on the message itself and for its own sake.
5. *Contact:* the language used for the initiation, continuation and termination of linguistic encounters – the interaction management referred to above (3.2.2) – arises from focusing on the contact element of the situation.
6. *Code:* focus on the linguistic code itself results in a metalinguistic function, e.g. the whole of descriptive linguistics has, or ought to have, a purely metalinguistic function as the primary purpose of its use of language.

Jakobson's model displays very clearly the problems of attempting to set up some kind of taxonomy for the functions of language. It is, in one sense, an advance on the earlier three-function model simply because it contains twice as many categories. But this is exactly where the danger lies. It does not seem inconceivable that we could keep on creating new functions forever but still not have a satisfactory system in the end, simply because many utterances are, even in context, multifunctional.

Following Jakobson, several alternative systems have been proposed (many summarized and added to in Robinson, 1972, pp. 42-56) but we shall consider only one – Halliday's – before concluding this chapter and moving on to the next.

3.4.2.2   *Halliday's Language Functions*

In a series of papers Halliday (1973) explored the relationship between function and use in child and adult language and proposed a theory of sociological semantics in which he demonstrates the collapse of the seven functions of child language (pre-school children that is) into three macro-functions which serve adults.

The child, he argues has seven language functions which correlate very closely, initially in a one-to-one way, with form, e.g. a child wishing to ask for a sweet is likely to say 'I want. . . ' rather than the multitude of possible utterances available to the adult. Because of this very close connection between language form and social function in the child, Halliday (1973) suggests 'The language system of the very young child is, effectively, a set of restricted varieties. . . What the child does with language tends to determine its structure' (p. 27). We shall return later to the notion of 'restricted language' and limit ourselves here to proposals for modelling the unrestricted use of language by adults; a substantial problem, since 'Every adult linguistic act, with a few broadly specifiable exceptions is serving more than one function at once' (ibid., p. 34).

During the course of maturation, Halliday suggests, the seven discrete functions of child language are 'gradually replaced by a more highly coded and more abstract, but also simpler, functional system' (ibid, p. 36.). This system contains only three macrofunctions – the ideational, the inter-personal and the textual – which to some degree supplement and cut across the three traditional functions. We shall consider each in turn:

The *ideational* function of language corresponds closely to the cognitive function discussed about (3.2.2 and 3.4.1) but is broader, since it also includes, under the general heading the 'expression of experience', the evaluative and affective aspects of attitude, value, emotion and feeling. The ideational function of language, then, is 'concerned with the expression of experience including both the processes within and beyond the self – the phenomena of the external world and those of consciousness – and the logical relations deducible from them' (ibid., p. 99).

The *interpersonal* function subsumes the indexical and interaction management functions described above (3.2.2), since it 'expresses the speaker's role in the speech situation, his personal commitment and his interaction with others' (ibid.). It is this language function which 'serves to establish and maintain social relations', through which 'social groups are delimited, and the individual is identified and reinforced, since by enabling him to interact with others language also serves in the expression and development of his own personality' (Halliday, 1970, in Lyon (ed.), 1970, p. 143).

The *textual* function is concerned with the structuring of the speech act – the choice of grammatically and situationally appropriate sentences and the ordering of the content in a cohesive and logical manner suitable for the interaction as a whole.

The integration of these macrofunctions of language or, more properly of the grammar, within a theory of situated language use hinges on the relationship of the semantic component to the social on the one hand and the linguistic on the other. As Halliday sees it, the input to the semantics is social in contrast with its output which is 'linguistic' (ibid., p. 100). The theory, then, depends on an intermediate level of structure — the semantic — between the general social 'uses of language' and the general linguistic 'forms of language', i.e. without such a specifying element, any form could be employed for any use. The macrofunctions are seen as the mechanism which converts 'meanings' into 'grammatical systems' and ultimately into grammatical structures and speech acts. Perhaps a diagram might make the relationships clearer (Fig. 3.11 based on diagram in Halliday, 1970, p. 101).

FIGURE 3.11   *Situations and Language Systems*

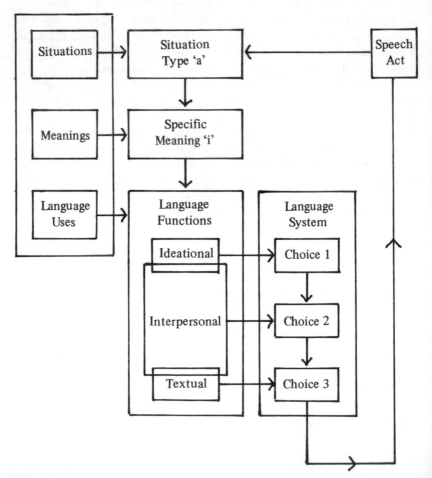

We have taken some liberties with Halliday's model in order to integrate it with earlier suggestions – let us hope that in doing so we have not misinterpreted him.

In place of his term 'general', we have used Pike's term 'etic' and similarly 'emic' for 'specific'. The diagram is to be interpreted in the following way, reading from left to right: from all possible social situations a set of types can be isolated (in this diagram only one is depicted); similarly for all possible meanings one which corresponds to the specific situation is chosen; next, from all possible uses of language one, modified by the remaining two, function is chosen; next, each function demands choices from the total linguistic system of the language and the combination of these creates the speech act chosen for the specific situation.

3.4.3   Summary

We have been surveying the notion 'functions of language' and have, in doing so, moved away from the traditional three-function view – cognitive, evaluative, affective – to a more abstract model. This, though containing three terms, differs in important ways from the older view, since it not only includes many of the sets of language uses referred to earlier under the heading of Communication Content (3.2.2) but also makes a bridge between sociologically-orientated linguistics and descriptive linguistics on the one hand and philosophy on the other. Specifically, the ideational function appears to correspond to the 'nucleus' in Seuren (1969), the proposition in Fillmore (1968) and Searle (1965), while the interpersonal correlates with their 'operator', 'modality' and 'illocutionary force' respectively.

3.5   CONCLUSION

In this chapter, we have been examining the component parts of functional models of language, comparing linguistic, information theory, anthropological, sociological and social-psychological approaches to the description of situated language use. Next we considered how information is conveyed by language – what channels are available in face-to-face communication – and what the information exchanged consists of. The answer to the questions 'how?' and 'what?' turned out to be far more complex than at first seemed possible and it was only with difficulty that we were able to suggest tentative correlations between channel choice and information content. When we turned to the situational constraints under which the user of a language is forced to operate, we found an even more complex set of interrelated factors, any one of which, it seemed, might, by changing itself, cause a change in the 'meaning' of the speech event. This led us to the final section of the chapter in which we reconsidered the notion of 'function' and offered as a final tentative outline of the production side of the speech event Halliday's model with its three macrofunctions — ideational, interpersonal and textual — encompassing the vast array of language uses available to the user and acting as the interface between the extra-linguistic situation and the semantics of the language on the one hand and the grammar (in the broad sense of the whole code system) on the other.

We have made some progress but are still faced by two large issues — such a complex system must be rule-governed and we have yet to specify what such rules would be like and where within the models we have been outlining they would operate — and we have, all along, limited our definition of 'communication' to a dyadic interaction, without facing up to the fact that social groups, more often than not, consist of more than two members and social groups themselves can communicate with other groups to the extent of world-wide mass communication.

Hence in the next chapter, we are committed to attempting to consider the notion of rules of language use and of examining interaction within and between larger groups than the relatively simple one-to-one, speaker-hearer participation of the dyad.

4
Functional Models of Language
-Rules and Dynamics

In the previous chapter, we listed what appear to be the major components and functions of a model of language in use. We did not, however, attempt to specify the rules which are required to relate our notions of language as a system to the functional model we are aiming at. In this chapter, therefore, we shall be concerned with outlining the kinds of rule by means of which or in accordance with which language interacts with elements outside itself (see Feibleman and Friend, 1945).

A further limitation to our treatment so far, of functional models of language, has been that, almost entirely, our attention has been focused on interaction within the dyad. This may have helped to give a clearer picture of the elements involved but has inevitably had the effect of obscuring the more complex issues involved in the explanation of communication among many, rather than between a pair of, individuals.

There are, then, two major aims in this chapter. First, to consider what rules for language use might look like and second, to expand the model to cope with groupings of users larger than the individual speaker and interlocuter. This will take us, via groups, roles, domains of use, codes and codeswitching, to bilingualism: the borderland between micro- and macrosociolinguistics.

4.1   TYPES OF RULE

Before considering the rules involved in a functional model of language, we need to specify what exactly is intended by the term 'rule'.

One definition of a rule might be along the lines of 'a formal statement which relates elements of an abstract system to a model of that system'. Such a view would be consistent with the usage of many philosophers of science (e.g. Nagel, 1961, pp. 90f.). The function of a rule is to assign content of an empirical kind to a system by relating the abstract calculus of the system to the concrete data of observation and experiment. Hence, a set of rules is the means by which systems are manifested as models. How such rules are expressed will depend on the type of system involved and the intentions of the investigator. We shall, therefore, consider two contrasting pairs of types of rule — descriptive versus prescriptive and categorical versus variable — before moving on to the rules of speaking which relate a system of language in use to a model of situated language.

4.1.1   Descriptive and Prescriptive Rules

The commonsense meaning of the term 'rule' — some principle to which an action conforms or is intended to conform — implies two contrasting attitudes. A rule may be *descriptive*, in the sense that it attempts to describe what actually happens or, alternatively, it may be *prescriptive*, laying down 'laws' about what ought or ought not to happen.

Traditional grammar and rhetoric have tended to emphasize rules of the second type, prescribing that the user of English, for example, ought to say 'It is I' rather than 'It's me'. Often such prescriptive rules have their origin in Greek or Latin convention and, more often than not, bear little relation to actual present-day English usage (see Palmer, 1971, pp. 13-26).

Linguistics, in this century, has attempted to take a descriptive rather than a prescriptive orientation to its data and sought to build up a body of rules based, not on ill-founded attitudes but on empirical evidence derived from the observation of actual, though in fact somewhat idealized, speech.

Prescriptive rules are not, however, without interest to the sociolinguist, since they do, after all, embody formulations of attitudes to language use which, even if ignored in practice by users, are indicators of social views of 'correctness' that influence such behaviour as stereotyping and hypercorrection: both important variables in style-shifting. Indeed, where the sociolinguist is involved in the application of his discipline in, for example, language planning, he will find himself needing to adopt a position of 'enlightened prescriptivism' based on evidence derived from empirical observation (see an extended discussion of the issues involved in Language Planning in chapter 7).

However, just as the orthodox linguist has as his primary goal the discovery of descriptive rules which govern the structure of the code, so the sociolinguist is essentially concerned to specify the descriptive rules by means of which social interaction through language is made possible (see 4.2).

4.1.2 *Categorical and Variable Rules*

An essential distinction between the rules of the physical sciences, logic and linguistics on the one hand and those of the social sciences on the other, can be seen in the *categorical* or invariant nature of the first and the *variable* or probabilistic nature of the second. The distinction is an important one and derives directly from the view of the systems of the first group as closed, in contrast with the openness of the second (see 2.3.1 above).

A closed system can be related to its models by means of categorical rules which, if correctly formulated, always apply. In logic and in linguistics, two very similar types of categorical rule have been used – *formation rules* in logic and *base rules* in linguistics and rules of *inference, conversion* or *transformation.* The difference between the two is probably most easily seen in the rules of a transformational-generative grammar. The base rules, like the formation rules of formal logic, have the function of defining sets of well-formed formulae – the kernel sentences of the earlier TG models, for example (Chomsky, 1957). The transformational rules, in contrast, act upon well-formed formulae by converting them, in some way, into different strings of symbols (which in a grammar eventually convert into sentences in a phonemic transcription), e.g. the passive transformation of the 1957 model, which converts active sentences into passives.

An open system, by contrast, is related to its models by means of variable rather than categorical rules, which apply only in a probabilistic manner. A variable rule will typically state, not, *if x then y*, but, *if x in the context of a. . . f then there is a p% probability of y.*

4.1.3 *Summary*

The 'rules' which we are seeking for language in use will be descriptive rules, in part categorical like those of logic and linguistics and in part variable like those of the social sciences This is inevitable, since socio-linguistic rules must, of necessity reflect the closedness of the system which constitutes the code and at the same time the openness of the system which makes up the socially situated use of the code. We shall expect to find categorical rules consistent with the mechanistic explanations expressed in the mechanical models of the physical sciences and, in addition, variable rules consistent with the probabilistic explanations and pattern and functional models of the social sciences (see 1.1 earlier on types of scientific description and 2.3.1 on language as a system).

4.2   RULES OF LANGUAGE USE

One statement of the aims of sociolinguistics (Fishman, 1970, p. 3) emphasizes the importance of the discovery and the specification of sociolinguistic rules in a very clear way: '. . . sociolinguistics seeks to discover the societal rules or norms that explain and constrain language behavior and the behavior toward language in speech communities'. The rules for language use or the *speaking rules* (Hymes, 1971), refer to or define the *communicative competence* of the user in terms of his ability to select the appropriate code and mode for specific settings and activities. Such rules will, because of the complex nature of the language system — partly open and partly closed (see 2.3.1 on this distinction) — be in part the invariant categorical rules of the code and in part variable rules more like those of the social sciences. We shall outline below two important attempts which have been made to draw up rules for particular aspects of language use: the rules governing speech acts suggested by Searle and those concerned with the appropriate choice of address form in English proposed by Ervin-Tripp (1973).

4.2.1   *Rules for Speech Acts*

We have already noted the work by Searle (1969) on *speech acts* in relation to the 'strong claim' of sociolinguistics (1.5.1). We need now to consider his further claims that 'speaking a language is performing speech acts' and that 'these acts are in general made possible by and performed in accordance with certain rules for the use of linguistic elements' (ibid., p.16).

Searle's original inspiration derives from earlier work by Austin (1958) in which the distinction is drawn between *constative* and *performative* linguistic acts, the second being later expanded into the notion of the *illocutionary* act (Austin, 1962) — the defining characteristic being that 'saying it makes it so'.

Searle makes use of this idea by distinguishing, within the act itself, the propositional content and the statement of that content element employed by the utterer. We shall need to consider these terms in a little more detail, since the use of illocutionary acts or speech acts implies rules of different kinds.

Propositional content is intended, by Searle, to express the common shared meaning which links apparently different speech acts, e.g. the utterances 'will John leave the room?', 'John will leave the room', 'John, leave the room!'. 'Would that John left the room', 'If John will leave the room, I will leave also' all share, in spite of their surface differences of form, a common proposition — the speaker, in each case, *refers* to a person

'John' and *predicates* the act of leaving the room of that person (Searle 1965, repr. in Giglioli (ed.), 1972, pp. 140f.).

The statement of the proposition, Searle contends, is a 'part of performing certain illocutionary acts' (ibid., p.141), i.e. the choice of linguistic features for the expression of the content.

The distinction between content and expression is, of course, a very ancient one but what makes Searle's approach different and valuable is the way in which it ties in well with the linguistic notion of deep and surface structure (Chomsky, 1957, etc.), i.e. the relationship between the underlying 'meaning' and the subcategories realized in the actual production and reception of speech acts by users of language. In addition, Searle proposes a 'function indicating device' which consists of rules for specifying the kind of *illocutionary force* the act is intended to have – a mechanism, that is very reminiscent of the transformations of TG. It is the idea of the rules contained in this mechanism, that we must consider next.

Two types of rule are proposed – regulative and constitutive – to distinguish those which *regulate* an already existing form of behaviour, from those which *create* the behaviour. For example, in a conversation between two people, let us call them A and B, communication is impaired, if both speak at once. This fact can be expressed in a *constitutive rule* – 'if A speaks when B is speaking (and the converse) communication will be impaired' – which cannot be broken, since the truth of the statement of the rule can be verified by observation. The same fact can equally be expressed by a *regulative rule* – 'A and B should not speak simultaneously' – the truth of which cannot be verified, i.e. it cannot be shown whether it is true or not, that A and B *should* behave in a particular way. Put slightly differently, constitutive rules are descriptive and regulative rules, normative or prescriptive, in the sense in which we have been using these terms above (4.1).

It is not our intention to list the rules suggested by Searle (see Searle, 1969, p. 126f., esp.) but it may be useful to show how their formal character differs from the rules of TG exemplified above (4.1.1)

Regulative rules can be expressed in terms of having an underlying imperative:

   if X *then* do Y

Constitutive rules, in contrast, are more likely to have the form:

   X counts as Y,

i.e. a constitutive rule defines and indeed creates the activity to which it applies, while a regulative rule merely makes the operation of the activity efficient (Searle, 1965, p. 139). Searle's own example of the rules of games shows how crucial not merely to the efficient playing of a game the rules are but how, without the rules, there would, indeed, be no game to play.

Yet another convergence of philosophical and linguistic interest can be seen here; the attempts, by numbers of linguists, to include, in the deepest and most abstract levels of their grammars, notions of 'performatives', e.g. the underlying form of 'I am tired' being 'I declare that I am tired'.

4.2.2   Rules of Address

We have been building up a formidable picture of the enormous range of elements from the language code available to the speaker and the great variety of situational features with which the linguistic choices have to be correlated and it must appear impossible to state in any ordered way, how it is that socially appropriate speech acts are ever produced but, as we shall see, two particular types of rule – alternation and co-occurrence – facilitate choice and make cohesive speech possible.

Ervin-Tripp (1973) suggests two types of rule – *alternation* and *co-occurrence* – as a partial answer to the question 'how is it that the speaker is able to choose socially appropriate formal linguistic items in speech events?' and the corollary, 'how, once the appropriate choice has been made, do similarly appropriate choices continue to be made, during the course of the interaction?'.

Alternation rules, as their name implies, control the choice of linguistic elements from the total repertoire of the user and represent the sociolinguistic equivalent of the paradigmatic axis of linguistics. That is, where a single context permits a choice from a set of elements, these are described as being in a paradigmatic relationship with each other – the suffixes of Latin conjugation and declensions; the ability of most English consonants to 'fill' the 'slot' – in the environment / – *en* /, giving *pen, Ben, ten, den... when* – is seen as parallelled in sociolinguistic description by such items as *sir, professor, Fred,* etc. which form the address system of the language.

Co-occurrence rules, in contrast, are syntagmatic – in effect, sequential – regulating the consistent choice of forms which, in sequence, reinforce a chosen alternative. In linguistics, the normal subject + verb + object order of English declaratives – *Brutus killed Caesar* – provides a clear example. In Latin too, the lexical items *Brutus, Caesarem necavit* express the English sentence above, irrespective, in principle at least, of the order in which they occur. In sociolinguistic descriptions, syntagmatic relationships can equally be found, e.g. the choice of the address form *professor,* for example, implies later uses, not only of the same term but orders

modified into requests, probably 'careful' pronunciation, choices of
'standard' grammatical structures and lexical items and so forth.

These two types of sociolinguistic rule will be illustrated below, by the
choice-rules of the address system in English, a system of formal linguistic
items which, as we shall see, has extremely powerful influence as a marker
of the differential status and role of the participants.

Whereas many European languages are able to mark status by choice
of pronoun in address – *tu-vous, du-Sie, tu-Lei,* etc. – the loss of the
thou-you contrast in modern English, except, of course, for such ritualized
speech acts as prayers, forces a less obvious set of choices on the speaker of
the language. Since *you* is no longer a marker or status, the alternatives
appear to be First Name (FN), Surname (S), Title (T) as well as avoidance
of a term (∅). Thus in a dyad, ignoring initials, nicknames and the like,
twenty-eight combinations each marked with a '+' seem to be available,
as displayed in the matrix below (Figure 4.1).

FIGURE 4.1   *English Address in Dyads*

A addresses B using / B addresses A using	FN	S	T	FNS	TFN	TS	∅
FN	+						
S	+	+					
T	+	+	+				
FNS	+	+	+	+			
TFN	+	+	+	+	+		
TS	+	+	+	+	+	+	
∅	+	+	+	+	+	+	+

Clearly, some combinations are extremely rare – the reciprocal use of
Title + First Name (TFN); 'Good morning Mr. John' 'Good morning
Mr Henry' – but others are equally clearly markers of a specific social
relationship – 'Good morning Smith' 'Good morning Brown' has very
strong indications of maleness as a characteristic of the speakers rather
than femaleness. There must be rules underlying these choices. We try to
illustrate them below.

It has been suggested that the choices within the address system of

English, for example, might be represented in terms of a model like the logical algorithms of computer programming (Ervin-Tripp, 1973) making use of the conventional diamond to represent a *yes-no* decision point and a rectangle an order to carry out a particular action; in this case (Figure 4.3) to choose one of a number of address forms.

A simple algorithm (Figure 4.2 below) for operating a record player will make the method and the conventions clear (National Computing Centre, 1973, 8/2). A word of warning is necessary, at this point, on the existential status of models of this kind, and indeed, linguistic models in general, restating what was said earlier (2.3.1.1) that such models are 'as if' models. Ervin-Tripp (op.cit. p.305) states the position extremely clearly:

> The diagram is not intended as a model of a process, of the actual decision sequence by which a speaker chooses a form of address or a listener interprets one. The two structures may or may not correspond. In any case, the task of determining the structure implicit in people's report of what forms of address are possible and appropriate is clearly distinct from the task of studying how people, in real situations and in real time, make choices. The criteria and methods of the two kinds of study are quite different.

In brief, models of this kind *specify* the component elements involved in choice but do not and cannot represent the decision-making process itself, since that is a task which falls clearly within the domain of psychology and neurology not sociolinguistics (see for example Gurney, 1973, pp 53-60; Morton, 1964).

This model is based on that suggested by Ervin-Tripp (ibid.) but contains a few minor adjustments. In the original model there was no way of avoiding a name or title except in the case of a child whose name was not known to the speaker. Since avoidance of an address form and the dependence on 'you' seem so common in English, the feature 'Desire to avoid Naming' has been added to the model and a number of rearrangements have been made to accommodate it.

Some notes may be required for the full interpretation of this diagram. The term *adult* may well be defined differently by individuals and groups — presumably, in Western society, school-leaving age, 16-18, marks the boundary between child and adult.

Status-marked situations may override normal selections, e.g. though one may be on reciprocal first name terms with one's Head of Department and would therefore normally address him by his first name in a meeting of Senate or the Board of Studies — both status-marked situations — the chosen address form will be 'Professor X' not his first name.

FIGURE 4.2

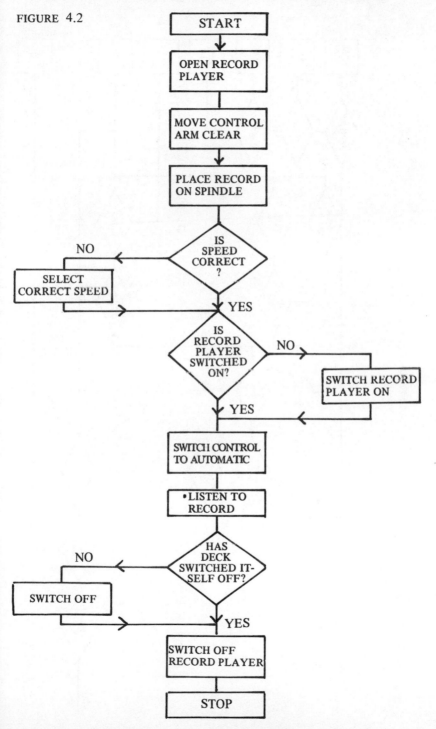

FIGURE 4.3

American Address

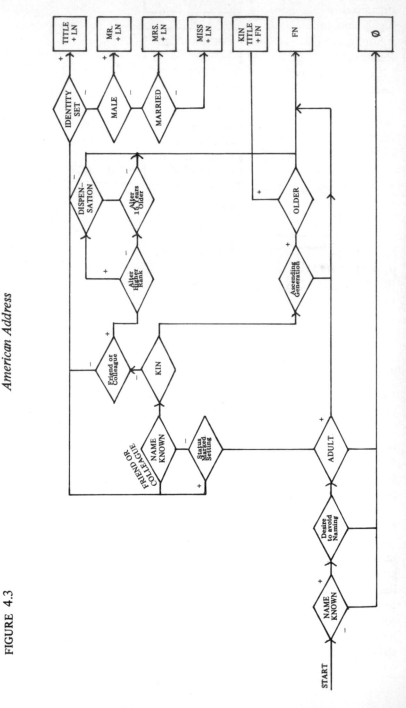

Rank refers to the status position of individuals within a hierarchically organized work group. Military ranks are, of course, the clearest and most highly institutionalized system of this kind but teacher-pupil, superior-subordinate, customer-shop assistant, etc., i.e. many of the Secondary Relationships of the social sciences (see 4.2.1 above).

Identity set refers to the occupational and courtesy titles given to possessors of certain statuses – Doctor, Professor, Father, etc.

Ascending generation is a notion required to prevent the choice of 'cousin' as an address form in present-day English (Elizabethan English, for example, permitted such a choice – 'dearest coz') but permit the use of 'aunt' or 'auntie'.

Two further points need to be made about these rules. Firstly, they are by no means universal. Different societies and different groups within the same society are likely to adopt different systems; necessarily so, since address terms, being markers of social relationships, can only form a homogeneous system within a homogeneous social group; a point which we shall expand upon below, in our consideration of the language uses of groups of various kinds (4.3.2). Secondly, should anyone doubt the rule-governed nature of this system, let him conduct the simple experiment of continuing, in a status-marked situation, to use the reciprocal first name form with his superiors and let him recognize the instant discomfort which will accompany such a decision!

4.2.3   Rules of Discourse

We commented earlier (1.3.1.3) in the discussion of the data of linguistics that the vast majority of descriptions of language have taken, as the upper limit unit of investigation, the sentence. A sociolinguistic description of language in use would, of necessity, need to take into account larger stretches of speech of which individual sentences or, perhaps more properly, utterances would form component parts. It is intended to present an outline of the models of discourse – language in use above the level of the sentence – in the final chapter of this book, so what is to be found here is a statement of the kinds of rule which regulate coherent discourse.

The distinction between categorical and variable rules has already been made (4.1.2) and a study of the rules suggested by sociolinguists tends to give the reader the impression that all are variable, sociolinguistics appearing to be primarily concerned with variation and with the creation of probabilistic explanations couched in rules which are themselves subject to variation and error as predictors of actual language use. Such a view is, however, mistaken. Labov (1970), for example, has demonstrated that, although many of the rules proposed for the explanation of sociolinguistic phenomena are indeed variable (see 2.4.2.3 earlier), there are others which are invariant. These are '. . . categorical rules which, given the proper input, always apply' (Labov, 1970, p.206), for example, Searle's rules for promising (Searle, 1969, ch.3), Sinclair and Coulthard's rules for the interpretation of interrogative clauses in the classroom (Sinclair and Coulthard, 1975, pp.30-3) and the sequencing, interpretation and production rules controlling discourse (Labov, 1970).

Labov suggests that these rules apply, not to the utterances themselves but the relationships between the *actions* performed by the utterances (ibid., p.208), i.e. in an ongoing linguistic interaction, acts relate to acts — often, though not exclusively manifested in actual utterances — and give rise to three types of rule: sequencing, interpretation and production.

Sequencing rules govern the order in which acts occur and link the rules of *production* which control the speaker's output with the *interpretation* rules which permit the hearer to understand the speaker's acts. Note that we are referring to acts *not* utterances as the minimal units of communication, since, as Labov (1970) insists, there '. . . are no simple one-to-one relations between actions and utterences', e.g. the teacher's utterance 'will you be quiet?' has the *form* of a question requiring a yes/no answer but woe betide the pupil who interprets it as having an interrogative *function.* The action performed by the utterance is one of ordering not enquiring.

Central to Labov's suggestions is the assumption that each individual has his own personal orientation, his own world-view built up from his own experiences. This orientation is in part different from and in part shared with other individuals: a point which we have already touched upon in our comments on the notion of the degree to which repertoires are shared by the participants in a communicative situation (3.1.1). Specifically, in a dyadic interaction between two individuals — labelled 'A' and 'B' — three types of event may be proposed. *A-events* which involve things which A knows about but B does not. *B-events* which are the converse. *AB-events* in which the knowledge is shared.

An example, and one which constitutes 'one of the simplest invariant rules of discourse' (Labov, 1970), may be given here: 'If A makes a statement about a B-event, it is heard as a request for confirmation'. Labov gives a number of examples which by their very oddity strengthen the validity of the rule, e.g. A: 'I feel hot today'. B: 'No', an example which native speakers of English would immediately recognize as a deviant piece of discourse. His rules are, naturally, more complex and comprehensive than this simple example would appear to suggest and connect well with the similarly motivated efforts of Searle to create or discover rules for the correct use of speech acts.

The distinction between A and B events has also been noticed by social psychologists in their work on types of interactive behaviour (see, for example, Argyle, 1969, p.171f.).

The attempt to create shared knowledge – AB-events – has been termed *converging behaviour* and its converse, the avoidance of the creation of shared knowledge, *diverging*. There is, in addition, the question of influence: *reciprocal* behaviour where one or both participants influence each other's behaviour in contrast with *non-reciprocal* or *parallel* behaviour where there is no influence. Reciprocal behaviour can, clearly, be subdivided depending on whether the influence is one-sided – A influencing B or the converse – or mutual. The two sub-types have been termed *asymetrical* and *symetrical* respectively.

It is interesting that much the same distinctions should have been arrived at by philosophers, social psychologists and sociolinguists and at very much the same time. It is also clear that we can now begin to propose rules which, even though they do not force participants into saying or doing a particular thing in an absolute sense, specify what the individual is likely to do, or more properly what he must do, if he wishes his actions to be interpretated by his interlocutor(s) in the way he himself intended. We are, of course, free, at least in principle, to say and do as we wish, i.e. to break the rules but at the cost of altering the nature of the interaction in which we are involved. It follows, then, that rather more of the rules of sociolinguistics turn out, given as Searle (1969) consistently puts it (p.126) 'normal input and output conditions obtain', to be categorical in nature and hence, expressible in terms which are compatible with the rules of logic and of orthodox linguistics – a further indication that not all 'performance' need be left out even of a model of the code.

4.2.4   *Summary*

In this section we have been looking at some of the rules which have been suggested for language use. We have of course not been able to list all the necessary rules, since no such set yet exists. What we have been able to do is to show how three rather different kinds of rule have been proposed by scholars from contrasting disciplines all of whom are converging on what is essentially the same problem: the specification of the rules which permit the ideal speaker-hearer to function as an active member of a speech community. A full specification of such rules would constitute a definition of the *communicative* rather than the merely *linguistic* competence of the individual and would be required to cope not with the idealized and isolated Chomskian 'speaker-hearer' but a speaking-hearing individual in action in communicative situations. This issue and the problem of discourse will be taken up again in Chapter 8 but the next section by considering groups, roles and codes will move our discussion forward towards the problems involved in larger scale interaction above the level of the dyad.

4.3   GROUPS, ROLES AND CODES

Up to this point, the context of language use that we have been considering has been the extremely limited one of the two-person interaction. Now we must move on to the more complex phenomena of intragroup communication between larger numbers of participants.

We might approach this topic by stating a number of assumptions. We assume that each individual is a member of several different types of group, within each of which he will have a *status* — an institutionalized or merely tacitly accepted place in the hierarchy of the group — to which will attach more or less *prestige* — influence or glamour, which will give a certain weighting to the opinions expressed by the status-holder. We further assume, that each status will have assigned to it particular *roles* — structured and rule-governed ways of participating in the activities of the group — that for each role there will be *norms* of behaviour, to which the individual actor will be; to a greater or lesser extent, expected to conform and that some of these norms will be norms of linguistic behaviour — appropriate language — *codes*. Finally, we see language as functioning in recurring situations — *domains* — in which role playing by the participants, in part, consists of the expression of appropriate behaviour, through the choice of the appropriate code from the linguistic repertoires of the individuals involved.

These terms will need to be defined more closely and their interrelationships specified with more precision below.

4.3.1   *Types of Group*

It is traditional, in the social sciences, to distinguish two contrasting types of relationship, each of which gives rise to differently organized kinds of group. We shall see that this dichotomy has strong correlations with sociolinguistic factors, particularly code-choice, not only in intra- but also inter-group communication, whether the choice be at the stylistic or dialect level of a single language or at the level of choice between or among languages in a multilingual speech community.

The defining characteristics of the two types of group fall under a pair of headings — physical and social — some of the constituents of which have already been touched upon in earlier discussions of face-to-face interaction:

Primary relationships are typified by close spatial proximity of long duration involving a small number of participants. Normal too is an agreement on goals, extensive knowledge of the other participants, an intrinsic valuation of the other participants and of the relationship – they are valued, in themselves, for what they are, rather than for what they are worth, in some utilitarian sense – and the individual tends to feel free and able to express himself spontaneously, hampered only by purely informal controls. In psychological terms, such relationships demonstrate an essential *solidarity* of attitudes and values – a factor of prime importance for code choice and use.

Secondary relationships conversely, are typified by spatial distance, short duration and larger numbers of participants. Disparate goals, extrinsic or use-orientated valuations, limited knowledge of the other participants and a feeling of inhibition, brought about by the operation of formal controls on the behaviour of those involved, characterize secondary relationships, as they express *power*, rather than solidarity.

We can therefore think in terms of primary relationships within primary social groups or, to use a term frequent in sociolinguistic description, *domains* – the family, containing mother-father, husband-wife, son-daughter, brother-sister relationships for example (see figure 4.4 below). Equally, secondary groups – the nation, the shop, the industrial organization – contain such relationships as ruler-subject, customer-shop assistant, manager-operative and so on. Naturally, the secondary group, by virtue of its sheer size, may well be divisible into smaller secondary or even primary groups, e.g. a work team (primary) of, say, six members, within a production unit (secondary) of say sixty, within a 'shop' of say 300, within a factory with a total work force of perhaps more than a thousand. Such a fact makes the strict application of the dichotomy between primary and secondary somewhat problematic, since, faced by competition from a rival organization, the whole staff of the factory may be imbued with a feeling of solidarity, which would manifest itself in agreements on goals, greater freedom of expression, etc. But, with this proviso in mind, we shall continue to make use of the distinction, because of its considerable value as a marker of linguistic choice – we are, after all, still attempting to correlate linguistic with social structure, the basic goal of sociolinguistics.

Figure 4.4 below (based on Davis, 1957, p.306) summarizes what has been said here and provides a number of examples of relationships and domains.

FIGURE 4.4

Social Relationships

	Characteristics		Examples		
	Physical	Social	Relationships		Domains
PRIMARY	Proximity Smallness Long in duration	Common goals Intrinsic valuations Extensive knowledge of participants Freedom Informal controls Essential solidarity	friend- friend		play group
			parent- child husband- wife		family
			teacher- pupil		school
SECONDARY	Distance Large size Short duration	Disparate goals Extrinsic valuations Partial knowledge Constraints Formal controls Essential power	officer- subordinate		armed forces
			employer- employee		corporation
			performer- spectator		concert

Some comments might be made here. It will have been noticed how many, though not all, of the primary relationships are dyads, thought of as primary in the sense that they have an enduring influence on the behaviour of the members (Krech *et al.*, 1962, p.214), while secondary relationships tend to be larger and, because of the limited knowledge of the participants about each other and the extent of the constraining influences involved, lead to a narrow interpretation of the roles each plays – *stereotypes*, in which the possibility for individual variation is severely limited. We shall see, in a moment, how important this is for linguistic choice.

A second dimension has also been suggested for the classification of social groups and one which cuts across the primary-secondary dichotomy above – the contrast between membership and reference groups.

In addition to social groups to which an individual may belong, there may be other groups to which he aspires. Both of these may act as *reference groups*, i.e. groups with which the individual identifies, to the extent of adopting the norms as his own, for the evaluation of his behaviour and as a source of personal goals and values (Krech *et al.*, 1962, p.102.). Such groups are of considerable interest to the social and behavioural scientist, since mobility is frequently preceded, and the desire for membership signalled, by the adoption by the individual of the *perceived* norms of behaviour amongst members of the group – style of dress, make of car, type and location of home and linguistic features.

4.3.2   Codes

We suggest above that the individual in society plays many roles, in many social situations, and that these roles contain with them norms of behaviour, some of which are norms of language. We are now able to expand a little on this. The individual may be described as possessing a set of codes – each appropriate to a set of role relationships, within the context of a set of domains – which constitute his *repertoire* in an analogous way to the individual pieces of music which make up the repertoire of a performer. The skilled social performer draws upon a repertoire of social skills, which include linguistic codes and the problem which faces such a performer, in an encounter with others, is to choose, from his repertoire of skills, the roles and codes which best suit his purposes. Indeed, it is just this learning of how to choose, which lies at the root of the socialization process in the child (Fichter, 1971, p.218) and, to the extent that societies contain individual members with differing inherent potentials and access to learning situations, it must be expected that individuals and groups will control repertoires which may differ from each other both qualitatively and quantitatively, perhaps to the extent of choosing different languages for the same social purposes (we shall consider this in chapter 5 under the heading of 'bilingualism').

It is possible too, to suggest some correlation between the kinds of relationship and domain described above and typical linguistic code choices with which they co-occur.

A useful distinction between *personal* and *transactional* linguistic interaction has been proposed (Gumperz, 1966) which correlates fairly strongly with primary and secondary social relationships. Personal inter-action predominates in primary groups: 'among friends, within peer groups, and within the family circle in periods of relaxation' (ibid., p.36), in contrast with the transactional nature of interaction in domains such as the shop, the bank, a visit to the doctor, etc. What is crucial here is the way in which, during a transactional interaction, the participants '. . . in a sense suspend their individuality and act by virtue of their status . . . as salesmen, customers, banktellers, physicians, rather than as Tom Hansen or Inger Stensen' (ibid., p.35) and choose stereotyped behaviour patterns which, if substantially departed from, would at least be noticed and quite possibly make the completion of the transaction impossible. There will be then, a strong probability of the choice of 'informal' linguistic features in solid-arity-marking primary relationships and an equally strong likelihood of more 'formal' features, the exact form of which may at times be predict-able, in secondary relationships. In brief, code choice and domain are intimately interconnected and hence the choice of code must be rule-governed — further support for what we have been saying above.

In addition to the connection between linguistic codes and inter-personal relations, there is the powerful indicator of social mobility in hypercorrect usages on the part of those attempting to join reference groups of higher social status (Labov, 1966c) and the converse, the retention of archaic features by individuals, as an indication of their unwillingness to accept the norms of some more economically successful group (Labov, 1963).

4.3.3   *Networks*

We have already considered the notion of 'channels', in the sense of means, medium, mode of communication and have indicated how several means are simultaneously available to the communicator (3.2.1) but now, as a part of our consideration of language use in small groups, we need to look at another side of communication — the notion of 'channel' in a broader sense, which we shall, following the normal social-psychological usage, term *nets* or *networks*. By a network we mean the pattern of channel usage between individual members of a group. It is to be expected that the patterns of communication within a group will vary in a stateable way which correlates with group structure, function and so forth. At one extreme, a group may have a strictly hierarchical power structure, which only permits communication with the immediate superior and immediate subordinate – the armed forces are a very cléar example of this – at the other, a group of close friends may permit a completely open system, in which all may communicate with all, without restriction.

Considerable work has been carried out by social scientists on the description of communication networks, particularly in industrial contexts (see for example Simon, 1945, revised edn. 1965, pp. 154-71) which has important implications for microsociolinguistics. We shall examine two concepts that have arisen in the course of this kind of research and indicate how they are relevant to our present topic.

First of all, let us turn our attention to networks within small groups. Laboratory exercises, designed to test the relationship between group effectiveness and communication net (Leavitt, 1951), demonstrate several configurations, some of which are illustrated below:

There are, of course, other networks which could be constructed, e.g. one in which A has a subordinate B, on whom the spokes of the 'wheel' converge and whose role is to 'filter' information from C, D and E before it is passed on to A. Some brief comments might be appropriate here on the four networks illustrated below.

The 'all-channel' net has been shown to facilitate certain kinds of problem solving and to provide the most satisfaction to the members of the group. It has 100 per cent connectivity, i.e. since there are no restrictions on who may communicate with whom – 20 channels – and hence no 'leader'. Indeed, for a leader to emerge, the structure of the net would need to be changed to reduce the connectivity by placing the leader in a more central position; to move in the direction of A in the wheel.

The *circle* has half the connectivity of the all-channel net – 50 per cent with ten direct channels – but, in principle, each participant can commun-icate with each, though in all but two cases, those adjacent, only indirectly. This configuration actually mirrors rather well a common situation in organizations in which, in spite of the availability of internal telephones, physical proximity tends to increase communication, a fact which might well have been predicted from our comments earlier on the relationship between solidarity and physical propinquity (4.2.1).

The *'Y'* with its eight channels – 40 per cent connectivity – was found, under the experimental conditions of small-scale problem solving in five-man groups, to be the least prone to errors but later experiments involving more complex problems reversed this finding and showed that the circle tended to be faster and more efficient (Shaw, 1968).

The wheel — eight channels, 40 per cent connectivity — was shown to be most efficient at solving simple problems, since the role of the central individual is to process information as it comes in and to make decisions but inevitably, the more complex the task the harder becomes A's job until, far from being starved of information as those on the outer rim of the wheel can be, he becomes saturated with it and hence, less efficient and ultimately, quite unable to cope.

FIGURE 4.5   *Networks*

(a) *The 'all-channel' net*   (b) *The circle*

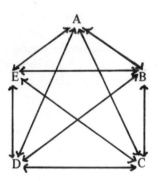

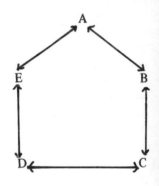

(c) *The 'Y'*   (d) *The Wheel*

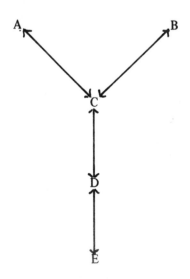

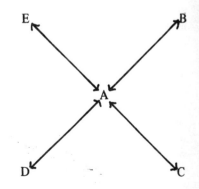

We have, of course, only touched upon a very complex problem here but we have done so to emphasize the existence of an area of research which has the clearest implications for the microsociolinguist. If linguistics is to broaden its scope to include descriptions of the language use of social groups, we cannot afford to ignore the fact that there already exist experimental techniques which have produced data which we can reinterpret in sociolinguistic terms. In a way, we are in the position; vis-à-vis social psychology, that Labov was in relation to sociology when he followed a sociological survey of the social structure of part of New York City collecting sociolinguistic information (Labov, 1966b.), i.e. able to follow up existing research and rework its data. In short, microsociolinguistic research must come to terms with what has been achieved in social psychology and adopt and adapt some of its techniques in the search for a 'socially realistic linguistics'.

If we now move our attention to communication networks within larger groups than the five-man problem solving teams discussed above, for example to the networks within industrial, commercial or military organizations, we need to notice a primary distinction between formal and informal channels, i.e. between those networks which have been set up intentionally and those which have grown up in an *ad hoc* way, not as part of a planned process but through the role relations which constitute the social structure of the organization.

The formal network will control the direction and rate of flow of much 'official' oral communication, as well as memoranda, letters, reports, records and documents of all kinds — a rich area of textual research for the sociolinguist. To a considerable extent, the formal channels of communication within an organization reflect the hierarchical power structure but there is rarely a perfect one-to-one match between the two, since informal networks tend to provide alternatives which bypass the officially laid down procedures.

Such an informal network, based as it is on solidarity rather than power, frequently cuts across formally established groupings within the organization, creating and sustaining cliques of various kinds. Again, the sociolinguist, by specifying the linguistic form and content of messages passed between members of such cliques, is likely to be in a position to provide supporting evidence for the descriptions of organizations produced by social scientists, since group membership is almost certain to be indicated by language — ingroup features, with phonological and lexical features which at once define the group and exclude interlopers.

4.3.4 *Summary*

The search for a more exact understanding of the context of language use
has led us into a discussion of types of social group and social relationship
and then into the related linguistic area of code choice and its correlation
with group membership and the expression of social relationships. In this,
we have argued that there is a close connection between primary social
groups and relationships, manifested in solidarity and individuality-
expressing code features, in contrast with the choice of power- or
transaction-expressing codes within secondary groups and relationships.
Finally, we examined some aspects of intercommunication within groups
— networks and their relationships with group structure and function —
and the existence, in larger organizations, of formal and informal networks
— correlating with power- and solidarity-expression respectively.

  We need now to accept the fact that no individual plays only one role,
participates in one single social relationship or belongs to a single group
and therefore no language user is monolingual, in the strict sense of
possessing a single code. This implies code-switching as the linguistic
correlate of role-switching; the subject of the next section.

4.4   CODE-SWITCHING

One of the assumptions of earlier models of language on which we have
commented (1.4.1) and which we must surely now reject is the monolithic nature of language. What we have been saying above, about the
relationship between role and code, must lead us to a redefinition of
language as some kind of 'bundle of codes', from which the role player
chooses. We should not be alone in this, since some psychologists, and no
doubt other social scientists, would include the language used by an
individual in their definition of role itself '. . . what the occupant of a
given position *does and says*' (Sarbin, 1968, p.546, original emphasis). In
place of the view of language as a homogeneous object, we must put
forward some notion of language as a set of role-related, and in part role-
defining, codes, grouped together as the repertoire of an individual, the
combined repertoires of a group and perhaps as the sets of repertoires of
formally or functionally related languages. In short, the individual user is
to be seen as a chooser amongst codes and it little matters, in terms of pure
description, whether the codes are styles, dialects or what are normally
thought of as autonomous languages, since any or all of these can be
involved in the code-switching behaviour of the language user.

  If this view of code-choice is accepted, it will be clear that the difference
between intra- and inter-language switching is only one of degree and not
of kind and that the notion of bilingualism is no more than a special case

of such switching. We shall now discuss types of code-switching, during which we shall begin to move across the border line between micro- and macrosociolinguistics.

4.4.1   Code-Switching in Monolinguals

We may approach the description of code-switching behaviour in monolinguals by first considering the growth of differentiated role behaviour and specific language uses in the small child of pre-school age. It is not intended here to examine in detail the process of mother tongue acquisition, since this complex field has been and is being studied by substantial numbers of linguists and behavioural scientists but we shall attempt to focus on the growth of communicative competence in the child, manifested in the development of code-switching skills.

It is no exaggeration to say that the first eighteen months or so of a child's life are, from the sociolinguistic point of view, extremely limited. He operates entirely within a single domain – the family – playing an extremely circumscribed set of roles – son/daughter, sibling – within a very limited set of role relationships and hence, is able only to handle a small number of codes, tied closely to basic wants. Figure 4.6 below illustrates, in diagrammatic form, the situation of the young child in a nuclear family with one sibling.

The child then learns how to communicate with the three members of his immediate family, switching roles and, necessarily, the codes that co-occur with those roles, as he does so. Even at this stage, there is a great deal of evidence of stylistic variation between the codes, e.g. anecdotally, no one can have failed to notice how differently the child sets about achieving the same purpose with mother than with father. Lenneberg (1967, p.137) gives a fascinating example of an extreme case of the three-year-old child, with deaf parents, who is already 'bilingual'; adopting a clearly different kind of system for communication with the parents from that used with siblings and others. Twins, too, frequently develop a markedly separate system for communication with each other (Hörmann, 1971, p.270) – a special case of the influence of family structure on the language acquisition opportunities of the child. Inevitably, the role norms and code norms that accompany them will vary to some extent from social group to social group in a society and hence, the greater exposure to a wide range of roles and domains, the larger the repertoire the child will acquire. It is exactly this point that Bernstein (1966) develops in the theory of Restricted and Elaborated Codes, by means of which he seeks to explain the educational disadvantage at which large numbers of British working-class children are placed. We do not intend to discuss the theory here — there are many adequate summaries in existence (e.g. Robinson, 1972, pp.154-85) — preferring to move on in our brief survey of language acquisition.

FIGURE 4.6   *Role Relations*

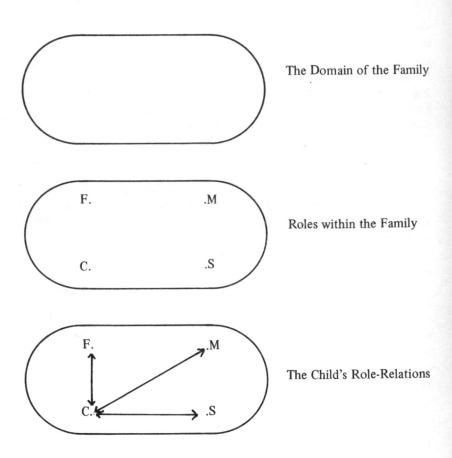

The Domain of the Family

Roles within the Family

The Child's Role-Relations

As the child matures, his single domain of language use, the family, is joined by others — the informal, and perhaps, formal playgroup, the kindergarten and finally school — each containing new roles, relationships and codes. At school, in particular, several new factors come into play. The learning of vocabulary, a crucial aspect of code differentiation, though not of course the only one, shifts from a process which has been termed (Gurney, 1973, p.83f.) *syntagmatic* — the word 'red', for example, might be responded to by 'car' — to *paradigmatic*, in which a term elicits an item which can substitute for it – 'red' elicits 'green', 'car'; 'lorry' and so forth (we have, of course, already made use of these terms earlier in the chapter, in our discussion of Social Rules: 4.1.3), and the process continues through the course of the life of the individual.

Now, it would be ideal, at this point, to produce a description of the ways in which groups contrast with each other in their code-switching behaviour, as they change from role-relation to role-relation and domain to domain but such a description is unfortunately still impossible, dependent as it is on a far more precise specification of the components of domains, the nature of role-relationships and the correlation of codes with these factors. However, it is possible to make one or two rather general points, which lead on to the discussion of code switching amongst bilingual individuals and in bilingual societies.

Although a description of code-switching depends on the production of 'rules of speaking' which do not themselves yet exist except for rough outlines and rules for narrowly delimited situations, it is possible to state one or two principles which will permit us to link monolingual style and dialect switching with bilingual language switching.

First of all, it seems certain that the sources of code-shifting must be the factors referred to earlier as 'situational variables', in the wide sense of the term suggested by Hymes (3.3.2.1), that influence the decision on the form and content of the selected code. Most, if not all, societies appear to distinguish types of code which are appropriate for use in particular categories of situation, with certain topics, in certain role-relationships and so forth, often labelling them 'formal', 'informal' and the like. As far as the mother tongue communities of English are concerned, there is little problem in deciding whether a text is 'formal' or not, since there is a very close correspondence between 'formal' usage and the linguistic characteristics of the standard language but where 'English' consists of a continuum of codes, without clear natural breaks between them and with extremes which may not be mutually intelligible, description becomes extraordinarily complicated (see 5.3.1). Part of the difficulty arises because of the vague terminology, linguistic and sociological, which we have been using – language, dialect, standard, non-standard, formal, informal – and which we must attempt to clarify by means of some kind of typology that isolates codes from each other in terms of their possession or lack of specific attributes (6.2).

Secondly, in some speech communities, the interconnection between situation and code is so highly institutionalized that a functional division reflected in two strikingly different language structures has arisen. We refer to the notion of *diglossia* (5.3), the real social borderline between monolingual and bilingual code-switching phenomena.

4.4.2 *Summary*

We have been considering in this section the notion of code-switching amongst monolinguals and have stressed the point that such behaviour, the paralleling of role and code changes, differs only in degree from bilingual switching, changing between languages. In adopting this attitude, we simultaneously attack the concept of language as a monolithic structure and refer back to our earlier comments on *register* (1.4.3.1) which we might now redefine as a role-related code, i.e. a change in register is the formal linguistic marker of a change of role and the converse.

4.5   CONCLUSION

In this chapter, we have attempted to specify the nature of the rules for language in use, to expand our analysis to include larger groups and their communication networks and to introduce the concept of code-switching.

We noticed that we had been operating with a rather vague definition of the term 'rule' and suggested one which would be acceptable to most philosophers of science and particularly to students of 'systems'. The distinction between the different types of rule, most importantly that between the categorical rules of closed systems and the variable rules of open systems has been stressed and the inevitable need for rules of both kinds in the creation of a model of language in use pointed out.

It is encouraging that there is such a convergence of interest in the rule-governed nature of the social use of language, exemplified by the speech act rules of Searle, the address rules of Ervin-Tripp and the discourse rules of Labov, all of which relate in an intriguing way to the contrasting types of interactive behaviour isolated by social-psychological research (Argyle, 1969).

In the attempt to widen the scope of our description beyond the dyad, we next considered groups, roles and codes of various kinds and the types of communication networks available to groups, giving the example of small problem-solving groups in which the shape of the network has been shown to have an important influence on the success or failure of the group in solving its allotted task. An interesting correlation was found between personal linguistic interaction in primary, and transactional inter-action in secondary groups which related 'informality' of language with 'solidarity' in social relations in contrast with the 'formal' language of the 'power'-orientated relationship.

The recognition that roles and codes were closely interrelated led us quickly to see that role-change implied linguistic change (and the converse) and that the phenomenon of code-switching, seen amongst monolinguals as 'stylistic' variation, differed only in degree and not in kind from the language-to-language shifting of bilinguals. This forces us to reassert our rejection of the monolithic concept of language, a notion which can no longer survive in the face of clear evidence of stylistic shifting even within the idiolect and even in the language of the pre-school child. We have now to see language as a set of repertoires of codes rather than a homogeneous object. In this case, any purely linguistic definition which seeks to distinguish languages from dialects for example, must fail especially since 'borrowing' between languages is such a common feature of international contact and since there actually are individuals who can communicate in more than one 'language'.

The outcome of the chapter must be a feeling of considerable dissatisfaction with much of the terminology of linguistics when it attempts to define as discrete units what are clearly non-discrete phenomena. We shall therefore attempt, in the next chapter to explain the behaviour of the bilingual both as an individual and as a participant in a language contact or continuum situation.

Since we outlined the layout of this book earlier (1.4.3) as essentially proceeding from micro- to macro-, it might be as well to state here just where we have got to. The bilingual is clearly the dividing line between micro- and macrosociolinguistic investigation. A micro- approach to his behaviour would stress such psychological aspects as fluency, accuracy in usage and in switching, while the macro- would seek to place the bilingual, or rather the usage of the bilingual, in its appropriate domains and would raise questions concerning the relationships between mother tongues and other languages in a given society. We shall in chapter 5 focus our attention on the micro- aspects of bilingualism and turn, in chapter 6, to the macro-issue of typological definition and, in chapter 7, of the more political side of sociolinguistics – language planning.

5
Code -Switching
-Bilingualism and Diglossia

In this chapter, we shall consider the bilingual individual both in psychological and social psychological terms as a code-switcher and role-player but also as a member of a society in which the widespread use of more than one language is common. We shall, in addition, look at two special cases of code-switching phenomena — diglossia, in a stable and in an unstable continuum situation, and this will lead us on to a more precise definition of types of code — language, dialect, creole, pidgin, etc. — a necessary pre-condition for the macrosociolinguistic consideration of language policy in contrasting nations.

5.1   THE BILINGUAL INDIVIDUAL

Before considering the bilingual individual, it is important to disambiguate some of the terminology involved, particularly the notions of 'mother tongue' and 'foreign language' or 'first' and 'second language'.

For most individuals, the first language learned — the mother tongue — is also the most used and, conversely 'second languages' tend also to be 'secondary' in terms of use — auxiliary languages. But there are cases of individuals in language contact situations — migrants especially — in which the mother tongue loses its position as primary medium of communication, is limited to hearth, home and friendship and is displaced, in other domains, by the dominant language of the host community. Such a situation is common to immigrant and refugee groups — Indo-Pakistani immigrants in Britain, Turkish workers in Germany, Eastern European refugees in Western Europe as a whole — and therefore we need to distinguish order of learning — the diachronic aspect — from degree of present use — the synchronic (proposed by Whiteley 1964, p. 184, on whom the table below is based), and to provide terms and symbols for these distinctions.

FIGURE 5.1   *Language: Order of Learning and Using*

TIME FOCUS	LANGUAGE	SYMBOL
Diachronic	First Language	L1
	Second Language	L2
Synchronic	Primary Language	PL
	Secondary Language	SL

We shall not wish, of course, to be held to a literal interpretation of
L2 as 'second language' and thereby be forced into speaking of an
individual's L3, L4, etc. We much prefer L2 to stand for any language or
languages learned after the L1 and equally, to assume that SL means
'auxiliary', just as 'bilingual' can stand for 'multilingual'. In any case, as we
shall see, it is by no means easy to discover 'how many' languages an
individual uses nor to be precise about the ranking of importance each has
for that individual.

5.1.1   *The Notion of Bilingualism*

The assumption that languages were objects, between which there were,
ideally, clear boundaries implied that any utterance could be assigned
unambiguously to a specific language. Items which clearly 'belonged to
another language' could be accommodated, within this view, in terms of
having been 'borrowed' or having just 'slipped in', through 'interference'.
The assumption and its attendant terminology is most unfortunate, since
it fails to account for 'switching' between languages, a common phenomenon amongst bilinguals, and implies that such behaviour constitutes 'noise',
which reduces the efficiency of the communicative act in which it occurs.
There is plenty of evidence to show that the reverse is the case, i.e. that
'language mixture', far from making communication for bilinguals with
substantially shared repertoires more difficult, actually facilitates it. An
example (attested by myself) of an utterance by a six-year old child of
Italian speaking parents, supports this assertion – anyone in contact with
similar situations can amass large quantities of similar anecdotal evidence.
The child, though using Italian at home, operated entirely in English at
school in Britain, hence needing to describe a school event in Italian, he
was faced by problems of lexical selection; school is 'in' English, in the
sense that, though there are some Italian equivalents – playground, playtime – the child does not know them and, in some cases, there is no
equivalent entity in Italian schools – dinner-lady. The child, therefore,

produced an utterance that communicated perfectly adequately with his parents: 'Oggi a scuola a playtime, Mark Jones è caduto dal climbing-frame nel yard e Mrs Smith la nostra dinner-lady ha fasciato il suo ginocchio'. Clearly it makes little sense to describe this as 'Italian syntax with massive lexical interference from English. A more interesting approach is to accept the utterance as it is and observe how the composite Italian-English system operates. We might note at what points in the structure English lexical items occur, judge their influence on the phonemic system and phonetic realization of the utterance and attempt to derive rules which will, at least partially, predict internal switching of this kind. Such an approach, it will be recognized, is far more likely to lead to satisfactory models of bilingual behaviour than the covertly prescriptive assumption that the English features are some kind of regrettable lapses within otherwise correct Italian. The attempt to create rules for interlingual switching will be made later on in this chapter (5.4) but the issue has been raised here for the dual purpose of linking our earlier comments on monolingual — intralingual — code-switching with the concept of bilingualism and the phenomenon of continua of codes, which we shall illustrate later by reference to the creole-English continuum in the Caribbean.

5.1.2   *Compound and Co-Ordinate Bilingualism*

Until about 20 years ago, most interest in bilingualism had been shown by psychologists, who, almost without exception, devoted their efforts to describing the relationships between bilingualism and intelligence or mental illness. Linguists and psycholinguists had only begun to take an interest in the topic, the two classic studies being by Weinreich (1953) and Ervin and Osgood (1954). From these grew the realization that bilingualism was, in fact, an instance of the concept of 'co-existent systems' proposed by Fries and Pike in 1949 (see 2.4.1.4) for the explanation of stylistic variation in monolinguals. To reiterate what has been stated earlier, multi-code usage is normal linguistic behaviour, whether it be intra- or inter-language switching and, in rather simplistic terms, it might be better to think of the bilingual, not as an oddity but as an ordinary individual, whose repertoire happens to contain codes which, in others, would be labelled as separate languages. However, put in this way, the notion of bilingualism vanishes in the triviality of recognizing that all speakers adopt varying styles to suit varying purposes — a truism which is hardly calculated, in itself, to advance our understanding of language use.

The crucial question which faces the describer of bilingualism is whether the bilingual individual possesses one or two systems. In answer to this, Ervin and Osgood, following suggestions made by Weinreich, proposed

FIGURE 5.2   *A Linguistic Model for Bilingualism*

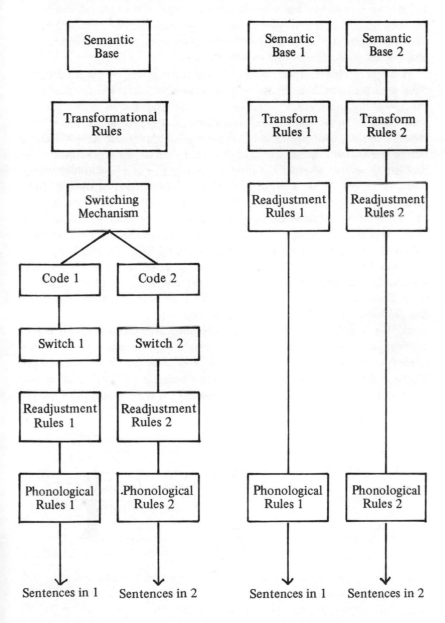

that bilingualism should be viewed as a scale running from the *compound bilingual,* in whom two languages form a merged system to the *co-ordinate bilingual,* in whom the two language systems are kept distinct. In TG terms, the compound has a single semantic base connected to two input and two output mechanisms, while the co-ordinate has two semantic bases, each connected to language specific input-output systems — Figure 5.2. above gives an outline of the two models.

A major problem, apart from the existential status of the models (an issue we have considered above in general terms; 2.3.1.1), is the nature of the switching mechanism — assumed in our diagram to occur for the compound after the transformational rules, i.e. here, language 1 and 2 are closely related — but presumably in the case of the co-ordinate bilingual, before the semantic base — perhaps in some kind of 'ideas generator'. The problem is severe, whether the model is thought of as a psychological or a linguistic model; either way, the nature and rule content of the switching mechanism needs to be specified. We shall return to the issue later as part of the discussion of code-switching and confine ourselves here to comments on the very serious implications such a model has for yet another cherished axiom of descriptive linguistics — the indivisibility of the linguistic sign.

It has been accepted, at least since de Saussure, that the analysis and explanation of language must hinge on the specification of the relation-ships between (1) linguistic signs — their form and meaning — and (2) their referents — the 'objects' to which they refer, and ultimately to their users. The linguistic sign has traditionally been thought of as consisting of *expression* — the 'image acoustique' roughly 'phonemic shape' — and *content* — the concept, which together refer to some 'object'. We might illustrate this by reproducing de Saussure's example of 'tree', making use of an *ad hoc* convention, that of using capitals for the concept:

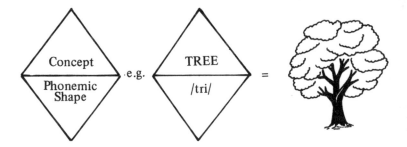

Clearly, in this case, where the user of the sign is a monolingual, and the comments above on code-switching must make us wonder whether such beings actually exist, the relationship between the acoustic image and its concept, which will constitute the sign, and its referent is straightforward. What though of the bilingual? We can try to fit the sign into the two models shown in the first illustration, using an Italian-English bilingual in both cases.

The Co-ordinate Bilingual

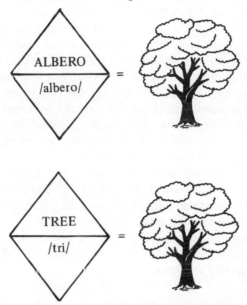

This user has two signs for the same referent and, it seems, two concepts and phonemic shapes for the physical object definable along the lines of 'perennial plant with a single self-supporting trunk of wood, usually without branches for some distance from the ground'. Actually, it is possible that the two signs refer to different objects ALBERO/ /albero/ to the umbrella pines of Italy and TREE/ /tri/ to the vaguely deciduous object of our illustration.

The Compound Bilingual

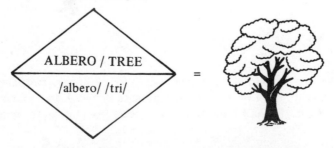

If the compound bilingual has a fused semantic base, his signs must necessarily be fused too but, if this is the case, how does he unscramble the component parts of his signs and produce, not a totally unpredictable mixture of Italian and English, but one or the other and, should he wish, a mixture, as the occasion demands? That his signs are fused is implied by the whole notion of compound bilingualism, as is the divisibility of signs as the user generates sentences but this conflicts with the Saussurrean belief of the nature of the sign – a change in one element automatically creating a change in the other. It might be pointed out too that this is not solely a problem of bilingual description, since the same break-up of the sign seems imminent in monolingual usage of homophones and homographs. A partial solution might be to suggest a model of the compound bilingual's signs, in which the concepts are fused into a kind of super ALBEROTREE concept to which the two acoustic images, /albero/ and /tri/, are attached but this does little to cure the inherent difficulty; the sign is still divided and there is no mechanism to prevent the production of utterances like 'Io I ho have gia just visto seen un a albero tree'! Clearly, we now are in urgent need of a statement on the switching mechanism which permits the production of unmixed utterances and the processes which allow such a mechanism to be suspended (see 5.4).

A third type of bilingual, suggested by Weinreich (1953, p. 9f), the subordinate bilingual, though a far from uncommon individual, presents similarly intractable problems:

The Subordinate Bilingual

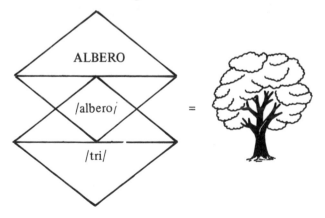

Unlike the compound bilingual who, by acquiring two languages simultaneously, has two L1s, the subordinate bilingual, in common with the co-ordinate, has an L1 and an L2 but differs from him in the sense that his complex sign contains a single concept which, as it were, 'calls up' his L1 word, which itself 'calls up' the English /tri/. For him, often taught the L2 by translation methods, /tri/ 'means' /albero/ and hence his Italian sign ALBERO/ albero is itself a sign of a sign – in semiotic terms a *metasign.*

The subordinate bilingual's method of generating sentences in his L2 involves, then, the equation of a lexical item of the L1 with a lexical item in the L2 – a quite different process from the concept-item procedure adopted by the compound or the co-ordinate bilingual and one which certainly seems to parallel the earlier stages of the learning of a second language. In fact, the three types of bilingual do appear to mark stages in learning, beginning with the subordinate and moving on towards the co-ordinate, as the learner starts to feel that he is actually managing to 'think in the language', rather than 'translate from the mother tongue'.

It might now be asked whether there is any psychological evidence for the existence of these models in the minds or the brains of bilinguals, in addition to self-rating measures of various kinds. There is some experimental evidence which tends to support the hypothesis, particularly the results of semantic differential tests (Osgood et al., 1957). If, as is suggested, the compound bilingual has a single conceptual-semantic system, any change in the meaning of a word in one language should be matched by an equal change in the meaning of the equivalent word in the other but, since the denotative meaning – the conceptual or cognitive meaning – cannot easily be altered, such tests must rely on changing the connotative – associative or emotional – meaning of words (Leech, 1974, pp. 10-27 gives a summary of 'seven types of meaning' which may be useful here). For the co-ordinate bilingual no such change would be predicted and several series of experiments have produced results which appear to support the dichotomy between the two types (Lambert and Jakobovits, 1961).

We have, so far, been ignoring a crucial aspect of bilingualism; the relationship of language to culture in such an individual, since, parallel to the question of the relationship of linguistic code to linguistic code in the bilingual individual, there is the relationship of culture to culture. In short, there are presumably biculturals, just as there are bilinguals and further, might such biculturals form a continuum along a compound co-ordinate scale? This proposal will be given consideration below (5.2.1) and later, in the context of the social use of codes in multilingual societies (5.2), but first, some effort must be made to examine the nature of the switching mechanism, on which the description of bilingual language use must ultimately depend.

5.1.2   Bilingual Code-Switching

We have been describing bilingual behaviour rather as if there were no problem involved in switching from language to language, as if, that is, the switching mechanism, whatever it is, were always in perfect working order and yet we observe how 'mixed' utterances occur or, to put it in a more prescriptive way, the bilingual makes 'mistakes'. As long ago as 1957, it was suggested (Lado, 1957, p. 1) that explorations in the area of languages in contact (Weinreich, 1953 and Haugen, 1953) demonstrated 'that many linguistic distortions heard among bilinguals correspond to describable differences in the languages involved', i.e. differences between the monolingual forms of language and forms used by bilinguals were largely to be explained by the phenomenon of 'interference' from the L1. It was assumed that such interference derived from the carry-over of L1 patterns at all levels, linguistic and cultural, into L2 usage. We shall exemplify this claim below by examining phonological interference, recognizing as we do, that the processes suggested are intended to apply equally to the code as a whole and to the cultural aspects of language use.

5.1.2.1   Phonological Interference

The fact of 'sound substitution' has been long recognized in linguistics (Bloomfield, 1933, p. 445ff.) although a precise definition of the phenomenon was not achieved until 1953 (Weinreich, 1953, p. 14): 'Interference arises when a bilingual identifies a phoneme of the secondary system with one in the primary system and in reproducing it, subjects it to the phonetic rules of the primary language'. A simple example may help here. The 'loan-word' rouge, phonemically / ruʒ / and phonetically [bu: ʒ] in French, will be identified by the English user in terms of the French [ƀ] being equivalent to the English /r/ and realized normally as [ɪ]. The French /u:/ will be identified with the English /u:/ but reproduced as a more centralized and lengthened vowel than the French, i.e. as [ü:]. The / ʒ / of French will be equated with the English / ʒ / but, because of the phonotactic rules of English, which exclude it from initial position and often replace it finally in a word, the phoneme may well be replaced by the more common / dʒ / cf garage, beige, etc.

Four major types of phonological interference have been suggested — the over- and under-differentiation of phonemes, reinterpretation of distinctions, and phone substitution — each of which we shall illustrate below:-

Underdifferentiation; if L2 contains phonemes which do not occur in the L1, these may not be recognized for what they are, e.g. Italian has no /i:/-/ɪ/ contrast, although long and short vowels do occur but only as wholly predictable allophones which do not affect meaning. The Italian user of English may well, out of context, be unable to distinguish in production or reception, the contrasting meanings of 'he *beat* his wife' and 'he *bit* his wife', for example. Conversely, the lack of phonemic contrasts carried by 'double consonants' in English – except for marginal cases like *holy* and *wholly* in some speech – may lead the English speaker of Italian to fail to distinguish *casa* /kasa/ *house* and *cassa* /kassa/ *cash-desk* or *fato* /fato/ *done* and *fatto* /fatto/ *fact.*

Over-differentiation; this is the reverse of the interference type described above – the identification of a phonetic contrast in the L2 with a phonemic distinction of the L1, e.g. the existence of written double consonants in such English words as *little, bigger, banner,* etc. may lead the Italian to pronounce them as /littel/ and so on or the recognition of aspiration in initial voiceless plosives in English lead the Hindi speaker to assume and therefore over-emphasize, the phonetic differences between the /k/ of *kin* and *skin,* producing strong aspiration in the first case and none in the second, on the analogy of k^hal/ *akin* and /kal/ *rare.*

Reinterpretation of distinctions; the notion of the phoneme as a set of distinctive features may lead a bilingual to seize upon a phonetic feature, in his L1 an integral part of a phonemic contrast, which he then makes use of in attempting to make a distinction in the L2. Though English has, and Italian lacks, the /ɑ:/ – /æ/ distinction – RP *bard-bad* – fronted allophones of /a/ do occur, in many dialects of Italian, before 'double consonants'. The English speaker of Italian may therefore hear and produce the difference between *fato* and *fatto* in terms, not of the crucial single-double consonant contrast but by using a vowel close to /ɑ:/ in *fato* and one close to /æ/ in *fatto.*

Phone substitution; where the realization of a phoneme in the L2 is recognized as a variant of the 'same' phoneme in the L1, a sound-for-sound substitution may take place, e.g. the English user of French is aided in his recognition of the French [ʁ] as a realization of the /r/ phoneme by having heard similar realizations in rural north-eastern English cf. *rouge.*

5.1.2.2   *Interlingual Identification*

In each of the four cases of interference above, we have been suggesting a common feature – the identification of an L2 phoneme by a bilingual in terms of his L1 system, i.e. he hears 'x' and assumes it to be 'y' which he therefore uses in his attempts at producing 'x' in the L2. It should be possible to show this in a rather crude diagram below:

FIGURE 5.3   *Interlingual Identification 1*

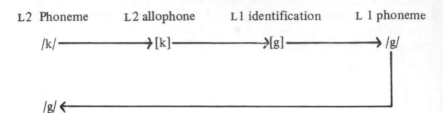

The English speaker of Hindi hears the unaspirated /k/ of /kam/ *work* as a /g/, since initial unaspirated /k/ does not occur in English (in RP that is; many northern British dialects permit it) but unaspirated /g/ does, he therefore uses /g/ in his realization of /kam/ producing /gam/ — a 'nonsense word' in Hindi.

However, this model is really rather too crude as an explanation of interference. For instance, it fails to explain in any clear way why it is that one of the features of /k/ should have been singled out and others ignored. A purely phonetic answer is hardly enough, and so we need to re-examine the model suggested in Chapter 2 (2.4.2.1 Figure 2.2) particularly at the level of the Phonological Component.

Phonological rules have the formal structure of context sensitive rules (Chomsky and Halle, 1963, p.332) and one function of converting binary phonological features into the many phonetic features which constitute actual speech sounds (Botha, 1971, p.225f.). It is now possible to revise Figure 5.3 to indicate a little more clearly the mechanism of interlingual identification at the phonological level.

What we are suggesting above is that the English speaker of Hindi hears the phonetic features of the Hindi phone and selects, on the basis of the phonological rules of English, the phonetic feature which he assumes to be the significant distinctive phonemic feature in Hindi, i.e. he, as it were, 'filters out' those features which either do not occur or are insignificant, in phonemic terms, for English. Hence, he interprets the Hindi allophone of /k/ as an English allophone of /g/, for the reasons we gave earlier — a misinterpretation of the contrast. In short, one contrast is sufficient and he selects the wrong one. The diagram shows the reception — decoding — process but once the identification has been made, the arrows can be reversed and the same figure used as a model of the transmission — encoding — process of speaking Hindi 'with an English accent'. The numbering of the features selected is, of course, quite arbitrary and merely for the sake of the example — a fuller treatment would list the Hindi and English features and contrast them.

FIGURE 5.4   *Interlingual Identification 2*

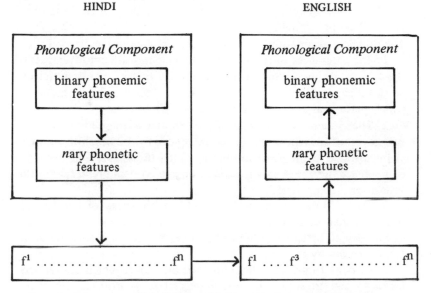

In principle too, such interlingual interpretations of surface phenomena can take place at all levels of the grammar and, as such, constitute the interlanguage – the Anglicized Hindi – used by this speaker, a notion which we shall expand in the next section.

5.1.2.3   *The Concept of the 'Interlanguage'*

Part of the difficulties we are having in explaining bilingual language behaviour derives from the fact that, despite protestations that our descriptions are objective and that we no longer accept the idea that language is a monolithic object, we are, in fact, proceeding in a thoroughly prescriptive and monolithic way. Unless we recognize that the utterances of the bilingual, even those of the learner in the early stages of learning the L2, are just as much language as the L1 Hindi or English at which we presume he is aiming, our understanding will not advance beyond listing 'mistakes' and seeing in his output 'broken English' or 'pidgin' this or that. What is needed is a reorientation towards the data, i.e. to describe 'not by adjusting a grammar of standard English so as to enable it to generate all the actual sentences of the . . . [text] , but by finding the grammar which most adequately describes the structure . . .' (Thorne, 1965, p. 51.). This interestingly enough was initially a proposal for dealing with an extraordinarily deviant variety of English – that of the poet E.E. Cummings – but one which was rapidly extended to the description of idiosyncratic dialects in general and to the discovery of the structured nature of learners' errors in particular, through the process of what became known as, 'error analysis' (probably the best summary, is to be found in Corder, 1973, pp. 256-94).

The principle assumptions of error analysis may be summarized as:

1. The utterances of the L2 user of a language are not utterances of the L2 nor are they those of the L1 but the surface manifestations of an 'interlanguage' — a linguistic system, the formal characteristics of which place it at some point between the L1 and the L2.

2. The system, in part isomorphic with that of the L2 in part not, is rule-governed and constitutes the knowledge of the L2 which the user has at his disposal at the point in time at which the data is collected — his competence in the L2; an 'approximative system' representing his 'transitional competence'.

3. Since forms which are isomorphic with those of the L2 may occur by chance, the errors made by the user are the clearest indication of his system, being the result of hypotheses about the structure of the L2, tested out by the learner.

4. Deviant forms need to be divided into those which are random-lapses — and those which are rule-regulated — mistakes and errors. Errors and mistakes alone are thought of as indicators of the underlying system.

5. The learner's system may or may not be changing — some are in rapid change, others have, as it were, 'fossilized' in the individual, yet others are relatively 'fixed' in the form of pidgin, creole, vernacular and other varieties of the L2 (see 6.2 for an expansion of this point).

Underlying these assumptions is a crucial re-evaluation of the language of the bilingual, at whatever stage in learning he is, as a unique and autonomous communication system which can be described just as the newly discovered language of a newly discovered people might be described, since that is exactly what it is — the language of a speech community, albeit consisting of a single communicator, with its own rules which require explanation in its own terms, not in terms of their 'deviation' from some other system. It is as unrevealing, it is argued, to describe Provençal as though it were 'bad French' as to describe an L2 variety of English as 'bad English', although a bilingual's 'interlanguage' may be properly described as 'good' or 'bad' in terms of its communicative efficiency (see 5.2). There are, naturally, substantial problems involved in the description of interlanguages but some texts have been analysed and some success may be claimed (Bell, 1973, 1974).

Two further points may be made, before we move on in our discussion of bilingualism. First, all L2 varieties are now to be accepted as 'real languages' amenable to the normal processes of linguistic description – another move in the direction of objectivity in relation to its data, which has been a prime goal of linguistics throughout this century. Second, the notion of the inter-language and the revaluation of the status of errors implied by it has fundamentally important implications for language teaching, since it directs the teacher towards a correction, not of surface phenomena – the 'symptoms' of L2 usage – but of the underlying conceptual system from which they arise.

5.1.2.4 *Summary*

We have been considering the bilingual individual and have made the distinction between the compound and the co-ordinate, a dichotomy which led to the realization that the concept tended to undermine an important axiom of descriptive linguistic – that the linguistic sign is indivisible – and hence raised issues, common to linguistics as a whole, not merely to the problem of bilingual description. Under the heading of 'code-switching', we considered the mechanisms involved in the use of more than one language by the individual and proposed that the language of the L2 user should be seen as an autonomous linguistic system and described as such, without overt or covert notions of prescription intervening.

What is required now is a shift of attention from the bilingual individual and the system which he possesses, to the uses which bilinguals make of their languages – the adoption of a social-psychological and sociolinguistic, rather than a purely psychological or linguistic, approach to the question.

5.2   BILINGUALISM AND DOMAINS OF USE

It will be readily accepted that the comments made above on code-switch-ing in monolinguals, its relationship with role-relations and its siting in domains of various kinds applies with equal or indeed with greater force to the code-switching activities of bilinguals (cf. 4.3.1). If we accept that the repertoires of individuals and groups of individual monolinguals differ from each other in the range of appropriate codes and roles with which they are able to deal, similar, though greater differences, must occur within the communicative competence of bilinguals in their L2. For this very reason, the definition of a bilingual as one who has perfect control over more than one language (Francis, 1958, p. 590) who is, to use Halliday's term, an 'ambilingual' (Halliday *et al.,* 1964, p. 77f.) breaks down, except for the rare individual, at the upper end of a proficiency scale in two or more languages. We need to recognize that bilingualism constitutes a range of skills, extending from the monolingual at one extreme, through the subordinate and co-ordinate bilingual, to the compound bilingual, whose mastery of both languages is never seen to be deficient. It seems realistic to explain the varying abilities of the bilingual in whom change and development of the interlanguage are still going on, as moving from co-ordinate to compound but, and this is the point, not at an equal rate in all linguistic or social skills. In order to communicate efficiently, the speaker needs to control, not only the linguistic code but the choices of channel through which the code is actualized, the situational variables which modify such choices and the sociolinguistic rules which permit cohesive discourse and sustain or create social relations. The achievement of mastery over such a range of diverse skills can hardly be expected to occur instantaneously and so, in some spheres, a bilingual will have a compound-like control, in others co-ordinate, in yet others even subordinate. If I may use my own ability in Italian as an example, it might be possible to make the point more clearly.

As an Italian-English bilingual, in Italy I should have rated myself, in domains in which I frequently used Italian, as close to the compound end of the spectrum but my ability was virtually tied to the spoken mode, though I read Italian with some speed and accuracy, my written Italian was very poor. Similarly, the normal domains in which the tourist finds himself, plus several common to the native Italian householder and employee presented little difficulty but most of these were transactional not personal (see above 4.2.2); I could operate as a teacher of English in Italy but would have been hard put to play the role of an Italian son, for example.

From this, there follows the absolute necessity of defining bilingual skills in terms of the social skills which the bilingual individual possesses and particularly, since we shall need to draw upon the notion, when considering bilingual communities, the domains in which one language, rather than another is normally employed.

We have suggested a crude domain division for my own use of Italian and English — English in all domains and Italian available in those which expressed secondary relationships and employed essentially transactional language. Such an approach permits the building up, for any bilingual or bilingual group, of a listing of domains and their typical code choices — a *dominance configuration* (Fishman, 1966) — which might be illustrated for a hypothetical Asian immigrant in Britain in a table of the following kind:

FIGURE 5.5   *A Dominance Configuration*

DOMAIN	LANGUAGE	
Family		P
Friendship		P
Religion	A	P
Shopping		E P
Work		E P
Government		E
Agencies		

A : Arabic
E : English
P : Punjabi

Such an individual, a Punjabi Muslim, has pretty clearly defined relationships between domain and typical language choice but in several – religion, shopping and contacts at work – two languages occur, depending, in the first case, on the stage of the service in the mosque whether the classical Arabic of the Koran or Punjabi is used, in the other two, the L1 of the shopkeeper and co-worker respectively. This, however, only partially represents the situation. The choice of English or Punjabi may not depend solely on the L1 of the interlocutor – topic, as we saw earlier in this chapter (5.1.1), may be crucial – the discussion of a complex process at work may be easier, even for L1 users of Punjabi, if carried on in English or, and here we return again to the issue raised earlier, in a mixture of the two (the point is taken up again below in 5.4).

A dominance configuration, even for a single individual bilingual, is, then, somewhat difficult to produce, since it entails the correlation of language choice with all of the situational variables discussed earlier. Even so, the concept is a useful one, allowing some kind of explanation of language choice, both in the individual and in the group, which, if extended over a period of time, can be made to indicate, just as the Guttman Scale and the Bailey Wave (2.4.3) indicated, waves of change -- in this case the expansion and contraction of language use – passing through a society.

5.2.1   *Bilingualism and Biculturalism*

The preceding section leads in to the broader issue which links the interests of anthropology and sociolinguistics; the relationship between language choice and culture. To recapitulate, we have been talking quite happily about the compound bilingual 'having a single concept system' but surely this implies a single cultural system too? Indeed, the existence of mono-linguals and of two types (extremes rather) of bilingual suggests, in

principle, six sets of relationship between language and culture which
can be portrayed in a 3 x 2 matrix — Figure 5.6:

FIGURE 5.6   *Bilingualism & Biculturalism*

CODE	CULTURE	
	monocultural	bicultural
monolingual	+	?
co-ord. bil.	+	+
comp. bil.	?	+

The monolingual requires little comment, since the monolingual-
monocultural individual is clearly the norm in human society and the
monolingual-bicultural cell seems self-cancelling — such an individual
appears to be quite contradictory.

The bilinguals, however, provide three interesting types, the compound-
monocultural bilingual appearing, in the light of evidence, to show that
bilingualism to a considerable extent entails biculturalism, which like the
monolingual-bicultural individual, is most unlikely (see discussion in Jakobovits, 1970, pp.85-90).

The monocultural-co-ordinate bilingual is likely to be one who has
learned the L2 for utilitarian purposes, access to the technological
information available in the language, the pursuit of research in academic
subjects, etc., who, in an extreme form, would be a subordinate bilingual
(see 5.1.2), perhaps limited to a reading knowledge of the L2, using it as a
'library language'.

The bicultural-co-ordinate bilingual, conversely, is more likely to have
learned the L2 for integrative reasons — getting to know the people,
tourism, etc. — and to have studied the literature, history and other aspects
of the culture of the L2 speech community. Some individuals of this type
may even demonstrate what has been termed a kind of 'bilingual schizo-
phrenia', feeling themselves to change personality as they change languages
(Ervin-Tripp, 1967).

The bicultural-compound bilingual is presumably exemplified by the
second-generation immigrant, who has acquired two L2s and two cultures,
that of the home and that of the host society, simultaneously but is it
not possible that such an individual actually has, parallel with his
compound bilingualism, a compound culture — perhaps the cultural
correlate of the interlanguage described above, an interculture — made up
of elements from both cultures, fused into a cohesive whole (Pearl and

Lambert, 1962)? The question is of the greatest importance in societies with large immigrant groups, e.g. race relations in Britain needs to consider whether the immigrant child is heir to two distinct or one new culture, since on this hinges such notions as 'integration', 'assimilation', 'accommodation' and views of the nature of a multi-racial society (Patterson, 1969, pp. 111-13 and Rose *et al.,* 1969, p. 24f.). Clearly too, such issues are of considerable interest to the sociolinguist since the interrelationship between language and culture and the social meaning of linguistic choice is central to the whole field of microsociolinguistics and has ramifications in the macro-areas of language planning and of education, particularly language teaching. We shall return to these macrosociolinguistic questions later, during the consideration of language policy in linguistically heterogeneous nations (7.3).

5.2.2   *Summary*

We have, in this hasty survey of bilingualism, reached the crossover point between the social-psychological aspects of bilingual usage in specific domains, noting the ramifications that code choice in such contexts may have on the cultural make-up of the individual, and are now ready to move on to look at the larger scale, more sociologically orientated, area of the institutionalization of code choice, beginning with the special case of diglossia.

5.3   DIGLOSSIA

True monolingualism, in an absolute sense of the term, would imply the existence of a single, monolithic, undifferentiated code system used by a society in which each member played a single insulated role manifested by a single mono-style code – a totally unrealistic situation, even, as we have seen for the very young child. But to base our explanation of language use on the truism that, in this sense, all users are 'bilingual' is hardly likely to be very illuminating. There are undoubted differences between codes, both at the micro- level of individual usage and at the macro- level of social use, which it is the task of sociolinguistics to specify and describe.

We have been discussing bilingualism in both the personal and the social sense of choice between different languages but have been avoiding the whole question of the social valuation of such choices which, as we shall see later, has implications for the sociolinguistic typologies in which such terms as 'vernacular', 'pidgin' and so forth are defined (6.2.2) and for the whole field of language planning which is concerned with decisions on which codes are to be used in 'official' functions of various kinds (7.2.2).

There are some societies in which there is a 'socially based and culturally valued functional differentiation' between the codes present in those societies (Fishman in Fishman *et al.*, 1968, p.50, note 16), i.e. there is a consensus that one variety has a 'high' status and another a 'low' status. Normally in such a situation there is a functional division between the two; the H being reserved for 'formal', 'public' use, often legally recognized as the Official Language of the state and marked by formal linguistic features more complex and more conservative than those of the L enshrined in a respected and perhaps ancient literature in contrast with the 'unofficial' status, 'hearth and home' use of the L with its variable and frequently 'reduced' structure limited to the spoken channels of communication. For such a situation the term 'diglossia' has been coined (Ferguson, 1959) exemplified, initially by such apparently diverse speech communities as Arabic, English and French Creole, modern Greek and Swiss German. More recently, however, investigations of seemingly diglossic communities have led to a redefinition of the term and the recognition that it is possible for there to be three sets of relationship between bilingualism and diglossia; bilingualism alone, diglossia alone and both bilingualism and diglossia (Fishman, 1970). We shall consider and give examples of all three below and indicate how the dynamism of social and linguistic change can produce cases which fall between the three.

5.3.1 Bilingualism without Diglossia

It is by no means usual for the whole of a society to contain large numbers of individuals who belong to more than one speech community – who have, that is, two L1s – but is far from uncommon for certain sections of a community to operate in more than one language in the course of everyday social interaction. Belgium, particularly along the Dutch-French language boundary, provides a clear European example. The situation is, however, not diglossic, in spite of the fact that there is often a functional division between the roles that the individual Dutch speaker is likely to play in that language and in French, since there is no agreement amongst Belgians that either language is H or L and, indeed, the co-equal National Official status of both is a clear legal statement of this fact.

5.3.2 Diglossia without Bilingualism

A necessary condition for the existence of diglossia without bilingualism appears to be the existence of a relatively rigid social system in which group membership is achieved by birth and which cannot be easily lost. An extreme case of this would be where the elite choose to isolate itself from the rest of the population with whom it communicated, if at all, through interpreters, preferring to make use of some high status foreign language for intra-group communication, e.g. the pre-1914-18 European elites of several countries using French or German rather than the local language. A similar situation can, of course, arise in the Third World where an elite may choose to operate in the language of the previous colonial rulers and either avoid contact with the masses or else communicate with them in some pidginized variety of the H – a point which will be taken up again in chapter 7 on language planning.

5.3.3   *Diglossia and Bilingualism*

A rare but possible situation in which a large proportion of the population can operate in more than one nationally recognized code is that in which not only is there a functional division between the codes, but an agreement that one is to be more highly valued than the other. This situation of bilingualism and diglossia seems to be examplified by Paraguay (Rubin, 1968) where Guarani acts as L and Spanish as H, and by the Swiss German-Standard German of the German speaking cantons, by the 'colloquial'-'classical' of the Arab world and by the Demotic-Katharevusa of Greece. There are important implications involved in bilingual-diglossic speech communities in respect of language planning in general and education in particular which we shall consider in chapter 7.

5.3.4   *Summary*

Bilingualism, then, is the result of the use of more than one code by an individual or a society. Diglossia is the result of the valuation of such functional divisions and hence bilingualism and diglossia can occur separately or together in a speech community. But, given that social change implies linguistic change, there are communities which are moving from diglossia towards bilingualism or bidialectalism and in which, parallel with the breaking down of a previously highly stratified social system and the creation of a more open and egalitarian society, the originally clearly-differentiated forms and functions of H and L are merging to produce in place of the earlier discrete codes a continuum in which codes merge into each other, e.g. the 'post-creole' continuum of the Commonwealth Caribbean, the topic of the next section.

5.4   LINGUISTIC CONTINUA

We have been asserting, in this chapter, the continuum nature of bilingual usage and wish here to take up again a point made earlier (2.4.3) about the difficulty of handling linguistic data from speech communities in which variation extends along some continuous spectrum of types — where, as de Camp puts it (de Camp, 1971, p.354), '. . . given two samples of . . . speech which differ substantially from one another, it is usually possible to find a third intermediate level in an additional sample. Thus it is not practicable to describe the system in terms of two or three or six or any other manageable number of discrete social dialects'. The problem for the linguist in such a context is to explain, as economically as possible, the structure of the underlying system to which all conform and the rules by which any individual speaker actualizes his own variety in interaction situations. More than this, an adequate description would contain rules which indicated how it was that speakers could switch 'up' or 'down' towards the terminal points of the continuum as they vary their code choices from within their repertoires in response to external constraints (cf. Hymes' taxonomy, 3.3.2.1).

A sample of data might help at this point to bring the enormity of the problem into sharper focus. In Guyana, there exists the kind of continuum we have been discussing above, ranging from a variety of English virtually identical to metropolitan standard English to extreme varieties of Creole English. This may be exemplified by the eighteen possible renderings of the sentence 'I gave him one'; presented below in a phonemic transcription:

FIGURE 5.7   *A Guyanese Continuum 1*

1	aɪ	geɪv			wʌn
2				hɪm	
3				ɪm	
4				i :	
5	a	gɪv		hɪm	
6				ɪm	
7					
8		dɪd	gɪv	i :	
9		dɪ			
10		dɪd	gɪ		wan
11			gi :		
12					
13		dɪ	gɪ	hi:	
14	mɪ				
15				i :	
16		bɪn			
17			gi :		
18				æm	

(Based on Cave, 1973, p.4f.)

How, one wonders, can such data be accounted for without recourse to idealizations which conceal much interesting information on the one hand, or individual descriptions of eighteen idiolects which would conceal the systematicness of the data on the other?

One solution would be to attempt to correlate each version with sociological categories of age, sex, socioeconomic class membership, education and so on (cf. 2.1.2.1) but this approach is dubious on two grounds – it is not possible to tell which characteristic or combination of characteristics is responsible for a particular code feature and sociological criteria are themselves continuous rather than discrete and hence not directly usable without error (see de Camp, 1971 p.354f. for discussion of these points). A further difficulty arises when it is recognized that style-shifting implies the ability on the part of each user to control more than one of the codes exemplified in the table above – one user's 'informal' speech being identical with another's 'formal' – and that such switching can occur not only between but even within the same speech act (see 5.5 below for some discussion of the rule-governed nature of code-switching).

It would, of course, be possible to write context-free transformational rules which would generate all eighteen possibilities plus, unfortunately, several which do not and presumably cannot occur, e.g. */aɪ bɪŋ gɪv æm wʌn/. A fragment of such rules might look something like this:

$$\text{GIVE + past} \rightarrow \left\{ \begin{matrix} \text{geɪv} \\ \emptyset \\ \text{bɪn} \\ \text{dɪ(d)} \end{matrix} \right\} + \left| \begin{matrix} \text{gɪ(v)} \\ \text{giː} \end{matrix} \right| \right\}$$

Another alternative would be to present the data in some kind of matrix form and attempt to arrange the parameters so as to produce an Implicational Scale (see section 2.4.3) as in Figure 5.8.

Some interesting facts emerge from what appears to be a rather confused situation. We might look first at those entries which are identical – 2/3, 5/6, 8/9/10 and 13/14 – in order to restate the data which has been concealed in the process of producing the matrix.

In each case, the distinction is between a 'full' and a 'reduced' form – /hɪm/; /ɪm/, /hiː/ ; /i/, /dɪd/; /dɪ/ and /gɪv/ ; /gɪ/ – and hence we should be well within our rights to propose, as a hypothesis only of course, that such a distinction marks, as it does in standard English, a shift of style from 'formal' to 'informal' and hence, the 'eighteen ways of saying 'I gave him one' are by no means of equal stylistic level. Some forms also correlate well with geographical provenance – 8-12 being 'typical' of African and 13-18 of Asian speech – and the whole set descending from the highest to the lowest socioeconomic strata of Guyanese society.

One or two are judged by native speakers of the creole (I am especially indebted to Miss J. Trotman of Georgetown for her comments) to be 'real howlers' – no.2 in particular – and others to be interesting transitional stages between communities – the /dɪ/ of 13 and 14 for instance which marks the movement in the speech of some Asians away from the expected /bɪn/ towards the /dɪ/ ~ /dɪd/ of the African versions of the creole.

FIGURE 5.8   *A Guyanese Continuum: Scale 1*

	A	B	C	D	Key		
1	0	0	0	0	A	:	*forms of 'I'*
2	+	0	0	0			+ : /a/
3	+	0	0	0			−: /mɪ/
4	+	0	+	0			0: /aɪ/
5	+	0	0	−	B	:	*Past marker*
6	+	0	0	−			+ : /dɪ(d)/
7	+	0	+	−			−: /bɪn/
8	+	+	+	−			0: /Ø/
9	+	+	+	−	C	:	*forms of 'him'*
10	+	+	+	−			+ : /(h)i/
11	+	+	+	+			−: /æm/
12	+	+	+	−			0: /(h)ɪm/
13	−	+	+	−	D	:	*forms of 'gave'*
14	−	+	+	−			+ : /giː/
15	−	−	+	−			−: /gɪ(v)/
16	−	−	+	+			0: /geɪv/
17	−	−	−	+			
18	−	0	−	+			

With this in mind, it is possible to adopt an approach which 'edits out' varieties which appear to be marginal and to produce an implicational scale for the remainder. Such an approach, it is recognized, is weak and unsatisfactory but can to some extent be justified in pedagogical terms as a step towards a normalization of creole speech, a step which must be taken if education in continuum areas is to come to grips with the sociolinguistic complexities of the situation in which it finds itself.

A revised table. (Figure 5.9 below) presents us with data that can be handled with relative ease with an implicational scale. For ease of reference the original utterance numbers have been retained:

FIGURE 5.9   *A Guyanese Continuum 2*

1	aɪ		geɪv	hɪm	wʌn
6				ɪm	
7			gɪv		
11	a		gi:		
12		dɪ			
14			gɪ	i:	wan
15					
16	mɪ	bɪn			
17			gi:	æm	
18					

A division suggested above between 'Asian' and 'African' versions of the creole can now be demonstrated by an almost perfect implication scale based on the three parameters the use of /æm/, /bɪn/ and /mɪ/, 'hallmarks' of Asian speech in contrast with their non-use by Africans. Such a scale has the additional value of simultaneously laying out the socioeconomic class membership of the speakers who would typically produce each utterance and indicating the direction in which change towards the superordinate variety (standard English) is naturally taking place amongst the Asian community. The use of a feature is marked with '+' and its non-use by '–' in the appropriate cell. Of 'African' varieties only 12 is used as an example, since neither they nor standard English make use of any of the three parameters. The scale is not quite perfect because of the non-occurrence of any tense marker in the last and most extreme example – no.18 – and since on these features 15 and 16 are the same, one has been omitted.

FIGURE 5.10   *A Guyanese Continuum: Scale 2*

	æm	bɪn	mɪ
12	–	–	–
14	–	–	+
15	–	+	+
17	+	+	+
18	+	–	+

A similar scale can be constructed for the African versions which will distinguish varieties within it and the type as a whole from Asian and standard forms at the same time. Four parameters appear to be adequate – the use of /dɪ/, of a form of 'gave' without a final consonant, of /i:/ for 'him' and /a/ for 'I'. This scale, unlike that in Figure 2.6, is perfect for the data and the parameters chosen and, like Figure 2.6, one pair of utterances, indistinguishable on terms of the four features chosen is represented by one, i.e. 11 is identical to 12 except for the vowel of 'give'.

FIGURE 5.11   *A Guyanese Continuum: Scale 3*

	dɪ	gi:/	gɪ	i:	a
1	–	–	–	–	
6	–	–	–	+	
7	–	–	+	+	
11	+	+	+	+	

An interesting feature of this scale which is apparent from the sudden jump between 7 and 11 is the hypothetical form, which may indeed occur although the hiatus between the adjacent vowels makes its unlikely. It suggests – *\/a gi: i: wan/ or /a gɪ i: wan/ – a clear example of the way in which an analysis of this type may have a feedback into fieldwork in suggesting to the investigator the possible existence of as yet unattested forms.

5.4.1 *Summary*

The attempt by creolists in particular to deal with linguistic data which previously was either ignored or submerged by idealization has led in recent years to the realization that not only do creole-language speech communities contain a continuum of codes which merge into each other and between which there are no clear-cut dividing lines but that this situation is in fact the norm for language – an ever changing pattern of code choices and functions reflecting and facilitating social change in the community which uses it.

How the individual is able to switch from one code to another is considered in the next section in terms of bilingual interlanguage switching but it is to be understood that the whole notion of continua and of code-switching must be thought of as applying to codes in the widest sense of the term, i.e. to intralanguage – stylistic and dialectal – switching as well as to interlanguage – bilingual, in the common usage of the term – switching and in any case, as we shall see in the next chapter, the terms 'language', 'dialect' and so on still lack precise definition.

5.5 RULES FOR BILINGUAL CODE-SWITCHING

Implicit in what has been said above on bilingual usage is the assumption that the individual is able to switch from one language to another – or from one style to another in the case of the monolingual – in a rule-governed rather than a random way. It is this assumption that we must now consider as we attempt to formulate rules which constitute the switching mechanism which we saw was a *sine qua non* for bilingual usage.

5.5.1 *Types of Rule*

In somewhat crude terms, two very different types of rule for code-switching might be attempted – *sociolinguistic* rules which would match linguistic choices with social constraints, at the micro- level of individual use or the macro- level of national language choice and *psycholinguistic* rules which would relate choice to psychological constraints, inherent in the verbal planning which preceeds speech. We shall concern ourselves here with the second type, since from the arguments presented earlier which insisted on the difference between languages and dialects and styles being seen as one of degree rather than kind, it follows that the social constraints which can be called upon to explain stylistic variation in the monolingual are equally those which can explain bilingual usage – age, sex, status, setting, topic, etc.; Hymes' factors subsumed under the acronymic heading SPEAKING (see 3.3.2.1 on this). The kind of rule in which we are interested in this section is a probabilistic rule which explains not why topic X is typically discussed in language Y in society Z – sociolinguistic rules would seek to do this – but how it is that, even within the same utterance, bilinguals 'mix' their languages and produce speech acts like *So wir gehen essen maintenant n'est-ce que pas?* (overheard in Strasbourg) or *Can one buy zucchini in inghilterra?* (produced by myself in conversation with an Italian L2–English L1 speaker).

5.5.2 *Verbal Planning*

Psycholinguistic research indicates clearly that prior to the actualization of speech the semantic content of the intended utterance is encoded by means of some kind of verbal planning process, that the 'chunks' of language involved co-occur fairly closely with the unit *Tone Group* (Halliday, 1967 and see 3.2.1.3 earlier for a mention of this in relation to communication channels) or *Sense Group* (O'Connor and Arnold, 1961, p.3) and rarely exceed in number of words the 'magic' 7 + 2 (Miller, 1967). Indications of the verbal planning process in action can be readily seen in the hesitations, pauses, back-trackings and the like of spontaneous speech (Goldman-Eisler, 1968, esp. p.127f.) which, in the utterances of the bilingual, permit the switching from one language to another, even, as we point out above, within the same 'chunk'.

We assume, then, that verbal planning consists in essence of matching 'meanings' with code items and the encoding of these in an integrated form as a 'message'. If this is the base, the bilingual has, in principle at least, two or more lexical items, for example, for the expression of the 'same' meaning (the situation is of course far more complex than this bald statement makes it seem – see the discussion earlier in this chapter) or, conversely, one language may lack a lexical item to express a particular meaning which the speaker wishes to convey. Our earlier example of the child discussing, in Italian, events at an English school demonstrates the phenomenon well – the 'sandwich word' wedged, as it were, between structural items of the 'other language' (Clyne, 1967, esp. pp.84-95).

5.5.2.1   *Sandwich Words*
A common feature of bilingual speech is the extent to which L2 lexis occurs within the general syntax of the L1 – the 'franglais' which has so excited the purists in France, the wholesale adoption of English lexis in certain topics by Commonwealth nations in the Third World – the L1 providing the semantically empty framework which carries the semantically full lexis of the L2, e.g. *ek schoolmaster ko: Ti:n so: rupe Tankha: milTi: Thi:* – 'a schoolmaster used to get 300 rupees a month' (Hindi examples are from Setlur, 1973). 'T' is used here to represent the retroflex [t].

5.5.2.2   *Switch-Words*
The 'sandwich word' described above is the easiest to describe and probably the least interesting aspect of, code-switching behaviour amongst bilinguals. More intriguing are cases where an item appears to have triggered off a switch into the other language, perhaps only for two or three words, perhaps for the rest of the interaction. The English-Italian example above demonstrates this. The lexical item *zucchini* represents the concept of a vegetable for which the speaker had no English word, not knowing, at the time, that the English for *zucchini* was *courgettes*. The expected utterance might well therefore have been *Can one buy zucchini in England*?; a very ordinary example of a 'loan'. But in this case *zucchini* occurs not as the anticipated 'sandwich word' but as a switch which completes the utterance in Italian, assisted by the fact that *in*, though pronounced slightly differently, is common both in form and meaning in the two languages.

Two types of switching may be suggested – anticipatory and consequential – depending on whether the effect of the switch word precedes or follows it.

Anticipatory switching – like regressive assimilation, e.g. *absurd* pronounced /əp's̩ʒːd/ an item influences some part of the utterance preceeding it, in this case the devoicing of /b/ in anticipation of the voiceless /s/ – an English lexical item may trigger an earlier part of the utterance into English though the whole speech act is essentially in Hindi, e.g. *To: wo: hoard of whiskey To: Tumarre ghar me͂ he* – 'The hoard of whiskey is in your house' – in which the item *whiskey* might well be expected as a loan and to occur as a 'sandwich word' but here switches the preceding pair of words into English in spite of the existence of the post-position *ka* 'of' and a lexical item *jamak* meaning 'hoard'.

Consequential switching – the reverse of the situation above, like progressive assimilation – *absurd* pronounced /əb'zʒːd/ – influences items following the switch word, e.g. . . . *saːth rupe, it's too much* – ' . . . six rupees, it's too much' where the phonic similarity between the Hindi and English 'rupee' presumably switched the rest of the utterance into English.

There are naturally problems involved in deciding the motivation of a switch – the discovery of the switch word itself is by no means easy – especially when the cause may not be lexical but syntactic, e.g. *Oui. Vous êtes absolument right*; 'Yes. You are absolutely right' an utterance (personally attested) in which an L1 user of French with considerable knowledge of English answered a native English-speaker who, he knew, also spoke French. Here the switching mechanism is of considerable interest, since it is syntactic. Having intended the message 'Yes. You are absolutely right', there is no way of generating a grammatical French sentence using *être* – the complement *raison* must have *avoir* as its verb – and hence the speaker has two ways out of the dilemma, either he can begin the utterance again – *Oui Vous avez* . . . – or he can find a lexical item which will act as complement to *être*. The second alternative was chosen in this case and, interestingly, *right* is treated as a French lexical item pronounced with a French uvular 'r' [ʁ].

Why do bilinguals not resist such switching? Many do in fact but in communities in which more than one language is in habitual use by the majority of the population such switching is taken for granted since, as Haugen puts it, ' . . . they are accustomed to having bilingual speakers before them and know that which ever language they use they will be understood' (quoted in Rayfield, 1970, p.54) and in addition to the pointless effort involved in translating a direct quotation, for example, (who would bother in Britain to translate the French of 'President de Gaulle cried "Vive la France" '?) a switch can function as a stylistic device. Hence Fishman's term 'metaphorical switching' (Fishman, 1970, p.44) and the functional identity of bilingual language switching and monolingual register or dialect switching. Switching of this kind, then, has a rhetorical function serving to ' . . . emphasize a statement and add colour to speech' (Rayfield, op. cit. p.56), perhaps by repeating the statement in both languages — 'I'll never do it, jamais' — making a parenthetic remark or introducing taboo words or topics into the conversation.

5.5.3   *Summary*

Given that bilingualism is a special case of the wider phenomenon of stylistic variation, switching between languages has to be seen as different in degree only from switching within one language and indeed within a community in which most speakers are bilingual the concept of 'different languages' can be seen to have little validity except as 'different styles'. It is possible to see then in rules for language choice exactly the same parameters in operation as appear when attempts are made to correlate monolingual choices of linguistic items with situational constraints of an essentially sociological nature.

Particularly interesting in the case of the bilingual is the psycholinguistic problem which emerges when we attempt to explain how he keeps his languages apart and how this mechanism is at times suspended or overridden. The initial approaches to the answering of these questions appear to be to recognize the crucial influence of verbal planning and the regressive or progressive influences which a lexical item — and no doubt, but less easy to recognize, syntactic structure — can have on its neighbours; an influence which can 'switch' a whole segment of interaction out of one language into another. What is most fascinating about such phenomena is the way in which such switches often take place without the conscious recognition or later recollection of the participants — a fact which must make us yet again question the assumptions of monolithic language structure creating languages between which there are discrete boundaries.

5.6   CONCLUSION

This chapter began with some thoughts on the bilingual individual and closed with the same topic but from a rather different standpoint, having surveyed on the way the relationship between bilingualism and biculturalism and the problem of linguistic variations which fall together along a continuum of types between which no clear divisions can be drawn. We are now ready to question even more closely the assumption that the terms 'language', 'dialect', 'vernacular' and so forth represent definable entities whose characteristics can be listed — we need a typology and that is the aim of the next chapter.

6
Language Types
-Formal and Functional Typologies

During the course of the previous chapter, we considered the code-switching behaviour of those whose codes are normally labelled 'different languages' and hinted that there might be social meaning in the choice of one code rather than another. In this chapter, we shall pursue one notion involved in code-switching between languages a little further, and consider the types of language available for such choice before moving on in the next chapter to consider the large-scale functions of language at the level of the state as an introduction to the problems of language planning.

An extreme view of language can be that each individual uses an autonomous code which is different from that used by any other and although, in an absolute sense, this is true, little value can be derived from it as a means of explaining the forms and functions of language. More useful is to accept that some codes resemble each other in the forms they use or in the social functions they perform and the status which accrues to them as a result of performing those functions. This would permit us to type languages on two parameters — formal and functional — to create, that is, formal linguistic and functional sociolinguistic typologies.

6.1   FORMAL TYPOLOGIES OF LANGUAGE

The comparison of languages in terms, not of their historical antecedents, which was the great contribution of the nineteenth century, but of similarity of structure — phonetic, phonological, morphological, syntactic, lexical, to use the traditional labels — began in earnest in the late seventeenth century and has led to a number of notions which can be drawn upon to create three or four broad structural types to which, to a greater or lesser degree, any particular language will conform, i.e. no language is tied wholly to the use of one type of structure to the exclusion of the others.

Two fundamental systems can be seen in the internal structuring of languages — (1) *analysis*, in which items consist mainly of free morphemes, i.e. can function as words without the addition of any kind of affix, e.g. Chinese and Vietnamese, in which the word is an immutable monosyllable and (2) *synthesis*; in which items tend mainly to be bound morphemes, i.e. unable, as individuals, to act as words, e.g. Classical Greek, Latin, the Slav languages, Turkish.

An example from English may be useful here in which both analytic and synthetic structures can be found. Most English lexical items are analytic — *eat, dog, bad, fast* — but the language makes use of synthetic processes for the marking of tense, plurality, degree, etc. — *ate, dogs, worse, fastest,* etc. — and some items consist entirely of bound morphemes, e.g. *retain, deceive, institution,* since there is no word 'tain' or 'ceive', etc.

Synthetic processes are manifested in three major subsystems — agglutination, flexion or fusion, incorporation — each of which will be illustrated below:

1. *Agglutination*: typical of this type of structure is the form-invariable root + affixes, e.g. the Turkish root + suffix + suffix in *evlerimizde* 'in our houses' (*house* + plural + *my* + plural + *in* = *ev* + *ler* + *im* + *iz* + *de*) or the Swahili prefix + prefix . . . + root in *anamataka* 'he wants him' (*he* + present + *him* + want = *a* + *na* + *m* + *taka*). Agglutination also occurs quite frequently in English, e.g. the 'root' *reason* may be greatly expanded by the addition of affixes which modify both the meaning and the form class membership of the word — *un - reason - able - ness*.

2. *Flexion*: in contrast with the agglutinative structures above, flexional structures permit, not only the addition of affixes but the actual modification of the root, to the extent that root and affix become fused, e.g. Arabic *k – t – b* has some general 'meaning' of 'book', 'reading', 'writing' but, by the use of various types of affix — prefix, infix, suffix — and modifications to the root itself, a wide range of precise meanings can be created, e.g. *jiktib* 'he writes', *tiktib* 'she writes', *ʔaktib* 'I write', etc. Such structure is very typical of the Semitic languages but by no means confined to them. English provides a number of examples — *were* clearly contains the 'syntactic information' *be* + past + plural, just as *was* contains *be* + past + singular but it is well-nigh impossible to decide, in any principled way, which elements represent *be*, which *past* and which *number*.

3. *Incorporation*: the two processes above have demonstrated the fusion at the level of the individual lexical item of larger and larger linguistic units, a movement which culminates in the holophrastic 'single word sentence' of the incorporating or polysynthetic languages which, as Robins (1964, p.334,) puts it '. . . only differ from the

agglutinative and fusional types by carrying the processes to extremes and uniting within single grammatical words what in most other languages one would find spread out amongst several words'. Some New World languages provide examples of this type of structure, e.g. Nahuatl; *qanivatcar'oanivinjgu* 'did I drink at the house?' = *house* + *at* + past + drink + interrogative + *I*.

We noted above that no language is wholly isolating or agglutinative or the like in its structure but it is true to say that languages tend to favour one process rather than another, English being essentially analytic but making use of the synthetic processes of agglutination and flexion. In addition, linguistic change in general appears to be in the direction of analysis, i.e. towards the loss of affixes and the creation of the immutable and often monosyllabic lexical item, a trend which can be observed both in diachronic studies of language change over a long period of time – compare the steadily decreasing part flexion is playing in present-day Romance languages compared with the role it had in their common ancestor Latin – and in the pidginization of languages (see 6.4 below).

The formal typologies which can be derived from the comparison of language structures in terms of the processes listed above are of some interest but, for our purposes, less attractive than a typology which emphasizes, not internal form but the external social function of a language, i.e. a sociolinguistic typology which defined, with some degree of precision, such terms as 'standard language', 'vernacular', 'pidgin', etc. It is to such a typology that we must now turn.

6.2   FUNCTIONAL TYPOLOGIES OF LANGUAGE

The underlying assumptions of a sociolinguistic typology are that 'languages may be differentiated into types in terms of . . . attributes which demonstrate a consistent tendency to affect social attitudes toward them' (Stewart, 1962, p.17) and that these attributes may be ranked to produce an '. . . order of potential social prestige' (ibid., p.18). We shall consider the attributes necessary for the definition of sociolinguistic processes – pidginization and creolization.

Three models for the definition of sociolinguistic types have been proposed since 1962. We shall consider each, since the modifications to the original proposals are of some interest as an indication of the way in which thinking has developed in sociolinguistics during the last decade.

6.2.1   *Model 1: Stewart, 1962*

Stewart proposed a typology which depended on four attributes –

standardization, vitality, historicity, homogenicity — by means of which seven sociolinguistically defined language types could be isolated. The four attributes are worth looking at in some detail since they have formed the basis, unchanged or revised and extended, of the subsequent improvements to the model.

1. *Standardization* — whether or not the language possesses an agreed set of codified norms which are accepted by the speech community and form the basis of the formal teaching of the language, whether as L1 or L2. This feature has been referred to already above in the discussion of 'norms' of usage (4.1) and it is important to recognize the necessity for the codification not only to have taken place but also to be accepted before a language can be said to have been standardized. The existence of grammars and dictionaries, then, is a necessary but not a sufficient condition for standardization; there are, after all, linguistic descriptions of many of the world's languages but without the acceptance of these by their users and their use as the arbiters in the normative teaching such conditions do not materially alter the classification of existing non-standard languages. Naturally, standardization, being a feature imposed upon rather than inherent in a language, can take place at any time, e.g. the creation of the national language of Indonesia — Bahasa Indonesia — by the process of standardizing an existing non-standard variety of Malay — Bazaar Malay, originally a pidgin language.

2. *Vitality* — whether or not the language possesses a living community of native speakers, i.e. the L1-L2 distinction made above (5.1). Here again, change is possible. A language may lose its vitality as its L1 community dies out, e.g. the recent demise of the Gaelic language of the Isle of Man — Manx — or, conversely, a classical language, like Hebrew, or pidgin languages like Neomelanesian may gain a community of mother tongue users and become, in the case of the first, a standard language or in the case of the pidgin, a creole.

3. *Historicity* — whether or not the language has grown up or grew up through use by some ethnic or social group. The possession of this attribute clearly divides L1 languages from L2 and especially from artificial languages which are *ad hoc* creations. However, a pidgin language, though in origin artificial in this sense, has developed over time through use by social groups for whom it is not L1 but functions as a lingua franca, so, as it stands, the distinction is not quite so clear-cut as it at first appears.

4. *Homogenicity* — whether or not the basic grammar and lexicon of the language are derived from the same pre-stages of the language. It will be seen that while many or perhaps most of the languages of the world are homogenetic — French for example having developed from vulgar Latin — some are not and that the examples of such 'mixed' languages are by no

means confined to non-standard varieties – the pidgins and creoles for example – but include such standard languages as Swahili, Maltese and indeed English, with its essentially Germanic grammar based on that of Old English and its mixed Germanic-Romance lexicon.

FIGURE 6.1   *Sociolinguistic Typology 1*

ATTRIBUTES				LANGUAGE TYPE	EXAMPLE
1	2	3	4		
+	+	+	±	Standard	Standard English
+	−	+	+	Classical	Latin
−	+	+	+	Vernacular	Colloquial Arabic
−	+	+	−	Creole	Krio
−	−	−	−	Pidgin	Neomelanesian
+	−	−	±	Artificial	Esperanto
−	−	+	±	Marginal	'Household languages'

Key:

+ possession of attribute
− lack of attribute
± either + or −

6.2.2   *Model 2: Stewart, 1968*

In view of a number of problems which arose with the first model – its inability to distinguish 'vernacular' from 'dialect', thereby putting the majority of Asian, African and American 'tribal' languages on the same sociolinguistic footing as the geographical and social dialects of the standard languages of the world, e.g. Gondi being classed alongside 'Cockney' or Demotic Greek and emphasis on homogenicity which is necessarily a matter of degree – a revised model was proposed in which the attribute 'homogenicity' was dropped and replaced by a new attribute 'autonomy' (Stewart, 1968).

   1. *Standardization* – as above.
   2. *Vitality* – as above.
   3. *Historicity* – as above.
   4. *Autonomy* – whether or not the language is accepted by the users as being distinct from other languages or varieties. Clearly, where there are substantial structural differences between two varieties, French and English for example, no question arises as to the autonomy of the two systems

(problems connected with 'code-switching' however cast doubts on the absoluteness of this statement – see 5.1.2). But when there are substantial structural similarities, as there are between standard English and the regional and social dialects or between metropolitan English and its pidgin and creole varieties, disputes will occur between those who claim and those who deny autonomy for the 'lower' variety (see 6.3.3 below and 5.3 on 'diglossia').

FIGURE 6.2   *Sociolinguistic Typology 2*

ATTRIBUTES				LANGUAGE TYPE	EXAMPLE
1	2	3	4		
+	+	+	+	Standard	Standard English
+	−	+	+	Classical	Latin
−	+	+	+	Vernacular	Colloquial Arabic
−	+	+	−	Dialect	Cockney
−	+	±	−	Creole	Krio
−	−	−	−	Pidgin	Neomelanesian
+	−	−	+	Artificial	Esperanto

6.2.3   Model 3: Hymes 1971

While Model 2 was clearly an advance on Model 1, several problems also arose in its use. The subjectiveness of the category 'autonomy', the fact that partial standardization [i.e. the existence of a codification but its non-acceptance by users] and partial historicity, all seemed possible and therefore tended to blur the edges between the types. In addition, the notion 'marginal language', now unaccounted for, seemed in retrospect, to have been valuable as a coverall term for several non-standard, but actually systematic, varieties ranging from 'baby-talk', 'foreigner talk', to a number of L2 varieties 'Xized Y' and individual learner's 'interlanguages'. For this reason three new attributes – reduction, mixture and *de facto* norms – are suggested together with a restatement of the attribute 'historicity' (based on Fishman, 1971, and Hymes, 1971).

1. *Standardization* – as above.

2. *Vitality* – as above.

3. *Historicity* – whether or not the community is concerned to find for the language a '. . . 'respectable' ancestry in times long past' which leads to the attempt to '. . . create and cultivate myths and geneologies

concerning the origin and development of their standard varieties...'
(Fishman, 1971, p.230).

4. *Autonomy* – as above.

5. *Reduction* – whether or not the language makes use of a smaller set of structural relations and items in this syntax and phonology and a smaller lexicon than some related variety of the same language.

FIGURE 6.3 *Sociolinguistic Typology 3*

LANGUAGE TYPE	EXAMPLE	1	2	3	4	5	6	7
Standard	Standard English	+	+	+	+	–	±	+
Classical	K. James' Bible English	+	–	+	+	–		+
Vernacular	'Black English'	–	+	–	+	–	–	+
Dialect	Cockney	–	+	–	–	–	–	+
Creole	Krio	–	+	–	–	+	+	+
Pidgin	Neomelanesian	+	–	–	–	+	+	+
Artificial	'Basic English'	–	–	–	+	+	–	+
Xized Y	'Indian English'	–	–	–	±	–	+	?
Interlanguage	'A's English'	–	–	–	–	+	+	–
Foreigner Talk	'B's simplified English'	–	–	–	–	+	±	–

Key:
+ possession of attribute
– lack of attribute
± either + or –
? insufficient evidence

6. *Mixture* — whether or not the language consists essentially of items and structures derived from no source outside itself. This is a return to a modified version of the notion of 'homogenicity' suggested originally in Model 1 and while it seems most unlikely that there are any entirely 'pure' languages, it appears valuable to take account of the fact that some languages at different times in their development are more or less willing to 'borrow' from others.

7. *De facto norms* — whether or not the language possesses norms of usage which, though uncodified, are accepted by the community. A simple test of whether norms of this type exist would be to discover whether there were speakers who were thought by the community to 'speak well' — individuals whose competence could be used as a check on standards and who could therefore act as teachers of the variety.

6.2.4 *Summary*

We have been considering typologies which illustrate differences, not between the internal form and structure of codes but in their sociolinguistic attributes which influence social attitudes to them and the social functions which each is likely to be permitted to perform. It should be emphasized again that the scale points are, of necessity, arbitrary — attitudes being, in any case, extraordinarily difficult to measure — and that one individual or group is often likely to grant the possession of a feature to a code which is denied by another. However, in spite of this, we shall attempt below to exemplify the ten language types presented above by drawing upon the world-wide variations in 'English'.

6.3 THE RANGE OF ENGLISH

English, it appears, provides examples of all ten of the varieties categorized in Figure 6.3. It therefore seems useful to expand on the ten types and to give examples of them from world-wide English. Before this can be done however, it should be emphasized that the points on the scale are arbitrary (as all scale-points are), that there exists today a considerable degree of dispute concerning the status of certain types of English and that this arises, to a great extent, from disagreements as to the possession or non-possession of the attributes listed above. It should be recognized too that not only the formal characteristics but the functional status of a language or variety can change quite quickly, given the social motivation to make such changes, and that such planned change is the central issue of a topic of major import in macrosociolinguistics — language planning (see 7.3).

6.3.1   *Standard English*

Standard English can be defined (see Figure 6.3 above) as a variety of English which has been standardized, possesses a mother tongue community of users which is concerned to find a respectable history for the language, is autonomous, non-reduced, somewhat mixed and possesses, of necessity, *de facto* norms, as a result of possessing *de jure* norms as a standardized language.

The norms of usage for standard English, codifications of the grammatical, lexical and to a lesser extent phonological conventions of the dominant socioeconomic groups in the major mother tongue communities of North America, Britain, Central and Southern Africa, Australasia consist (as we have seen in chapter 2) of an essentially shared grammar, lexis and indeed rhetoric, alongside a considerable degree of tolerance of phonological variation.

6.3.2   *Classical English*

Given that there are older varieties of English which differ from the present-day standard only (in functional terms) in lacking vitality and which are afforded a high status – they enshrine the 'great works' of English literature and are the basis of the public worship of the Established and the Free Churches – it seems possible to accept that there does exist a type (or types) of English which might properly be labelled 'classical'. The implications of this for the teaching of English overseas, where the writings of such 'classical' authors may be the only acceptable model presented to learners are of considerable importance as factors tending to the creation of Xized varieties of English amongst detached L2 and L1 speech communities.

6.3.3   *Vernacular English*

The term 'vernacular' seems to be a most unsatisfactory one, since there are so many definitions of it (see, too, Labov's quite different use of the term in section 8.1.1.7, below). The most used, proposed by UNESCO, '. . . the mother tongue of a group which is socially or politically dominated by another group speaking a different language . . .' (UNESCO, 1953 p.46), is essentially a legal one and the definition above distinguishes the term from 'dialect' only in the possession of autonomy in the vernacular and its lack in the dialect. The essential problem is 'who is claiming autonomy for the variety?'

154 SOCIOLINGUISTICS

6.3.4 Dialect English

Just as with the notion 'vernacular' the problem arose of which group claims autonomy, so the same issue arises in regard to 'dialect'.

It would be an advantage if dialectologists were clear in their own definition of the term but even recent studies indicate that a common definition of dialects '. . . variant, but mutually intelligible, forms of one language, whereas *language* is assumed to imply a form of speech not on the whole intelligible to other languages' (Wakelin, 1972, p.1) dependent, as it still is, on the notion of mutual intelligibility is unfortunately not precise enough for our purposes.

There seems, too, little point in listing the 'dialects' of English, even if this were a feasible endeavour, since the subject of the whole of this book is, in the broadest sense, 'dialects' or, more simply and inclusively, just 'lects'.

6.3.5 Creole English

Creoles share many of the attributes of vernaculars and dialects but differ from them in the degree to which they are mixed and reduced in their structures. In comparison with the languages from which they have developed creoles demonstrate large-scale 'borrowing' — in the case of the English-based creoles from English and several West African languages — and 'reduction' in the sense that the grammar, phonology and lexis contains a smaller number of items and processes than that found in any of the contributory languages. An interesting feature of creole English (which will be discussed more fully in 6.4.2) is that the continuum situation in which they find themselves in relation to metropolitan English is rapidly increasing their structure and the proportion of English elements in it — a movement which must end in the redefinition, or the demand for the redefinition, of the variety as a dialect rather than a creole. Indeed, such a movement carries with it a denial of autonomy but, dialect status once having been achieved, leads on to a further demand for autonomy and vernacular status. The situation in the Caribbean provides fascinating examples of both processes in action simultaneously.

6.3.6 Pidgin English

It will be seen from Figure 6.3 that the crucial difference between pidgin languages and creole languages is their lack of vitality — a pidgin, unlike a creole, has no L1 speech community but has, in common both with creoles and other 'natural' L1 varieties, *de facto* norms of usage. Although, in origin, pidgins are L2 lingua francas, the fact of their use by social groups, particularly by linguistically heterogeneous societies where exogamous marriages are common, can lead to the growth of L1 communities of children for whom the language is the mother tongue – the pidgin has become a creole. It is possible too, for a pidgin to progress rapidly to the status of standard, given sufficient social and political effort, as in the case of Bahasa Indonesia referred to earlier.

6.3.7 Artificial English

An artificial variety of a language, like a pidgin, lacks both an L1 community and historicity and, again like the pidgin, shows considerable reduction but, unlike a pidgin, an artificial language is not only autonomous but has highly codified norms of usage. This is certainly the case with Basic English (Ogden, 1934) with its drastically reduced lexicon – 850 items – and its carefully codified textbooks and dictionaries. Basic also contrasts with a pidgin variety in the matter of mixture. Indeed the concentration on phrasal verbs of Old English origin, at the expense of longer single item verbs of Romance origin makes Basic less mixed than standard English.

In its intended global scope Basic can be seen as an attempt to normalize and codify the haphazard 'foreigner talk' described below and in this it contrasts strongly with the limited function artificial Englishes such as that agreed upon by air-traffic controllers and deck-crew in the international airlines.

6.3.8 Xized English

One interesting and little-studied variety of a language is that which arises when, for one reason or another, the motivation for or possibility of further learning is removed from a group of learners. It might be that the learners or teachers, or indeed, both, accept that a code efficient enough for their communicative purposes has developed and are prepared to settle for that. Where such a decision is reached early in the learning process, a drastically reduced system – a pidgin – results but where the fossilization occurs much later, a mixed but non-reduced variety is the result – an Xized Y. (Hymes, 1971, p.71). An example of this would be Indianized English or its converse Anglicized Hindi.

An Xized variety of a language may or may not have supporters who claim autonomy for it but if it does, the claim will, of necessity, be founded on a postulation of de facto norms of usage and may be supported by an attempt to create de jure norms – a codification of the norms of usage for the variety based on the practice of some socioeconomic or geographical group. An example of such a variety would be 'Indian English' — a 'full' version of English containing elements of Indian language systems (see Bansal, 1969). It is on the issue of the autonomy of varieties of English that there is considerable dispute at the present time, ranging from those who see incipient 'local Englishes' which are '. . . being taught and sanctioned by local custom' and regard these varieties as comparable to Scots or Australian English and equally viable as 'recognized and effective forms of world-wide English' (Perren, 1965, p.39), to those who deny the possibility of the existence of such a variety terming the entertainment of such a notion 'pernicious heresy' (Prator, 1968, p.474).

Xized varieties of English, whether autonomy is claimed for them or not, seem to be a common feature of the English of L2 users in English as a second language situation, just as the stable or unstable Interlanguage English (see below) typifies the English as a foreign language situation (see 5.3 on this distinction).

6.3.9   *Interlanguage English*

On the micro- rather than the macro- level, of individual rather than group usage, the Xized variety of a language finds its correlate in the Inter-language. Both are non-standard, both lack vitality and historicity and are mixed but the Interlanguage is further differentiated by being reduced, like the pidgins and creoles, but, unlike them, lacking even *de facto* norms of usage nor would anyone claim autonomy for them. They have, of course, norms in the sense that they are rule-governed activity but these norms are not common knowledge nor may they be cognitively accessible even to the user himself (see 5.1.2.3 on error analysis, and Corder, 1973).

Synchronic descriptions of language conceal a crucial factor; the natural state of language is change not stability and in the case of the concept of the Interlanguage the acceptance of this is of prime importance to distinguish the relatively stable from the relatively unstable variety.

In the second language situation — India for example — two extremes of Interlanguage can be isolated: the stable individual variety, judged against the incipient norms of the Xized English of the area and the unstable 'learner varieties' represented by the speech of those who are still engaged in acquiring the language as an L2 and in whose system change, perhaps very rapid, is still taking place (see comments earlier on 'error analysis' 5.1.2.3).

6.3.10   *Foreigner Talk English*

Two intentionally idiosyncratic varieties of English (Corder, 1971) used by

native speakers of English which deserve serious study by sociolinguists –
baby-talk and foreigner talk; in the sense of 'talk *to* babies and foreigners'
(Ferguson, 1971) – share six of the seven attributes above and may indeed
share a seventh, that of mixture. Both varieties and the earlier category
'marginal language', the *ad hoc* creation of linguistically mixed ships crews
(Reinecke, 1959) or Europeans in 'developing' countries and their house-
hold servants, are postulated on the assumption that there are parts of the
'normal' language which are in essence 'difficult' and that require reduction
on the part of the competent user of the language. Typically, changes
consist of a slower production, exaggerated emphasis, repetition, and so
forth. A hypothetical example of 'foreigner talk Italian' is given by Hall
(1964, p.377) as an example of pidginization – verbs in the infinitive, no
agreement between nouns and adjectives, no concord between subjects
and predicators and so forth and although there is little evidence to
support this suggestion, the similarity between European-based pidgin and
creole languages may, in part, derive from some tacit conventions amongst
the users of European languages on the procedures to be followed in
simplifying their languages for short-lived makeshift communication (see
6.4 on this).

A further curious aspect of these makeshift languages is that they are
L2 varieties of English used, initially at least, only by L1 speakers and
formed on the basis of hypotheses concerning the nature of L2 learning
or in the case of 'baby-talk' L1 acquisition and this being the case, such
varieties of the language deserve far more attention than they have so far
received.

6.4   THE PIDGINIZATION AND CREOLIZATION OF LANGUAGES

Pidgin and creole languages provide a fascinating example of the power of
sociolinguistic processes to mould available linguistic codes into satisfactory
media of inter-group communication and, as such, constitute a 'special
case' of what we have been discussing at some length earlier in this book –
the phenomenon of code-switching.

In terms of the typology suggested above, pidgin and creole languages are
identical except for the possession by the creole of vitality and its lack by
the pidgin i.e. the creole has an L1 community of users, while for the
pidgin there is no such community – all pidgin speakers are L2 users and
indeed, it is only the possession of *de facto* norms of usage that distinguishes it from a learner's interlanguage. One crucial shared feature –
reduction – links both pidgin and creole with other 'contact varieties'
which have arisen in response to the need for communication between
groups without a common language and separates them from the higher

status dialect, vernacular, classical and standard varieties. It may therefore be valuable to look at the process of pidginization and at the linguistic changes which it causes.

6.4.1 . Pidginization

Given a 'contact situation' in which two groups which share no common language wish to communicate, the growth of some kind of makeshift medium seems inevitable. At its most minimal, such a code might consist of a reliance on the non-verbal paralinguistic channels – gestures, body-movement and so forth (see 3.2 above) – initially crude and limited but potentially capable of development into a relatively complex and flexible system like, for example, that of the Plains Indians of North America (Beals, 1965, p.616). Most likely would be the combination of gestures and the 'acting out' of needs with frequently repeated elements from the languages of the users, in accordance with the conventions, overt or covert, of 'foreigner talk' (see 6.3.10 above). It is at this point that divergent views have been expressed as an explanation of why pidgin languages should arise from some but not all contact situations. Three major hypotheses have been proposed – 'baby-talk', polygenesis and monogenesis – each of which will be reviewed below.

6.4.1.1 The 'Baby-talk' Hypothesis

The 'baby-talk' theory assumes that the norms of 'foreigner talk' become the norms of teaching, i.e. the normal problems of learning compounded by the presentation to the learner of a deviant model by the teacher. This is a possible explanation for the appearance of short-lived 'marginal' languages but gives no hint as to the reasons why only *some* contact situations give rise to pidgins nor why pidgins (and creoles) in widely scattered areas and derived from different European and non-European languages should share substantial amounts of structure, not only lexical but also in syntax and in phonology. In essence, this theory suggests that a pidgin variety of a language consists of a 'frozen' or 'fossilized' inter-language (see 6.3.9 on interlanguages) which has become accepted as a medium for group rather than individual use.

6.4.1.2 Polygenesis

Just as the 'foreigner talk' theory of the origin of pidgins rests heavily on the notion of the 'reduction' of one language, so the polygenesis theory rests on the notion of 'mixture' of two or more. Crudely, a pidgin is seen as the result of the 'mixing' of the systems of the L1s of the two groups involved, to create a new hybrid system which contains elements of both but is neither – in zoological terms, a pidgin is a mule! Against this form of the polygenesis theory is the historical and actual evidence that, far from being the language of explorer to native or master to slave, pidgin and creole languages are, par excellence, the medium of communication between New Guinean and New Guinean, West African and West African, i.e. a genuine *native* lingua franca.

In order to account for this, it has been suggested that pidgins result, not from the mixing of two mother tongues but from the mixing of two or more interlanguages based on different and mutually unintelligible L1s. The basis of pidgin, then, is seen not as the European L1, simplified or otherwise by the first teachers, but as the 'transitional competences' of a number of those who had for a time been involved in contact but with the removal of that contact were forced to fall back on 'their knowledge of the language to date' and make that the basis of the system, i.e. to make full use of a reduced version of the L1 *as though* it were the 'full' form.

6.4.1.3   *Monogenesis*
The revised version of the polygenesis theory helps to account for one of the objections raised earlier but fails to answer the other. How is it that pidgin and creole languages of diverse origins are so similar? There must be some common element involved. The similarity between West African and Caribbean creoles might be explained by the common presence of Africans but what does 'African' mean in this context? It certainly implies less homogenicity of language than does the term 'European' – the other half of the mixture – since the West Africans involved in contact with European traders and slavers lived in an enormous area extending inland from the coast for up to 2,000 miles containing hundreds of languages representing several 'language families' (Greenberg, 1966, p.173, map A gives a hint of the complexity of the situation). Even if this were not the case, it is hard to see why there should be features common to pidgins of 'African origin' which recur in Pitcairnese or in Neomelanesian, in which no possible direct African influence can be supposed.

A proposed solution to the dilemma is found in what is, in a sense, an up-dating of the 'foreigner talk' thesis – the underlying similarities are traceable to a common European source. Either Europeans share common reduction techniques when speaking to foreigners, which is perhaps implausible, or else the European-based pidgins and creoles have derived from a common European-language pidgin whose conventions were adopted by later explorers as the basis of a system formed on their own mother tongues. There is historical as well as linguistic evidence to support the view that it was a pidginized Portuguese which acted as the initial European contact language during the 'geographical discoveries' of the sixteenth, seventeenth and eighteenth centuries and that other Europeans, following in the footsteps of the Portuguese, learned and relexified the pidgin (see Cave, 1973 for a tentative 'family tree' showing this).

6.4.2   Creolization

It has usually been assumed that creolization implies prior pidginization (Hall, 1962), i.e. a language system native to no one and functioning as a mere auxiliary becomes, sometimes rapidly, the L1 of some. But as de Camp puts it 'the beginning and end of this cycle is shrouded in uncertainty' (de Camp, 1971, p.349) and little attention has therefore been paid to the process by which pidgins become creoles, stabilize or die.

A major factor in the creolization of an existing pidgin seems to be the growth of communities which consist of families containing linguistically heterogeneous members. Typically as a result of migration and urban growth, children are born to parents who have no common language other than a pidgin which, unless the parents make a conscious effort to teach their own mother tongues to the child and avoid using the pidgin in his presence, is more than likely to become the child's L1. The existence of other children whose linguistic background is similar will lead to the use of pidgin outside, as well as inside, the home and it is this spread in the domains in which the language is called upon to operate that constitutes the 'expansion' process which finally makes the creole into a 'full' rather than a 'reduced' language as the pidgin is. Indeed, the native speaker of a creole, presented as he is with no alternative but the creole in which to express himself, can and will, make it as accurate and versatile a medium of communication as any other language. There will be linguistic signs of this expansion of scope — the lexis at least will be extended, either by the adoption of 'loans' from outside, e.g. the Krio ɔmɔlanke 'handcart' from the Yoruba (Jones, 1971, p.90) or by internal creation, e.g. the Krio term wantwant suggested for 'ambition' by Decker (1965). The grammar, too, is likely to extend in complexity as more precise expressions of temporal and spatial relations become necessary — typically this is seen in a growth amongst the stock of modal verbs on the one hand and prepositions on the other.

There seem to be several stages which a creole can reach, each of which can be illustrated by a number of examples:

    1. Virtual stability in relationship to other languages in the community, reflected in little or no linguistic change or expansion or contraction of domains of use. A clear example of this would be creole in Haiti, in which a kind of diglossia (5.3) has come about between the

'low', 'subordinate' creole and the 'high', 'superordinate' standard French.

2. Change is taking place which has resulted or seems likely to result in

(i) The extinction of the creole by the standard superordinate language. This has happened in the Dutch West Indies in the case of Negerhollands and is happening to Gullah in the islands off the coast of Georgia.

(ii) The evolution of the creole into a standard language. A contemporary case would be Bahasa in Indonesia but Afrikaans, Maltese and, it has been argued, most of the Romance languages after the fall of the Roman Empire may have a similar history.

(iii) The merging of the creole with the superordinate language. The 'post-creole continuum' (de Camp, 1971) of the Commonwealth Caribbean provides a striking example, e.g. Jamaican creole and standard English.

6.4.3 Linguistic Characteristics of Pidgin and Creole Languages

A surprising feature of pidgin and creole languages and one which is not limited to those with a common ancestry is the degree to which, in comparison with their 'parent languages', their linguistic structures are reduced – 'simplified' – in the direction of an analytic rather than synthetic system. The term 'simplified' is in quotation marks for a good reason: reduction leads not to the simplification of a language as a system of communication but, in the case of creoles at least, makes it more complex, since the smaller grammar, phonology and lexicon may be called upon to carry just as large a semantic load as the 'full' language and hence, each item has to bear a greater share of meaning.

One concomitant effect of shifting closer to a purely analytic or isolating system – an acceleration of the 'drift' (to use Sapir's term) which seems common to language in general over time – appears to be the growth of the use of grammatical tone, e.g. Krio (Sierra Leone) distinguishes 'large eyes' and 'greed' by tone alone – bíg yài (high low) in contrast with bìg yái (low-high)– and Jamaican creole negates the modal can mainly by tonal contrast – im kyàn guo 'he can go' and im kyáan guo 'he can't go'.

Another result of the trend towards isolating structures is the loss of morphological elements which distinguish number and case in nouns, pronouns and adjectives and tense – aspect relationships in the verb and their replacement by items which in the 'parents' are normally independent lexical items. For example, many English-based pidgins and creoles have *dem*, historically 'them', as a plural marker with nouns — *di buk* and *di buk dem* — and even with proper nouns — *Jan* and *Jan dem* 'John and his friends'.

In sum, pidgin and creole languages appear to be simplified when compared with the languages from which they have derived. There are 'extensive grammatical differences between the structures of H and L', and in the lexicon 'H items have phonemes not found in "pure" L items' and 'many paired items, one H one L, referring to fairly common concepts frequently used in both H and L where the range of meaning of the two items is roughly the same' — the quotations are from Ferguson (1959) and refer to the diglossia situation in which many pidgin and creole languages find themselves functioning as L (see 5.3 above).

6.4.4   *Summary*

Pidgin and creole languages can be seen as a special case of the accommodation which takes place when speakers of different codes come into contact with each other and an acceleration of the ever present trend in languages towards a greater use of analytic structures — relationships shown by whole words rather than by affixes. In terms of a sociolinguistic typology, creole and pidgin languages, stand on either side of the L1-L2 line, possessing *de facto* norms like the L1 varieties but being reduced in structure like most of the L2s. Historical linguistics too may find in the processes of pidginization and creolization a clue to otherwise puzzlingly rapid change in languages in the past (Southworth, 1971); a further example of the way in which sociolinguistic interests lead to a breaking down of the synchronic-diachronic dichotomy.

6.5   CONCLUSION

We have now reached the point where it is possible to provide fairly precise definitions for at least ten distinct types of codes, both in terms of their linguistic structure and the attitudes adopted by speech communities to them. Seven parameters — standardization, vitality, historicity, autonomy, reduction, mixture and *de facto* norms of usage — seem adequate for the specification of the component characteristics of ten types, ranging from standard to foreigner talk and taking in such intermediate types as pidgins, creoles, artificial languages, etc. It will become clear in the next chapter that, although there is no necessary correlation between the formal structural characteristics of a language and its sociolinguistic type, there are strong indications that sociolinguistic type has a powerful influence on social function (and no doubt the converse) and hence, on the crucial macrosociolinguistic issue of language planning – code choice, not at the individual, nor at the intra group level but at the intra-national and international level.

7
Language Planning
- Communities and Policies

It is intended in this chapter to continue the description of language use, focusing on the macro- contexts of national and supranational communication needs and the policies adopted by governments through which language choices are made. We shall examine the contexts, goals, policies and language types available to the ruling elites of 'developing nations' in particular, since it is in such societies that a variety of interesting linguistic and social problems are most clearly demonstrated and· a wide range of solutions attempted. We shall conclude the chapter with an exposition of the notion of national sociolinguistic profiles which capture, in symbolic form, the linguistic situations of nations and thereby permit the comparison of states separated in time and space and suggest generalizable characteristics of language choice and social function at the macro- level of sociolinguistic description.

7.1 LANGUAGE USE IN MULTILINGUAL SOCIETIES

A basic assumption of sociolinguistics is that individuals are to be seen as members of social groups, in which they play social roles within domains of various kinds, making use, as they do so, of appropriate behaviour, some of which is language. A fundamental research topic for the socio-linguist, then, is the discovery and delimitation of groups and the correl-ation of their constituent roles with typical linguistic choices. However, such a task can be approached from two contrasting standpoints − (1) by analysing the language use of individuals or that involved in small-group interaction, i.e. micro-, intra-group, description or, alternatively (2), by studying the typical language choices of groups as aggregates, in their macro-, inter-group, interactions within the context of society as a whole.

Where the linguistic choices involve code-switching between languages, a pair of contrasting micro-, macro- approaches can be adopted. The first, centred on the bilingual individual, would raise questions concerned with the ways in which it is possible for the bilingual to operate in more than one language and to switch between the various codes in his repertoire (see 4.2.2 on this); the second, centred on the group, would be interested in discovering how language was used to maintain and create social distance or co-operation, how elites gain control of the political machinery of the state or lose it to other elites. In short, this chapter is concerned as was chapter 5, with bilingualism but in its macro-, rather than its micro-aspect. This being so, the correlations which we shall expect to find between language use in such a large context will be with the theories of the social rather than with the behavioural scientist – economists, historians, educationists and political scientists – and the sociolinguist will need to justify to them, just as he needs to justify to the psychologist, the relevance of his interests and expertise to the fields in which they are acknowledged experts.

We shall begin with a discussion of the social contexts in which language planning takes place, but first there is a terminological problem arising from the ambiguity of the term 'bilingualism' that needs to be disambiguated before a clear discussion can take place.

'Bilingualism' refers both to the use by an individual and the use by a group or nation of more than one language, i.e. it subsumes within it the micro- and macro- aspects of multilingualism. A neat solution (proposed by Kloss, 1968) commends itself and will be used here:

Micro-level; individual phenomena may be designated by the use of the appropriate Latin-root terms, e.g. bilingual/multilingual individuals, bilinguals, bilingualism, etc.

Macro-level; group phenomena, conversely, may be labelled with the equivalent Greek-root terminology, e.g. monoglossic, diglossic, polyglossic groups, nations, states, federations, etc.

An example, a Belgian in Brussels may well use two distinct languages during the course of a single day – Dutch and French – and is therefore a *bilingual*. His usage will probably correlate closely with the power-solidarity axis – French functioning as the language of power in public, formal situations, with strangers, in contrast with Dutch at home, in informal situations, with friends – and hence, the society in which he lives is *polyglossic*, in the sense that more than one language is in common use (social function apart) within the confines of the state (see 5.3 earlier for the contrasting notion of *diglossia*).

We are, then, about to consider language use within polyglossic states some of which are also diglossic and all of which contain numbers of bilingual individuals.

7.1.1 *Linguistic Homogenicity and Heterogenicity*

Although, in an absolute sense, there is no such thing as a linguistically homogeneous social group or nation, since all individuals control repertoires of codes which differ, in some respects, from those controlled by others, for practical purposes it is convenient to accept that some differences between codes are thought of by the users of the code to be so great as to warrant the distinguishing label 'different language'. It is in this 'common-sense' spirit that we intend to approach the question of linguistic heterogenicity, as we recognize the crucial role in language choice, at the level of the state rather than the individual, of three key factors — the total number of 'different languages' within the state, the ratio of L1 users of each to the total population and the geographical and socioeconomic situation of each language.

7.1.1.1 *Total Number of Languages*

A major problem is immediately encountered when one attempts to count 'languages', since, as we have been stating all along, the difference between 'language', 'dialect', 'style' tends to be one of degree rather than of kind and more dependent on the attitudes of individuals and groups than on objective measures of any kind. Hence, estimates may well vary wildly, even for the same area and the same point in time, e.g. Wurm (1968, p.345), commenting on the linguistic diversity of the Highlands Districts of Papua-New Guinea, points out that 'the number of distinct languages encountered there could be said to be 48 or 26 according to what linguistic criteria were applied to distinguish between languages and dialects'. Much depends on achieving a consensus on the question of autonomy (see 6.2.2 above) — one of the contributory factors for example which has led to the wide acceptance of Swahili as a lingua franca in East Africa must be the agreement amongst Tanzanians and Kenyans that many of the local languages are closely related historically to Swahili, so closely as to be felt by some to be no more than 'dialects' of it. Conversely, the clear division between the Indo-Aryan languages of Northern India and the Dravidian tongues of the South can be recognized as one of the many causes of the linguistic disputes of the subcontinent.

7.1.1.2 *Ratio of L1 Users to the Total Population*

The choice of a national language (the term will be defined and discussed below) might appear, at first sight, to be a very simple one where there is a language which is spoken by a majority of the population of a state. However, the choice of such a language would necessarily place its L1 users at a substantial advantage, since their mother tongue would be the language of the government, of power, of control. The minority groups would feel themselves to be at a disadvantage and might well argue that independence for them had resulted in no more than an exchange of imperial masters and might well attempt to secede from the union and set up an independent state of their own in which their mother tongue would be the national language. We have seen the unsuccessful attempt at this in Biafra and the successful attempt in the creation of Bangladesh. In short, the choice of a majority language may, at least initially, serve the cause of political unity but at the expense of cultural unity and it is perhaps for this reason that occasionally a minority language is preferred.

An extreme case in which nationalistic consciousness has resulted in the choice of an indigeneous language with a tiny L1 community – nationalism at the expense of 'efficiency' – is Eire, where Irish Gaelic, with a mother-tongue community of no more than 3 per cent, was chosen as the national language. A minority language may also be chosen for other reasons – its pre-eminence as a lingua franca for example, as was Urdu in Pakistan, in spite of the fact that it was the L1 of only 7 per cent of the population and its homeland was outside the borders of the state in India, in Uttar Pradesh in particular (Das Dupta, 1970, p.124).

Indonesia too made a similar choice – Bahasa Indonesia, based on a pidginized variety of Malay, with therefore, by definition, no speech community of L1 users, in preference to Javanese with 40 per cent. The choice was a particularly interesting one from the point of view of sociolinguistics, since it represented the decision to adopt a pidgin language and adapt it for use as a national language, i.e. to convert it into a standard language. Israel made a similar and perhaps more striking decision in choosing a classical language with, of necessity, no L1 speech community, at the expense of Yiddish, which in 1961 could claim a 75 per cent community of L1 or L2 users.

7.1.1.3   *Demographic Factors*

The demographic distribution of a language, its placement by socioeconomic and geographical groups, is certain to be a major influence on its choice or rejection as a language with some degree of 'official' status. Other things being equal, a widespread language, the L1 or preferred L2 of a well-thought-of social or regional group will stand a good chance of adoption, particularly if it is already in use as a lingua franca within the state.

However, the situation is never so simple. We have been ignoring until now the question of who it is that makes the decisions in language planning in developing nations (and, the cynical would argue, in others too). The answer is the *elite*.

The notion of the elite and its relation to social class has been long debated in sociology (see Bottomore, 1962, pp. 188-96), so all that is required here is to adopt an operational definition which will suit our purposes. By an elite, we mean a group of 'professionals' found amongst the ranks of the *milieux dirigeants* (the ruling circles) '. . . top businessmen; . . . leading intellectuals; . . . political leaders; . . . high civil servants; . . . senior military men; . . . clerical and lay leaders of the church; and . . . officials of labor, farmer and other pressure groups' (Lerner and Gorden, 1969, p.77: the defining list for the French elite chosen for their study). Such a group need not be drawn from any particular social class and indeed, in a democracy, access to membership of the elite would be free to those whose educational achievements were judged adequate. In short, where there is equality of opportunity in education, there will be large-scale social mobility, which will be reflected in a growing complexity of the relationships between social and socioeconomic class and between class, status and the elite. The Third World is passing through a period of rapid change demonstrated by increasing mobility, modernization and urbanization which cannot but have the most powerful effects and demands on language, since the development from relatively static to dynamic societies, seen in the growth of mass culture, mass consumption and mass politics (the notion is Lerner and Gorden's, op. cit., pp.17ff.), can only be achieved if the means of internal and external communication are assured. We shall pursue the implications of this for language planning below.

7.2 GOALS

Whether the governing elite of a nation accepts the steadily increasing demand of the people for greater participation or attempts to stifle it, decisions on language policy have to be made. The elite, attempting to retain power or spread it wider by greater democratization, must fail if it lacks the linguistic means of carrying out its policies. The state must both (1) run efficiently and (2) give its citizens a feeling of 'oneness' which will promote national unity — fortunate is the nation in which a single language will fulfil both functions. These are the twin goals which we must now consider.

7.2.1   *Nationalism and Nationism*

It has been suggested (Fishman, 1971) that nations, particularly but not exclusively the 'developing nations' of the Third World, are faced by the requirements of satisfying the two potentially conflicting needs of nationalism and nationism — sociocultural and political integration respectively.

Nationalism; a 'new' nation is involved in a search for its own 'ethnic identity' as it attempts to overcome local, tribal, religious and other communal loyalties which clash with loyalty to the state. In practical terms, India needs to make its peoples feel Indian first and Punjabi, Tamil, Bengali, etc. second or, to bring the example nearer home, the EEC has to aim at making the member nations feel 'European' first and British, French or Danish second (see Bell, 1975). Nationalism is, then, the macro-aspect of what we have been considering earlier within the context of individual and small-group interaction; solidarity. At this macro-level, national solidarity is typically expressed by such outward signs as a national flag, anthem and perhaps a national language – a point to which we shall return in a moment.

Nationism: simultaneous with the need to achieve authenticity as a united people, the government of a new state has to arrive at operational efficiency – central and local government must function without undue delay and waste, health and education services must be provided for the citizens, commerce and communications must be fostered within the state and with its neighbours – power, rather than solidarity and integration at political, rather than the sociocultural level. The outward signs of nationism will be seen in state-operated postal, telegraphic and telephone services, transport, education, finance, justice and so forth and, crucial to the working of such complex systems and hence to the achievement of political integration, is a national language which can act as the vehicle of communication between the government and the people and between the government and other institutions outside the state.

As Kroeber puts it, writing on the distinction between nation and nationality, '. . . in nationalities and ethnic units, language is always a factor, and often the basic one' (Kroeber, 1963, p.36.). We shall see below how true this is and how difficult the balance between language choice in the service of nationalism and nationism is in actuality but before we examine the alternative language planning policies available to 'new' nations, we shall consider the context within which such planning takes place – the linguistic make-up of the individual states.

7.2.2 *National and Official Languages*

We have been using the terms 'national' and 'official' language above in a rather loose way which must now be rectified by some kind of definition, rather a problem, since many writers on language planning and most of the planners tend to use the terms as virtual synonyms. It is possible to follow Fishman (1971, p.32) and retain the term 'national language' for the code(s) chosen for the achievement of the goal of nationalism, in contrast with the 'official' which has the nationism function. Of course, in the

Americas, parts of Asia and Africa and most of Europe, the national and official languages are one, e.g. English in U.K., U.S.A., Australasia, but the choice of different languages for the two roles is far more common in the Third World and is exemplified by quite a range of alternative policies, some of which we shall consider below.

7.2.3   *Endo- and Exo-glossia*

Earlier (7.1.1) we considered the question of the degree of linguistic heterogenicity found in different nations but heterogenicity in itself may well be a less important factor than the source of the language(s) chosen as national or official by a state. A more revealing approach might be to contrast those nations in which the national, official or national-official languages are indigenous, with those in which they are not. Clearly 'indigenous' and 'imported' are not all-or-none categories and therefore need to be seen as terminal points on the now familiar 'continuum'. Drawing on the terminology of anthropology (*endogamy-exogamy;* Beals and Hoijer, 1965, p.480f.), Kloss has coined a neat pair of terms – *endoglossic* and *exoglossic* – to distinguish the choice of an indigenous language from that of an external language for some particular formal function. Given that a state need not be wholly endo- or wholly exo-glossic in its linguistic make-up and that goals and policies can and do change, we should expect to find 'mixed' situation and accept that our description is synchronic, in the classic sense referred to earlier (1.3.1), in spite of the fact that the object of description is an evolving dynamic system responding to and in part creating, external stimuli. We shall isolate three types of state and provide examples of each in which English has some key function.

7.2.3.1   *Endoglossic States*

The 'purest' form of endoglossia can be found in states in which the national-official language (NOL) is the mother tongue of the vast majority of the population and in which the only linguistic problems are those which arise in relation to the rights of indigenous minorities and immigrants and those whose variety of the NOL is non-standard. The United Kingdom provides a clear example: English is the NOL but there are indigenous linguistic minorities – the Welsh and the Gaelic-speaking Scots in particular, immigrants, Eastern European refugees, Southern European, Asian and Caribbean migrant workers – and social and regional dialects of long standing.

Another type of endoglossia is seen in states in which the NOL is the L1 of a number of the citizens, but not necessarily a majority, accepted by a general consensus – English in Liberia and Sierra Leone for example – or by a consensus of the elite, i.e. by imposition as in Rhodesia.

7.2.3.2   Exoglossic States

Typical of the ex-colonies of Britain and France in Africa is the choice of an exoglossic solution to language problems. Such states are often extremely linguistically heterogeneous – large numbers of non-standard indigenous languages, normally tied closely to specific social and often tribal groups – and, while some tribal languages may have gained wider currency as lingua francas within part or all of the state, few are acceptable as the vehicles of modern government. In such a situation, a common solution is to retain the ex-colonial language as sole NOL but to grant regional official status (ROL) to one or more local languages, e.g. Ghana, Nigeria, Uganda, etc.

Very occasionally, a state will adopt two external languages as NOL – French and English in Cameroun, or English and Afrikaans in South Africa – but such a decision is rare and arises, either from the federation of two ex-colonies, as in the first case, or by virtue of the existence of two large L1 communities, which together form a minority of the total population but constitute the elite, in the sense in which the term is used above.

7.2.3.3   Mixed States

Between the two extremes of endo- and exo-glossia, commented upon above, lie numbers of states which are part endo-, part exo-, in which the national and official functions are split between an indigenous and a non-indigenous language. More often than not, such a situation typifies Commonwealth Asia just as clearly as the exoglossic typified Commonwealth Africa. India provides an extremely clear example and demonstrates the extraordinary problems inherent in such a decision – Hindi as NOL, with English as a subsidiary OL and fourteen indigenous languages as ROL in particular states of the union. We shall need to consider in more detail the reasons for such a decision and the impact it has on Indian society (7.4:2) but first we shall survey the types of language planning decisions which can be made and relate them to the factors we have been discussing.

7.3   POLICIES

Three major types of policy have been suggested and labelled A, B and C respectively (Fishman, 1971). All three hinge on the notion of a 'Great Tradition' and its relationship to the twin goals of nationalism and nationism. It may therefore be of value, before considering the three types of policy, to examine the concept of a 'Great Tradition' and its influence on the planning decisions of the governments of nations.

Following Fishman (1971), a Great Tradition may be defined in terms of the assumed existence of a set of cultural features — law, government, religion, history — which is shared by the nation and can serve to integrate the members of the state into a cohesive body. Such a Great Tradition is almost certain to have as one of its manifestations and its major vehicle of expression, a language and frequently a literature, perhaps purely oral, which may for this reason commend itself as an appropriate choice for NL or OL. We have, in fact, already touched upon this in the earlier discussion of historicity; the concern shown by a community to find for a language '. . . a "respectable" ancestry. . . ' and to '. . . create and cultivate myths and geneologies concerning the origin and development of their standard varieties' (Fishman, already quoted above in 6.2.3) — a major defining characteristic of standard and classical languages and one which marks them off from all other varieties as defined by the sociolinguistic typology suggested above (see Figure 6.3)

7.3.1   Type A Policies

Where the elite has come to the conclusion that there is no available Great Tradition which can be drawn upon to unite the nation, language policy is likely to be directed towards the creation of an exoglossic state, by the adoption of the language of the ex-rulers as the NOL; an orientation which implies a greater valuation of the achievement of operational efficiency — nationism — than of ethnic authenticity — nationalism.

In the context of newly created multi-national or multi-tribal states in areas of great linguistic diversity in which few of the languages have been standardized or even reduced to writing, a type A policy seems the only possibility. But such a decision has important effects. The elite must already be proficient in the chosen language and may, in extreme cases, be incapable of direct communication with the mass of the population who, given the increased desire for participation, are certain to attempt to master the NOL — an ideal situation, if the elite is unwilling or unable to provide large-scale language learning facilities, for the growth of pidginized varieties of the NOL; as in Cameroun and Papua-New Guinea. Educational policy will inevitably stress the importance of the NOL at the expense of the indigenous languages, in spite of the fact that they will be the L1 of virtually the whole population, making competence in it the *sine qua non* of access to well-paid employment and ultimately to the ranks of the elite itself.

7.3.2   Type B Policies

The converse of type A policies are decided upon when the elite and in some cases the whole population, are agreed that there does exist a Great Tradition with a related language. An agreement which implies considerable sociocultural and often political unity and hence language policy can, by adopting the language of the Great Tradition as the NOL, aim at both goals – nationalism and nationism – simultaneously. In this case, an endoglossic state can be created with considerable hopes of success, since the NOL, being indigenous and accepted by the majority of the population, will serve the goal of nationalism by further uniting an already culturally united community and the goal of nationism by continuing to act as an already acknowledged lingua franca.

'Pure' examples of this policy can be found in Israel, Somalia, Ethiopia and Thailand, while Indonesia, the Philippines and Tanzania appear to be moving from a type A to a type B policy, by abandoning the old 'colonial' language – Dutch, Spanish, English – in favour of the indigenous NOLs – Bahasa Indonesia, Tagalog and Swahili respectively.

7.3.3   Type C Policies

While type A policies arise from the belief that no appropriate Great Tradition exists and type B from the belief that one does, type C policies result from the recognition that there are several competing Great Traditions, each with its own social, religious or geographic base and linguistic tradition.

The major problem with a situation of this kind can be seen in balancing the needs of nationalism against regional or sectional nationalisms and overall national efficiency against existing local political systems. Inevitably, rival elites representing the rival interests will spring up and, if dissatisfied enough, may take steps to take their region out of the federation – to secede and set up their own nation state.

Where sectionalism is further emphasized by physical distance and non-contiguity between the component regions of the state, national unity may well turn out, as it did in Pakistan in 1971, to be impossible to sustain.

Policy in a situation in which there are, as it were, too many Great Traditions must necessarily aim uncomfortably between the twin goals of nationalism and nationism. The regional, religious, ethnic or social sub-groups within the state must be permitted some measure of autonomy but not at the expense of national unity. Some kind of central government must be set up with an efficient medium of national communication but not at the expense of the regional administrations and languages. More often than not, the dilemma is resolved by the retention of the language of the previous rulers alongside one or more indigenous languages as NOL and the adoption of major local languages as ROL, with 'official' status within their own regions. Hence, a type C policy is, in effect, the 'temporary' adoption of a type A policy, tempered by the stated intention of changing to type B as soon as is practicable. The demands that such a policy make on the citizens of a state are enormous, since the implication is that proficiency in at least two and more probably three, languages is essential for all educated individuals. Indeed, unless a person is fortunate enough to be an L1 user either of one of the NOL or a ROL, his learning load will be increased to four.

7.4.3 *Summary*

Language planning is particularly concerned with the policies adopted in achievement of major social goals in linguistically heterogeneous nations. Heterogenicity of language can be seen to relate closely to the attainment of the ends of nationalism and nationism and to be a key factor in the choice of indigenous or non-indigenous languages for official functiõns within the state. The crucial difference between the role of English, for example, in Africa, in contrast with its role in Asia can be traced, without much difficulty, to the availability in the second case and the lack in the first, of an acceptable Great Tradition manifested in an accepted native language which can be drawn upon to unify the state at both the socio-cultural and political level.

7.4   LANGUAGE PLANNING IN THREE CONTRASTED AREAS

By way of extended illustration of the problems and policies involved in language choice in linguistically heterogeneous communities, we shall consider below the contrasting attitudes to English in three areas of the world — West Africa, India and Europe; more precisely, Anglophone West Africa, the Indian subcontinent and the EEC, the Europe of the Nine.

7.4.1 *West Africa*

Although the six nations which constitute Anglophone West Africa — Cameroun, the Gambia, Ghana, Liberia, Nigeria and Sierra Leone — differ from each other in important respects — size, population, historical background — there are substantial similarities which permit a general discussion of the linguistic problems of the area as a whole, and mark it off from other parts of Africa, from the Indian subcontinent and from Europe.

7.4.1.1   *Background*

Common to all six countries is the large extent to which they are linguistically heterogeneous – typically, several indigenous languages (vernaculars often not yet even reduced to writing) are spoken by relatively self-sufficient tribal or regional groups between whom communication is only possibly by means of a lingua franca. Typically, too, no single speech community commands a majority of the total population, though individual languages often dominate particular areas, e.g. the 9 million or so Ghanaians speak between them about forty-two mother tongues but four languages can be seen as dominating communication in the four largest population centres – Ga̰ in Accra, Akan in Kumasi, Ewe in Ho and Dagbane in Tamale. In addition, languages frequently cross the existing national boundaries – Akan in Ghana and Ivory Coast, Ewe in Ghana, Togo and Dahomey – a legacy of the nineteenth-century 'scramble for Africa' in the course of which tribal groups were split between new colonial territories.

On a larger scale, these West African nations can be seen to share another characteristic and one which has important implications for language planning – each has at least one common border with a Francophonic state, indeed the Gambia is totally surrounded by Senegal, and the Federal Republic of Cameroun consists of the previous British and French colonies of the same name.

7.4.1.2   *Language Policy*

In every case and as a result both of the linguistic heterogenicity and lack of an agreed Great Tradition, each of the six West African states has decided upon an exoglossic policy in relation to language. The commonest solution has been the retention of English as sole NOL and the adoption of major indigenous languages as the ROLs of particular areas, e.g. in Nigeria, English as the Federal Language and Ibo, Yoruba and Hausa as the ROL of the eastern, western and northern areas respectively.

Cameroun, because of its colonial past, stands out as the only state in which there are two NOL – English and French – which act as vehicles of nationism but without strenuous efforts at 'harmonization' – the creation, that is of a bilingual elite – can act against the goal of nationalism.

Up to this point, we have been implying standard English in our use of the term 'English', but a factor which makes Anglophone West Africa fascinating for the sociolinguist is the existence in each of the six countries of pidginized or creolized varieties of the language which, though crucial to communication between many groups, tend rarely to be promoted by the elite – WAPE (West African Pidgin English) in Cameroun and Nigeria, Kru English in Liberia and Ghana and Krio in Sierra Leone and limited, except in the last case, to social groups engaged in unskilled labour. Apart from the intrinsic interest that pidgin and creole languages have for the linguist, their existence has important implications for language learning, since the first contacts that many migrant workers in West Africa are likely to have with 'English' are with one of these reduced varieties, a fact which cannot but influence later learning of the standard variety or fail to influence local usage even by the local elite.

West Africa is typically exoglossic, having accepted that there exists no indigenous Great Tradition whose associated language might be pressed into service as the vehicle of nationalism or nationism. For this reason, the ruling elites of the states of West Africa have in all cases adopted type A policies, choosing the language of the previous colonial rulers — English or French, or in the case of Cameroun both — as the NOL. This language is required to act both as the medium through which official business, higher education, the managerial levels of commerce and external trade are transacted and, at the same time, as a neutral tongue, which exactly because it is the L1 of so few, acts as an equal barrier to all and hence, by what may appear at first sight a curious logic, an equally acceptable expression of nationalism.

The situation of English in West Africa has been succinctly summarized as '... consolidating itself as the language of public occasions rather than an all-purpose language... the vast majority... live practically all their private lives in their mother tongue but use English basically for business and official purposes' (Banjo, 1972, p. 4), i.e. diglossia plus bilingualism, in the sense in which the terms were used above (5.3.1) in which the domains in which English tends to occur will contrast in their 'formality', their expression of 'power' and their 'transactional' nature with the 'informal', 'solidarity' expressing integrative L1 mediated domains — crudely hearth, home and friendship; the social psychologist's primary groups.

In short, language policy in Anglophone West Africa is firmly exoglossic — no local language is envisaged in the forseeable future as becoming acceptable as a NL or OL; a very different situation from that of Commonwealth Asia (see below).

7.4.1.3 Educational Policy

Language policy necessarily influences educational policy, since it is in the schools that the governments of new nations must attempt to win the hearts and minds of the next generation and the success of such an enterprise depends equally on the teaching of literacy in the L1 and the ROL, lest valuable local cultures be lost in the transition from an essentially rural and static to a more urban and dynamic society and efficiency in the

NOL, in this case, English.

An almost inevitable result of the need to satisfy all three aims is the move, which we shall see too in India and potentially in Europe, towards a three language policy in education – the commonest learning load for the schoolchild being, in addition to his other subjects, the three languages – the mother tongue, the ROL and the NOL.

The demands on both learner and teacher are therefore enormous, particularly in the context of the provision of free primary education for all, typically made law in the early 1950s, and great expansion in all sectors of formal education during the next decade, which have highlighted the inadequacy of textbooks, buildings and many teachers, few states being able to cope with the increased enrolment and the concomitant demand for better qualified and greater numbers of teachers (Burns, 1965).

7.4.2   *India*

In this subsection we shall take India itself as an example but recognize that, *mutatis mutandis,* many of the problems and proposals examplified by Indian language policy are paralleled, not only in the subcontinent itself – Bangladesh, Pakistan and Sri Lanka – but further afield in South-east Asia as a whole – Burma, Cambodia, Indonesia, Laos, Malaysia, the Philippines, Singapore, Thailand and Vietnam – where independence and modernization have been approached through a mixed policy involving a combination of ends – and exoglossia (Fishman, 1971, p.51).

7.4.2.1   *Background*
Superficially, India resembles the West African nations in its linguistic heterogenicity – several hundred languages, some pre-literate tribal languages, others centred in particular areas and on major towns and cities – but the similarity is more apparent than real, since in India there is no equivalent to WAPE, Kru English or Krio but there are a score or so of ancient standard languages, each with a long literary heritage and the vehicle of a local Great Tradition. To some extent, there is the unifying factor of Hinduism, but by no means all Indians are Hindus, there are large Muslim, Buddhist, Sikh and Christian minorities. Nor does religion act as an overriding bond between the Indo-Aryan north and the Dravidian south – the major but by no means the only potential line of cleavage within the Union.

7.4.2.2   *Language Policy*
Faced by the need to overcome local nationalisms in favour of a greater Indian nationalism, the Government of India decided in its constitution to

raise Hindi to the status of NOL – the federal language – and give ROL status to more than a dozen indigenous languages at state level. However, such a policy has had the effect of strengthening an already existing North Indian nationalism and provoking a South Indian reaction to it and in addition would, in a pure form, leave the Union without an external means of communication. In the final formulation decided upon in India, Hindi is the NOL but English, the ex-colonial language, is retained as an 'auxiliary' NOL, until such time as the states of the Union all freely accept Hindi as the sole NOL. At that point in time, English will lose, or indeed will already have lost, its remaining internal communication functions and will become a solely external lingua franca.

The present situation, however, is far from this ideal, since many English speakers are unwilling to see their skill in the language reduced in value and hence their position as an elite weakened and speakers of Dravidian languages have argued that English at least disadvantages all equally, while Hindi, spoken natively according to 1971 census by over 30 per cent of the population and related historically to the major northern languages, places northerners at an unfair advantage over them (Das Gupta, 1970, p.46).

India, then, faced by a barely concealed power struggle between English speaking, Hindi speaking and Dravidian language speaking elites each, to a greater or lesser extent, involved in local regional, ethnic or religious factionalism has had to commit itself to the uncomfortable compromise policy between types A and B – a type C policy of accepting a temporary mixed endo--exoglossic situation and attempting to move towards a type B policy – the total internal replacement of the ex-colonial language – as soon as possible.

7.4.2.3   *Educational Policy*

Initially, educational policy in India accepted the need for all pupils to learn the NOL, the auxiliary NOL and the ROL, i.e. Hindi, English and the OL of the state in which the child lived. However, two major problems arose with this formula: children in states in which the ROL was also the NOL, e.g. Uttar Pradesh, where it is by far the majority language, would be required to learn only two languages and those whose L1 was not the ROL, entitled under the constitution to primary education in the mother tongue, would be forced, unless their L1 happened to be Hindi or English, to learn four languages. Worse would be the situation of the speaker of a pre-literate tribal language – Parji or Gondi for example – for whom teachers and textbooks could not even be found.

As a result, a revised Three Language Formula was devised: all secondary pupils are now required to study (1) the ROL or the mother tongue, where this is different from the ROL; (2) Hindi or, where this is the L1, any other Indian language; (3) English or any other modern European language. The intention of the formula is clearly to force northerners into studying a South Indian language as an aid to the breaking down of separatism and the increase of an overall Indian nationalism but understandably, many North Indians have preferred to choose an 'easy', related Indo-European language, rather than have to cope with the strikingly different structure of the Dravidian languages. In addition, teachers, particularly of minority languages, are hard to find and poorly rewarded and the formula, well-intentioned though it is, still discriminates against the linguistic minority groups. It is hard to see how the situation can be improved but at least from the very beginning India has a Commissioner for Linguistic Minorities, answerable to the President himself, who surveys the needs of linguistic minorities and attempts, through reports presented every two years, to protect their rights.

7.4.3   Europe

It would be wrong to assume that language planning is a problem unique or even specific to 'developing' nations; in a crucial sense the EEC – the Europe of the Nine – is just as much a new political unit, made up of the amalgamation of existing groups, as Ghana, Nigeria, Pakistan or India are and therefore as likely to be faced by problems of language policy as they are (see Bell, 1975).

7.4.3.1   Background
The EEC, roughly half the size of India and with less than half the population, presents a complex picture of linguistic heterogenicity, both in terms of individual nation-states with their own, often ancient, standard languages and of indigenous and migrant minorities. Adding to the already complicated situation is the fact that the EEC has the highest proportion of urban population in the world, following the USA and Oceania (UNO, 1969, table 10, p. 15) and a very sophisticated intra- and interstate communication and transport network which creates and to some degree controls, the need for international media of communication – a lingua franca or multilingualism – between the member states.

7.4.3.2   Language Policy
Given that four EEC languages each command over 20 percent of the total population of the Community – German, English, French, Italian – there is clearly no possibility of the choice of any single language as the OL. Each member nation has its own NOL(s); although in one case, Luxemburg,

the most widely spoken L1 is a variety of German and the leading OL French, i.e. in virtually every case, the states involved are endoglossic and pursue a type B policy.

At present, so far as the institutions of the Community are concerned, there are seven OLs — Danish, Dutch, English, French, German, Irish and Italian — but, given the goodwill of the Danes, Dutch, Irish and Luxemburgers, it might be possible to reduce these to four — English, French, German and Italian — retaining, of course the present national languages as the equivalent of ROL and the right for their speakers to have laws which are binding on them promulgated in their L1. What is probably more needed in the EEC at the moment is language for the achievement of nationism — an official lingua franca or set of languages with this function — rather than the long-term aim of a broader European nationalism.

Even if the EEC accepted a 4 OL and 7 ROL formula, the linguistic minorities would still remain and their rights would still need to be formulated and safeguarded. We have argued elsewhere (Bell, 1975) that the EEC, like India, could do worse than to appoint a Commissioner for its own linguistic minorities and could learn much from the successes of the Indian experience.

7.4.3.3   *Educational Policy*

It is hard to resist the Indian solution — a Three Language Formula — as a rational answer to the educational problems of language in the EEC. Such a formula might require all secondary students to study three languages: (1) the ROL, i.e. the present NOL — Danish in Denmark or English in the U.K. — or the L1, where this is different from the NOL — Welsh in Wales or German in North Italy; (2) one of the OLs of the Community, other than the NOL where this is an OL, e.g. English children having studied English under (1) would be expected to study French, German or Italian; and (3) any other modern European language, e.g. this could be another OL but some state governments might well choose or have already chosen to promote a minor indigenous language — Irish in Eire — in its place.

Such a policy would naturally be beset with the kinds of problems referred to above — lack of teachers and materials, the heavy learning load of those whose L1 was not already a NOL, the danger of diminishing interest in the cultures of small ethnic or linguistic communities. We are not attempting to propose a solution here — the purpose of this section is to make ourselves more aware of our own imminent language planning needs and to accept that others have faced similar difficulties and have, in response, created imaginative policies on which we would do well to draw.

7.4.4 *Summary*

In this section we have been examining, in a brief survey, the linguistic policies of three areas which superficially show strong contrasting characteristics – West Africa, India and the EEC – but which on consideration demonstrate common features. All three are linguistically heterogeneous and are faced by the common twin problems of nationalism and nationism. West Africa stands out from the other two in being forced to fall back on the non-indigenous ex-colonial language as its NOL, making use of the local languages only at the regional level. India has chosen an indigenous language as NOL but is, for the present, forced to retain English as a kind of auxiliary language. The EEC, in its search for operational efficiency cannot, it seems, cope without using at least four languages for interstate communication and all seven of the NOL of the member nations for legal enactments and as ROL.

All three areas present examples of the same problem – the linguistic minority, whether indigenous or migrant – and one which is likely to increase in scale and importance as the expansion of urbanization in the Third World and of migrant labour in Europe continues. In the face of this the three areas all seem committed to an essentially similar Three Language Formula for education – the study of the OL(s), the ROL, and some other language.

It must be felt at this point that different though the three areas are, some kind of general picture of language planning problems is beginning to emerge and that our discussion is being unduly hampered by the lack of a symbol system which will emphasize what there is in common between states and play down the inevitable differences. The next section will attempt to set up just such a system.

7.5 NATIONAL SOCIOLINGUISTIC PROFILES

In the course of this chapter, it must have become clear that a discussion of the forms and functions of languages in polyglossic communities tends to be extremely long-winded in the absence of some kind of symbol-system which can serve to represent the information available and make cross-national comparisons possible. Fortunately, a series of suggestions have been made (Stewart, 1962; Ferguson, 1966; Kloss, 1968) which we intend to adopt and adapt in this section.

Four key parameters may be suggested and symbolized – language *type* (as outlined in 6.2 above), *status* (also mentioned in 6.2), *ratio* of L1 users to total population (discussed in 7.1.1.2 above) and *functions* (touched on in 7.2 above) – each of which will be expanded on and exemplified below.

7.5.1 *Language Type*

Seven of the ten sociolinguistic types — standard to artificial inclusive — listed in Figure 6.3, can be seen to be of value in a discussion of language use at the national level and may be represented by their initial letters — S for standard etc., although C will need to be reserved for classical and K adopted for creole.

7.5.2 *Language Status*

Six stages of governmental attitude to a language have been suggested (Kloss, op. cit), extending from its recognition as the sole NOL to its proscription by the authorities. These may be represented by the following symbols:

SO; sole official language, e.g. French in France.

JO; joint official language — co-equal with at least one other, e.g. English and French in Cameroun, French, German, Italian, Romansh in Switzerland.

RO; regional official language — the OL of a constituent state or region of a federal state, e.g. Marathi in Maharastra, Ibo in eastern Nigeria.

PL; promoted language — lacking in official status but made use of by governmental agencies, e.g. WAPE in Cameroun, where in spite of not being 'official', the language is an important medium communication between government and people, particularly in face-to-face encounters and radio programmes concerned with community development, health, agriculture and so forth.

TL; tolerated language — neither promoted nor proscribed by the authorities — its existence is recognized but ignored, e.g. the languages of migrants in the U.K.

DL; discouraged language — proscribed by the authorities to some degree, at best discouraged by denial of autonomy (in the sense of the term above; 6.2.3) at worst by active suppression to the extent that speakers may fear to use the language in public for fear of reprisals, e.g. the banning of Scots Gaelic after the 1745 rising, and of the Norman-French patois during the German occupation of the Channel Islands in the last war.

7.5.3 *Ratio of L1 users to total population*

It would, of course, be possible to write in the actual percentage of L1 users but, in keeping with Kloss' suggestion, we shall divide the 0-100 per cent scale into six arbitrary ranks — 1 to 6 —from highest to lowest:

1. 100-90, e.g. English in Australia, U.K. and U.S.A.
2. 89-70, e.g. English in Canada.
3. 69-40, e.g. Dutch and French in Belgium.
4. 39-20, e.g. French in Canada, Amharic in Ethiopia.
5. 19-3, e.g. Afrikaans in South Africa.
6. less than 3, e.g. Irish Gaelic in Eire.

7.5.4   Language Functions

Three major functions of language within polyglossic states may be suggested – wider communication, education and religion – but the first two categories require some expansion:

WE; language of wider communication (external) – a state may make use of language for its contacts with other nations, e.g. the 'window on the world' function of English indicated by Nehru in the Indian context.

WI; language of wider communication (internal) – an intra- rather than an inter-state lingua franca, e.g. Hindi in India or Urdu in Pakistan.

MO; a language widely taught as part of the process of formal education but never used at any stage as a medium of instruction, e.g. Latin in U.K.

M1; medium of education at the primary stage of education, e.g. English is normally introduced at some point at the primary stage in Commonwealth Africa as the medium of instruction, though the actual time of introduction varies from state to state – from the beginning of formal education in Western Sierra Leone; later in Ghana and Kenya.

M2; medium at the secondary stage after having been introduced as a subject at the primary, e.g. in several East African countries English is taught as a subject at the primary level but replaces the L1 as medium of instruction at the secondary.

M3; medium at the tertiary stage, following its introduction earlier as a subject, e.g. Tanzania, where the three stages are marked by the use of three separate media of instruction – the L1 at primary with Swahili as a subject, Swahili as medium at the secondary with English as a subject and English as medium at the tertiary level.

M4; medium at the post-graduate level and used for the publication of scientific research and advanced textbooks, e.g. English because of its function as a medium of international communication tends to play a major role as M4 in nations in which the NOL has little currency beyond the borders of the state – the Scandinavian languages are a clear example. Many Asian states are typically in the situation of changing or having already changed to indigenous languages as media of instruction at all stages of their educational systems but are still dependent on a major 'world language', more often than not English, for advanced non-traditional intellectual activities, e.g. Hindi may well cope easily with such topics as theological and philosophical speculation but lack, for the present at least, the appropriate terminology and stylistic conventions for the natural, physical and social sciences – a point which we have already noticed under the heading of code-switching (5.5).

R; the language of public worship – in an endoglossic state the language of religion is certain to be either the NOL, a classical version of it or of the vehicle of an originally non-indigenous Great Tradition, e.g. the English of services in Catholic churches today (present-day standard English), that of the Established Church (essentially a kind of 'classical' English based on the language of the Book of Common Prayer and the King James' Bible) and the earlier use of Latin in Roman rite services prior to the Vatican decision in favour of the 'vernacular'. This decision has had a presumably unintended result in some exoglossic states – Papua-New Guinea, Cameroun – in which local pidgin or creole varieties, rather than standard varieties of English, have been taken as the basis of Dialogue Masses, catechisms, prayer books and so forth (Noser, 1965).

7.5.5   Summary

We are now in a position to create profile formulae which succinctly summarize the sociolinguistic characteristics of individual states and permit us to make generalizations and comparisons between states.

In order to demonstrate how such profiles work, we shall compare an Asian and a West African state and comment on the contrasts between them:

Sri Lanka (Ceylon):   English S PL 6 We M2
                         Pali   C PL 6 R
                         Sinhala S JO 2 Wi M1 M2
                         Tamil   S JO 4 Wi M1 M2R

The formulae may be glossed as follows:

   English – a standard language, promoted, spoken as L1 by less than 3 per cent of the population, vehicle of wider external communication, medium of instruction at the secondary stage (and beyond).

   Pali -- a classical language, widely used by Buddhists for religious purposes but, by definition, without an L1 speech community.

   Sinhala – standard, joint official, spoken natively by between 89 and 70 per cent of the population, functioning as an internal lingua franca and as the medium of instruction at primary and secondary level.

Tamil – as Sinhala except for a smaller speech community; 39-20 per cent; and with a religious function.

Ghana:		
	Akan	V RO 3 Wi M1
	Dagari	V PL 6 Wi
	English	S SO 6 We Wi M2
	Ewe-Fon	V RO 6 Wi M1
	Ga	V RO 5 Wi M1
	Moshi-Dagbane	V RO 6 Wi M1
	Nzema	V RO 6 Wi M1

The two profiles bring out fairly clearly the substantial differences in situation and policy of the two states and serve as examples of the more general contrast, on which we have already commented, between the 'typical' Asian and 'typical' West African Commonwealth nation, i.e. the relatively more homogeneous Asian situation which lends itself to endoglossic policies in which English is retained for specialist advanced educational purposes and as an external lingua franca, in strong contrast with the rather more heterogeneous African situation, where exoglossic policies are pursued and several indigenous languages have the status of regional official language, subordinated to the sole federal language – English.

7.6   CONCLUSION

This chapter has been concerned with the problems of language choice in linguistically heterogeneous nations; the major issue of macrosociolinguistics and the point at which the interests of the sociolinguist converge with those of the social scientist, particularly the social scientist involved in the planning of change in evolving societies. We have been stressing all through this book the need for the linguist to be objective in his descriptions, avoiding value judgements, describing but not attempting to prescribe norms of language, but it must have become clear in the course of this chapter that such an attitude to the data, appropriate though it clearly is for the descriptive linguist, can hardly serve as a basis for the applied linguist who is called upon to assist in the planning and implementation of social change of which language planning must necessarily be a part. In short, language planning is, by its very nature, an evaluative science seeking to discover and encourage the most suitable linguistic forms for specific social functions.

If we accept Aristotle's notion of language as a tool (see 3.1 on this), it follows that language '. . . can be evaluated, altered, corrected, regulated and improved and new languages created at will' (Tauli, 1968, p. 9) and that we shall need to reconsider very carefully the twentieth-century embargo on the making of value judgements in linguistics and question whether the earlier linguistic tradition of the nineteenth and preceeding centuries does not, in fact, offer, for the *applied* linguist, a more appropriate orientation to the data of language and language use.

It is important, however, not to appear to be claiming too much for the sociolinguist language planner. True, he can evaluate competing linguistic forms both in a purely linguistic and in a broader sociolinguistic manner (see Tauli, op. cit., pp. 29-44, and pp. 151-70 esp.) but he cannot guarantee that his evaluations or proposals based upon them will be accepted, either by the elite, whose task it would be to implement them or by the mass of the people, in whose usage the ultimate test of acceptance would be found. Language planners find themselves in much the same situation as management scientists '. . . very rarely in a position to take decisions themselves. They are employed to dig out and organize the relevant facts, analyse them, and then make recommendations. The decision-maker — manager or politician — takes the results of this work into account along with other information which he considers important. This usually consists of far more than quantifiable facts' (Jones, 1972, p. 56).

The planning of change is clearly an extremely complex operation in which language must play a crucial role as one of the many intricate subsystems within the overall cultural system of the society involved. The sociolinguist can therefore, together with other social scientists, specify and evaluate the forms and functions of language within the society as a part of this greater inclusive description on which the decision-makers will ultimately draw as they design their policies. We have touched earlier on the fear of being thought parasitical by the social sciences but it seems clear now that change, so typically a part of the character of this century, can only be planned and controlled through the combined efforts of scientists working together in an interdisciplinary way, and hence the sociolinguist, as linguist, has a unique contribution to make which, if he is willing to learn from the experiences of the human sciences should not be difficult to integrate into the kind of large interdisciplinary model suggested above. Indeed, such a model would contain within it descriptions of the total semiotic system made use of by society, within which language would be a part and the hope expressed by de Saussure that there would ultimately arise a *sémiologie,* which would study signs within the context of society as a whole, would be fulfilled.

8
Overview and Future Prospects

In this final chapter, we intend to restate some of the axioms of socioling-uistics and to raise questions about the adequacy of the theories on which work in sociolinguistics is based, to expand on two major issues which have earlier only been touched upon in passing — discourse analysis and communicative competence — and, in conclusion, to point out the ways in which sociolinguistic endeavour can be related to other fields of scholarship and drawn upon in practical ways by those who work in the applied sciences of social engineering in general and language planning and teaching in particular.

8.1. SOME AXIOMS AND ISSUES IN SOCIOLINGUISTICS

At the beginning of this book, as part of the discussion of the problem of variation in language, we suggested two key axioms of descriptive linguistics which seem to have been at the basis of most work in the field during this century (see 1.3.1). We shall now propose a number of axioms which appear to have a similarly general degree of acceptance amongst socioling-uists. Many of these axioms have been discussed in earlier chapters but have not yet been overtly formulated.

8.1.1 *Labov's Axioms of Sociolinguistics*

In a paper on the principles of linguistic methodology, Labov (1972) suggested eight principles or axioms on which sociolinguistic explanation should be based:-

1. *The Cumulative Principle* — the more that is known about language, the more we can find out about it. This has at least two implications which are of some importance for the future. First, 'new' knowledge about language must lead linguists into areas of study in which they are

strangers but in which they will often already find others scholars at work, e.g. as linguists probe the social bases of linguistic behaviour, they inevitably come into contact with the human sciences; a point which we have been emphasizing all along, which connects with axiom 3 below. Secondly, the attempt to integrate new knowledge will have implications for orthodox linguistics; a clear example of this will be seen below (8.2) in our discussion of the analysis of discourse.

2. *The Uniformation Principle* — the linguistic processes taking place around us are the same as those which have operated to produce the historical record of the language i.e. the distinction between synchronic and diachronic linguistics, one of the key assumptions of descriptive linguistics in this century, is denied by the sociolinguist (see 1.3.1 on the distinction). We showed in our survey of the use of implicational scaling techniques (2.4.3) and the application of such methods to the seemingly chaotic data thrown up in creole continuum situations (see 5.4 on continua), how the diachronic and the synchronic merge when an attempt is made to create a dynamic model of language in use and in flux. The point was well made by Turner (1966) when he drew the analogy between the Great Vowel Shift which so strikingly distinguishes Middle from Early Modern English phonology and the phonological systems of British (RP) and Australian English — 'Middle English spoken with an Australian accent is Elizabethan English' (Turner, op. cit., p. 107) — i.e. something very like the late medieval sound change has recurred in Australian English during the last 100 years. The remark should not, of course, be taken too literally but, *mutatis mutandis,* the similarity between the two processes lends considerable support to this principle of Labov's. The implications for linguistics are clearly that the historical and modern can now come closer together and the artificial barrier between them can be breached and finally removed, to the mutual benefit of both sides.

3. *The Principle of Convergence* — the value of new data for confirming and interpreting old data is directly proportional to the differences in the methods used to gather it. This axiom arises from the first and demonstrates, yet again, the need for linguistics to cross-check its methods and the data derived through them, with the methods of other sciences for which linguistic data forms a necessary part in their own search for structure and explanation. It is very much for this reason that we have not felt in any way embarrassed, in this book, to draw upon the assumptions and techniques of other disciplines than our 'parent' in our attempts to explain language in use.

4. *The Principle of Subordinate Shift* — when speakers of a subordinate dialect are asked direct questions about their language, their answers will shift in an irregular manner towards or away from the superordinate dialect.

This behaviour has already been noted earlier, in our comments on stereotyping and hypercorrection (4.1.1) and forms one of the character- istics of evaluative linguistic behaviour which is of considerable interest to the fieldworker attempting to collect evidence on attitudes to language, differing varieties, 'acceptable-unacceptable' usage and the like, within a speech community. The principle has value, too, in helping to explain what would otherwise have to be classified a purely random and unpredict- able usage where, for example, individuals or groups aim at the perceived norms of language of some reference group to which they themselves do not belong but to which they aspire (see 4.3.1 above on types of group and relationship).

5. *The Principle of Style Shifting* — there are no single-style speakers. This principle firmly denies the traditional monolithic view of language by asserting the nature of language, even in the individual, as a bundle of interrelated codes, differing from each other in formal make-up and in social function. This principle needs no expansion or exemplification here, since it has been inherent in this book as a whole and has been central to the issues discussed in chapters 4 and 5 in particular.

6. *The Principle of Attention* — styles can be ordered along a single dimension, measured by the amount of attention paid to speech. In simple terms, the more aware a speaker is of the language he is using, the more 'formal' it will be. This is well exemplified by the distinction between written and spoken language; the first, not being composed in 'real time' can be, and often is, revised and 'polished', so that the final version frequently bears little relationship to the first draft. Actual speech, on the other hand, is composed and transmitted in 'real time' together with the slips and revisions typical of normal spoken language. In speech, unlike writing, there is no way of erasing what has gone before; the first 'draft', as it were, is also the finished product, hence both the orthodox linguist's view of performance as 'degenerate' and the interesting way in which hearers fail to notice the actual 'defective' nature of much of what they hear. Labov argues (1966) that the phenomenon can be easily explained by postulating a small number of simple 'editing rules' by means of which the hearer reformulates the *utterances* he has received into the *sentences* intended by the producer. In operational terms, the principle of attention is of crucial importance to the sociolinguist in the field, since, without quantifying the degree of attention involved, he will be unable to distinguish one style of speech from another, except by a spuriously circular procedure. The circularity involved tends to be that of defining the use of certain linguistic forms as 'formal' or 'informal', or some other 'style', collecting data in which such items occur and then pronouncing the data to be an example of the particular style, which, of course, it is but in a very

uninteresting sense. Formality, and the like, is a label which properly applies to the *context* in which the language occurs. It is a sociological not a linguistic concept, a partial marker the occurrence of which is a particular kind of linguistic behaviour. Indeed, it is more accurate to insist that there is no such thing as, for example, 'formal' language, since what has been erroneously described in this way, in the past, is no more than one outward sign of a sociological or cultural phenomenon. Hence, for the sociolinguist, one of the major data-collection problems is to find language which correlates with others', forms of behaviour which, by themselves, are markers of 'formality' and the like, e.g. 'formality' in the western world is frequently marked by certain prescribed forms of dress, movement etc., which co-occur with recognizable forms of speech, e.g. perhaps a slower delivery, an avoidance of reduced forms – *n't*, *'ll*, *'n'* for 'and' – a preference for more complex sentence structures and, perhaps, for status-marked address forms etc. (4.2 discusses the notion of 'co-occurrence' rules).

7. *The Vernacular Principle* – the style which is most regular in its structure and in its relation to the evolution of the language is the vernacular, in which the minimum attention is paid to speech. (It should be noted, here, that Labov's use of the term is in contrast with our earlier functional definition in 6.3.3 q.v.) This principle often shocks those who hold on to the view that the 'purest' form of the language is the written or, if the linguist insists on describing spoken language, the formal speech of the 'best educated'. But it follows directly from the axiom above. The least influenced form of speech must necessarily be that created when the speaker is least conscious of speaking. This must be the most natural, since it is the least affected by external influences. Labov's fieldwork in New York City (1966) demonstrates the value of the principle in the clearest way. In attempting to elicit the most relaxed speech from his informants, he soon discovered that such data only appeared when the speaker was concentrating his attention on some task other than that of producing language, e.g. when asked to describe some emotionally charged event in which the informant had participated. Further, Labov found that such speech turned out to be remarkably homogeneous in form, not only for the single speaker but for the social group to which he belonged.

8. *The Principle of Formality* – any systematic observation of a speaker defines a formal context in which more than minimum attention is paid to speech. This leads directly to an issue to which we shall return below, the observer's paradox; to obtain the data most important for linguistic theory, we have to observe how people speak when they are not being observed. We wish to collect the 'vernacular'. In order to collect the vernacular, we need to observe speakers using it. If an observer is present,

the informant will not use the vernacular. How can the fieldworker, then, collect what cannot occur if he is there to collect it? We shall consider the practical, and ethical, problems raised by this paradox below (8.1.2).

8.1.2   Some Practical and Ethical Problems in Sociolinguistics

In so far as sociolinguistics is a social science dependent on the observation of the behaviour of human beings for its data, it shares with the human sciences several practical and ethical problems; problems which hardly arise if the data of linguistics is found by the analyst through introspection. We shall list some of these problems and suggest ways of overcoming them below.

The data-collecting interview contains within itself three major sources of error which, if not compensated for, can reduce or even totally destroy the value of the data collected, as sources from which valid inferences can be drawn; the informant, the fieldworker and the sampling techniques employed (see Samarin, 1967, pp. 140-50, for a discussion of specifically linguistic fieldwork techniques; and Webb et al., 1966, pp. 12-34 for a more general consideration of problems common to the social sciences as a whole).

8.1.2.1   Error from the Informant

At least four kinds of behaviour on the part of the informant can lead to error; the awareness of being tested, role selection, the interview itself as a stimulus to change, and the development of response sets.

The degree to which the informant is aware of being, in some sense, 'tested' relates clearly to Labov's principles 8.1.1.4-8 above. The sociolinguistic interview between an informant and a fieldworker is, after all, a rare and unusual kind of speech activity for most people. As Samarin (op.cit. p. 145) puts it: 'the only interview which people truly tolerate is the one that they themselves initiate or view as possibly being of benefit to themselves'. The sociolinguistic interview can hardly be described in this way, since the only participant certain to benefit from it is the fieldworker. The informant's involvement and interest must, necessarily, be far less than that of the fieldworker who is certain to be the only one with a clear understanding of the purpose of the interview. Worse, the informant is more than likely to equate this interview with others that he has had with the police, his bank manager or boss, situations in which he had to find the 'right answer' to each question, a behaviour pattern which he is almost certain to carry over into his relations with the researcher. He may even feel a certain resentment at being treated as a 'guinea pig' being 'experimented' with.

The assessment which the two participants make of each other at the beginning of the session will determine the role the informant – and to a lesser, though potentially as important, extent the fieldworker – decides to play. He will, no doubt unconsciously, select behaviour which will portray himself as the kind of person he feels he should appear to be. He will then select a role or set of roles which he considers appropriate, which will inevitably influence the linguistic data he produces. Several factors are at work here: the approach adopted towards him by the fieldworker, the familiarity of the informant with interviews and experiments etc., all of which will correlate with the personality, age, sex and social and educational background of the informant. Much will depend on the initial brief given by the researcher. One can easily predict the differences created by two approaches like:

(1) 'You have been carefully selected as a part of a scientifically chosen sample . . . it is of the utmost importance to the success of the project that you draw upon your own valuable and unique experiences in answering our questions . . . ' in contrast with (2) 'You are one of a random sample, drawn from the whole population of the country . . .'.

The first approach should make the informant feel that he has been sought out as an 'expert' for whom the fieldworker has a proper respect and appreciation, and in consequence he may well try his best to cooperate. The second approach, in contrast, devalues the individuality of the informant, reducing him to a mere statistic and making him feel that his answers are not inherently important, so that thoughtless or random responses will be as statistically insignificant as he himself has been made to feel. Of course, no research worker actually states his brief either in such a sycophantic manner as (1) or as brutally as (2), but the danger of creating damaging impressions is ever present.

The interview itself can be structured in such a way as to vitiate its results. It is, after all, a 'learning situation' in which earlier responses interact to create later answers which may contradict each other. A 'don't know', at an early stage, can set in motion a train of thought which colours a later response; equally, informants frequently feel that they are being inconsistent in their answers, showing themselves to be unsure and appearing foolish in the eyes of the fieldworker.

Some forms of interview, particularly paradigmatic linguistic interviewing, can lead to response sets which arise from the apparently irrational and irrelevant responses required. Samarin (op.cit. p. 140) has examples of informants producing strings of gibberish, either as a relief from boredom or through inattention!

8.1.2.2 *Error from the Fieldworker*

The fieldworker, like the informant, is also a human being and therefore a possible source of error. Two types appear to be particularly significant; (1) interviewer effects which lead to error in the informant's responses and (2) change in the interviewer himself.

The face-to-face nature of the interview situation makes demands on the reactions in the informant which 'spoils' the data he is trying to collect. He will need to have and to develop sensitivity to his informant and, particularly, must avoid producing negative reactions of the type described above. It is easy, for example, to question the value of dialect data collected by the university professor who is said to have begun interviewing an elderly farmworker with the words; 'Well now. I want you to speak to me just as you would to your friends, my good man'!

Just as the interview is a learning situation for the informant, so it is for the fieldworker; more so, since he, unlike the informant, has the experience and perhaps, too, analysed data of earlier interviews behind him, which can build up expectations of what he expects to find in the interview. He can dangerously bias the data by leading the informant into responses which he expects to hear. Indeed, it is by no means an empty question to ask if the fieldworker is, after a series of interviews, the same person as he was at the beginning.

8.1.2.3 *Errors from Sampling Techniques*

Sociolinguistics, like social anthropology and the other empirically-based social sciences, is still at the stage of development where data needs to be collected before significant gereralizations can be made. In its methodology, then, it must adopt and adapt much that is common to the fieldwork techniques of anthropology, sociology and so forth. We have seen earlier (1.5) how correlational the first work in the field was, attempting to demonstrate co-variation between linguistic and social structure and, drawing heavily on the correlation of linguistic forms with demographic characteristics, to isolate and describe regional and social class dialects. The fact that the emphasis has shifted over the last decade, first to stylistic variation and then to the more dynamic view of sociolinguistics as a discipline seeking the rule-governed bases of language use, still leaves the investigator in the position of needing data from which to deduce his rules or against which to check his hypotheses. Hence the very substantial experience in the field of the social scientists continues to have important implications for the sociolinguistic fieldworker; the errors likely to arise through faulty sampling being as applicable to a sociolinguistic survey as to one carried out by any other ethnographer. It is not intended here to go into detail on the problems of sampling, since there are several concise introductions to the topic (e.g. Moser and Kalton, 1971; Wakeford, 1968; Stacey, 1969) but to point out three which are of some importance to the sociolinguistic fieldworker; (1) restrictions in the population sampled, (2) the instability of the population in time and (3) in space.

It is clearly not possible, in most surveys, to question or collect data from the whole of the population in which the investigator is interested, nor, indeed, is it necessary to do so. The degree of confidence which can be placed on a partial sample has been known for some considerable time by social scientists and, hence, the degree of error which is to be anticipated (e.g. Galtung, 1967). However, there is a danger of over- and of under-representation, particularly if a door-to-door interviewing technique is adopted; those who typically answer doors will obviously be over-repre-sented – the young, the old and women. Even public opinion polls tend to fail to reach about 15% of the total population; 10% are likely to refuse to answer and a further 5% are permanently inaccessible for various reasons.

In addition, populations change over time: an important factor if data is collected over a long period and if an attempt is made to correlate information from earlier investigations with that collected later.

Even if the errors traceable to restrictions of access are allowed for, populations also vary in space, i.e. a nationwide survey runs the risk of falsifying its results through regional differences between its otherwise matched samples.

However, even though such sources of error cannot be avoided, their falsifying effects can be greatly mitigated when quantified by a competent statistician: a further plea for interdisciplinary teams to undertake socio-linguistic fieldwork, and a warning to us not to attempt to be linguist, sociologist, statistician, fieldworker and analyst all at the same time.

8.1.2.4 *Ethical Problems*

So long as linguistic investigation limited itself to the description of the closed system of the code (see 2.3.1 above for a discussion of language as a system) by means of the concepts and methods of the natural sciences, virtually no ethical problems arose. The object of analysis was either the data collected from a single individual who was quite aware of the investigator's purpose in using him as an informant, or the analyst was his own informant, in the sense that the data on which he was working came from his own introspection. But the moment language is seen as an open system and the goal of the investigation, the discovery of the rules of language use, particularly where the language use is the vernacular (see 8.1.1.7 and 8 above), data collection creates, in addition to the issues we have just been discussing, a serious ethical problem. The organism which we wish to observe and whose behaviour we wish to analyse is a human being like ourselves and equally worthy of respect and consideration (see Barnes, 1963, and Healey, 1964, for a survey of this issue).

It is possible to argue, at one extreme, that the total invasion of privacy by means of concealed recording devices and the large scale use of deception is justifiable 'in the name of science'. Alternatively, an investigator might feel that he cannot accept the idea of 'observations of private behaviour, however technically feasible, without the explicit and fully informed permission of the person [involved]' (Shils, 1964, quoted in Webb, op. cit. vi). Such an investigator might even object to the artificial creation of *rapport* by means of insincere warmth and interest which conceal the field-worker's real intentions. At its most extreme, it could be objected that even participant observation which lacks the prior disclosure of the purpose of the research is 'morally obnoxious . . . manipulation' (Shils, ibid.).

In sociolinguistics, the ethical problems posed by the technical possibility of obtaining badly needed surrepticious recordings of natural speech has, then, still to be resolved. We need ' . . . a specification of the multiple interests potentially threatened by social science research: the privacy of the individual, his freedom from manipulation, the protection of the aura of trust on which the society depends, and, by no means least in importance, the good reputation of social science' (Webb, op. cit. p.vii).

8.1.3 *The Problem of Theoretical Adequacy*

If we take a definition of a theory to be ' . . . a set of hypotheses structured by the relation of implication or deducibility . . .' (Galtung, op. cit. p.451), we can readily see that the adequacy of a theory depends on how well it is able to define these constructs or hypotheses. Two types of definition have been suggested (Torgerson, 1957, p.4), (1) in terms of other constructs — a *constitutive* definition — or (2) in terms of directly observable data — *epistemic* or *operational* definition.

A satisfactory theory will, of necessity, contain constructs of both kinds, thus ensuring both internal consistency and an external validity. The well-developed sciences — the natural sciences in general — typically have evolved theories of just this type in which constructs are related to the data, and rules of correspondence are set up to link the two types of construct as a coherent and empirically valid model. We have already implied as much in the earlier discussion of systems, rules and models in linguistics and have suggested that the orthodox view of the goals of linguistics, manifested in the theories and models of contemporary transformational-generative descriptions of the linguistic code, can be judged in terms which are equally applicable to the natural sciences (see particularly 1.1 and 2.3).

8.1.3.1   *Adequacy in Linguistic Theory*

Chomsky, initially in 1964 and then in 1965 in greater detail, proposed three types or degrees of adequacy which a satisfactory linguistic theory would need to fulfil: observational, descriptive and explanatory (see Chomsky, 1965, particularly pp. 24-27 and 30-37). We shall take each of these in turn and then consider how far such criteria apply to and are relevant to sociolinguistic theories.

Observational adequacy, the weakest form of adequacy required of a theory (not retained in the 1965 discussion), is achieved when a theory provides an analysis which is minimally consistent with observed primary data, i.e. the theory must, at least, contain constructs which are defined in epistemic or operational terms. We shall see below that even this adequacy is more difficult to attain than would at first appear when the methodology of the science depends on primary data gathered in the 'real world', but far simpler to satisfy when the data is itself substantially idealized and arrived at by means of introspection rather than by field methods.

Descriptive adequacy, the next highest form of adequacy, requires that a theory 'makes a descriptively adequate grammar available for each natural language' (Chomsky, op. cit. p.24) and such a grammar is seen as descriptively adequate 'to the extent that it correctly describes the intrinsic competence of the idealized native speaker' (ibid.). Such a grammar would seek to achieve both the internal consistency and the external validity remarked upon above, and would, in linking the constitutive and epistemic constructs together by rules of correspondence, fulfil the initial criteria (as set out in 8.1.3) for a satisfactory theory.

Explanatory adequacy, the highest of the three, is achieved when the theory succeeds '. . . in selecting a descriptively adequate grammar on the basis of primary linguistic data' (ibid.). A theory which satisfied this level of adequacy would, in fact, constitute a means of selecting between rival grammars in a principled way so as to choose the 'best' from those available. Explanatory adequacy would then be faced with the task of judging, by various criteria, how well the internal and external consistencies of differing grammars were expressed, i.e. it would be, in essence, a theory of theories.

In linguistics at present, observational and descriptive adequacy is claimed for several theories, and there is fierce controversy over the degree to which any one is better than its rivals; i.e. no theory has yet attained explanatory adequacy and this is, therefore, a major goal towards which theoretical linguists are working.

8.1.3.2   *Adequacy in Sociolinguistic Theory*

In the social sciences and the behavioural sciences, which encompass sociolinguistics in part and the sociology of language almost entirely, the problem of judging the adequacy of theories can be seen to be far more severe than in the more mature sciences. Essentially the same general criteria need to be applied, i.e. the general shape of a satisfactory theory, as outlined above (in 8.1.3), and the characteristic constructs and correspondences between them are equally valid whether the theory is one which seeks to explain an open or a closed system; but the empirical orientation typical of the human sciences makes the drawing up of such theories particularly problematical. It is not the case that these sciences lack observables and constructs. These are available in embarrassing profusion. What is lacking are correspondences of a clear kind between internally defined constitutive constructs and their equivalent epistemic counterparts derived from external empirical data. The problem is more easily stated than solved; relations between the two can be *presumed* but rarely *proved.*

A clear case of this can be seen in the difficulties we had earlier in our discussion of the relationship between linguistic form and social function (see 3.4.1), and is most evident in the 13 or more constraints listed by Hymes (1972) in his taxonomy of the situational components in play in face-to-face communication (3.3.2.1). In principle, a change in any one of these components can lead to a change in the social meaning of the interaction but, as we recognized earlier, we do not know yet whether this is actually true, whether some constraints are more powerful than others, or the precise effect on the linguistic form of a speech act a change in any situational element will have.

In simple terms, no sociolinguistic theory, so far, even attains Chomsky's lowest level of adequacy, the observational. The reason for this can be found in the nature of the primary data with which the sociolinguist chooses to work (we shall expand on this problem in the next section). Necessarily, too, no sociolinguistic theory achieves either descriptive or explanatory adequacy.

8.1.4   *The Primary Data of Sociolinguistics*

We take up again, here, a problem which was introduced at the beginning of this book (1.3.1.3) and which has underlain much of the discussion in it; the data with which the linguist works. It has been axiomatic in linguistics during this century (as we noted earlier; 1.3.1) that the data of actual speech – *parole, performance* – was not amenable to analysis, since it was too variable, indeed 'fairly degenerate in quality' (Chomsky, op. cit. p.31), consisting of 'fragments and deviant expressions of various sorts' (Chomsky, op.cit. p.201. note 14). Linguistics has, therefore, chosen to describe a more idealized form of data – *langue, competence* – and, within this circumscribed area has achieved spectacular successes. The sociolinguist, however, seeks a wider definition of his data and one which will allow him, at least, to correlate linguistic form with social function, and, at best, to create a theory of the situated use of language which will unite the explanations of linguists with those of other human scientists in the production of a broadly based semiotic theory in which man's skills as a user and creator of symbol systems will be described and explained.

What then is 'primary data' for the sociolinguist? Certainly neither the idealized data of competence nor the 'degenerate' data of actual speech — performance — but a kind of data far closer in form to that sought out by the ethnographer: '. . . socially meaningful behaviour within a given society'. There are, however, problems connected with such a definition of the data of sociolinguistic investigation: the degree to which the data is already idealized by the very process of collection, the extent to which the data can be used as the basis of valid generalization, and the relationship between data and theory. Each of these issues will be discussed below.

8.1.4.1 *The Problem of Idealization*
It must be recognized, at the outset, that it is quite impossible to collect 'raw' data. The process of collection, whether by observation, recording, introspection or any other method, is in itself a procedure which idealizes the initial facts of the observed event. For example, even an extremely detailed phonetic transcription of an utterance which included representations of the intonation and paralinguistic elements incorporated in it, and a specification of the context in which it occurred, would omit some features and would reflect preconceptions in the mind of the collector which would 'colour' what he 'observed'. A corpus would, then, consist of partially analysed data. It would be a representation of the event, but would clearly not be the event itself. This is by no means a problem specific to linguistics but one which is shared, of necessity, by any science which attempts to describe nondiscrete events in terms of discrete units of analysis. In terms of linguistics, the question is not whether raw data can be collected without idealization, but the degree of idealization which seems to be necessary for an adequate explanation of the phenomena in which linguistics are interested. We have seen that orthodox linguists have opted for a highly idealized form of data, and that the sociolinguist implies that a lower degree of idealization can and should be accepted.

This assumption requires of the sociolinguist that he deny the 'degeneracy' of actual speech. On the contrary he must show that most speech is, in fact, grammatical, and that the orthodox linguist has been avoiding data which could have easily been included in existing competence models.

Labov (1966) has demonstrated that the ungrammaticality of everyday speech is 'a myth with no basis in actual fact' (Labov, 1971, p. 165), that 'the great majority of utterances — about 75 per cent — are well-formed sentences by any criteria', and, further, that rules of ellipsis and universal editing rules can account for stammering and false starts, so that 'the proportion of truly ungrammatical and ill-formed sentences falls to less than two percent' (ibid.). If this is the case, it follows that introspection is not the only method available to the descriptive linguist, but is not even the most appropriate. Labov explains the discrepancy between his view of the grammaticality of everyday speech and that of Chomsky by pointing out that much of the data from which the orthodox linguist drew his assumption was gathered at conferences, i.e. at a time when the speaker was *most* preoccupied with his speech, attempting through it to express complex concepts and arguments. This data is, by definition (see 8.1.1 6 and 7 above), not the vernacular, and it is the vernacular which Labov claims should be the prime focus of investigation in sociolinguistics.

It is not possible to avoid idealization absolutely. The data we collect and seek to explain comes to our minds from the 'real world' through the filters of our senses and the cognitive processes by which we have become accustomed to the segmentation of 'reality'. The point is most clearly made in phonology where the contrast between the continuous acoustic phenomena of speech and the discrete units in which it is perceived has been long recognized. Shane (1973, p. 4) asks about the hearer of speech a question which is of general interest: 'If the speech signal is continuous, why should he hear it as discontinuous?'; and answers it: 'Probably because that is the only way the mind can organize language. We know that humans do perceive continuous phenomena as though discontinuous . . . In language the perceptual, the subjective, the discrete take precedence over the physical, the objective, the continuous' (ibid.). Abstraction and idealization cannot be avoided but the sociolinguist would wish to insist that idealization should be a little as possible, since the more idealized the data and the more abstract the description, the further from the reality it is intended to model the explanation becomes. However, this raises the question of the relationship between data and theory; an issue which we intend to take up below (8.1.4.3).

8.1.4.2 *The Problem of Generalization*

We have been arguing above that the sociolinguist is concerned to explain linguistic behaviour in its social context initially by means of the observation and recording of actual behaviour. We have also made the point that the sociolinguist wishes to work with data which is not too highly idealized, data which is as close as possible to the 'reality' of which it is a record. An immediate statistical problem arises here: how large a sample of informants are needed, and how much of their behaviour must be studied before generalizable statements can be made? This issue has been partly discussed above (8.1.2.3) where the problem was raised but no solution offered. The traditional fear of descriptive linguists has been that vast quantities of data would need to be analysed before any norms could be isolated (Hockett, 1958, p.444) and that without huge amounts of data all that could be achieved would be descriptions of single idiolects (see 1.3.1.3 above on this). Fortunately, and in accordance with Labov's Vernacular Principle (8.1.1.7 above), fieldwork has shown that a very small number of informants will provide in the course of relatively brief interviews adequate data in which extraordinarily regular patterns of usage correlating strongly with socioeconomic and stylistic variables occur. For example, in the survey conducted in Detroit (Shuy *et al.*, 1967) a mere 25 selected informants from a total sample of 700 were found to be enough to support the researchers' hypotheses concerning the relationships between linguistic and social variables, i.e. the major sociolinguistic norms of the population of a large city were discovered by selecting from a random sample of 0.035% of the total population a tiny set of individuals who themselves represented no more than 0.00125% of the 2 million or more inhabitants of the city.

It should not be thought, however, that the Detroit case is an isolated fortuitous example of general rules being derived from the analysis of a tiny sample. Labov's work in New York (1967), that of Trudgill (1974) in Norwich, and that concerned with multilingualism in Africa (Whiteley, ed., 1971) all support the belief that random sampling, followed by careful selection within that random sample of a very small number of informants, will throw up data which will be highly typical of the norms of the community as a whole. This has been shown to be the case not only where social stratification correlates with linguistic patternings of choices between varieties of the 'same' language, but even where the choices are interlingual, ie. code-switching between 'different' languages (see 4.4 and 5.5 above).

8.1.4.3   *The Problem of the Relationship of Data to Theory*

We commented earlier (2.4.2) on the contrast between the inductive techniques of structural linguistics and the deductive approach of transformational-generative linguistics. We need now to expand on this distinction, since it is crucial to the discussion of the relationship of data and theory in linguistics.

Francis Bacon (1561-1626) summed up the available methods of scientific investigation in an admirable analogy. He saw three approaches:

that of the spider which spins things from its own inside, that of the ant which merely collects, and that of the bee which collects and arranges. Unfair though this actually is to ants, as Russell (1946, p. 566) points out, the distinction between the spider-like deductive method and the induction of the bee illustrates the contrasting methods of transformational and pre-transformational linguistics. Our particular interest, here, is to consider which approach is the more appropriate for a sociolinguistic investigation.

The crucial distinction between the two approaches can be traced to two contrasting views of the nature of human knowledge. For the transformationalist, knowledge is discovered by intuition and introspection – a theory is postulated on the basis of informed intuition and is tested out by deducing the logical consequences of the theory and by putting them to an empirical test. Hence, the theory precedes the data and to some extent determines what is to be accepted as valid data. The effect of this in linguistics has been, as we have noted earlier on several occasions, to limit the field of inquiry of the discipline to that data which is generated by the grammar, and no other. A further important implication of the use of the hypothetical-deductive method of investigation is that the object of description must already be in the possession of the investigator, i.e. the procedure cannot, in its extreme form, operate where the linguist is not a native speaker of the language involved.

How does this fit into our conceptions of the goals of sociolinguistics? In one sense, the native user of a language can be thought of as possessing not only a linguistic competence which is amenable to description by the hypothetical-deductive method, but also a communicative competence (see section 8.3 below for an extended discussion of this concept) which should, in principle, be equally amenable to description by the same introspective approach. However, the vastly larger range of parameters involved in the discovery of the rule-governed system of actual language use makes the use of introspection unworkable at present, although, in the long term, a cognitive sociology of language will need to make use of the technique if it is to achieve the goal of discovering universal features which link, in a highly abstract manner, not only the underlying characteristics of seemingly diverse linguistic structure but the equally universal features of human language use.

At present, though, it seems that sociolinguistics is committed to the converse, data-oriented empirical approach which proceeds from data to theory by means of an inductive cycle (the term is from Cook, 1969, pp. 3f) based on the assumption that knowledge is arrived at from the evidence collected by the senses – data is observed, a pattern is perceived, on the basis of this hypotheses are formulated which form the initial shape of a theory which is then verified or denied by comparison with the observed data. Hence, induction represents the converse relationship between theory and data from deduction; data first then theory, i.e. facts to theory to new facts in a cyclical manner.

Induction has, then, the advantage of keeping relatively close to its data and insisting on the constant 'renewal of connection in experience' for which Firth argued in his linguistic theory in the 1930s (Firth, 1957 p. 22). Conversely, this approach has the weakness, in its extreme form, of creating no more than lists of phenomena, taxonomies which in themselves are not rules. Clearly, the next step is to attempt to discover generalizable relationships between units within taxonomies which will then form a basis for the creation of more abstract and ultimately universalistic rules. Sociolinguistics has, then, as its major aim at the present time, to discover initially for specific speech communities and ultimately for the universal notion 'speech community', the system which contains '. . . the set of community norms, operating principles, strategies, and values which guide the production and interpretation of speech, the community ground rules for speaking' (Bauman and Sherzer, 1974, p. 7).

8.1.5   *Summary*

We have been expanding, in this section, several topics which have either been touched upon or assumed in earlier chapters. Chief among these has been the question of the relationship of theory and data in sociolinguistic research and the appropriate means of relating the two. We saw how, for the foreseeable future, sociolinguistics is committed to a data-oriented empirical approach which arrives at explanation of phenomena by induction, rather than the deduction at present typical of work in 'orthodox' linguistics.

Such a methodology has its own strengths and weaknesses and, in particular, raises issues of a practical and ethical kind which arise in the course of the fieldwork, a necessary concomitant of the empirical approach to the explanation of the phenomena of language in use. Fortunately, the social sciences have substantial experience in this field on which the sociolinguist can draw and, even more fortunately, actual investigation has shown that very small samples of data can and do provide a sufficiently large base on which to formulate rules of a very high order of generality, even for a large speech community.

8.2   DISCOURSE: SITUATED LANGUAGE IN USE

We commented earlier (1.3.1.3) in our discussion of the assumptions and axioms of descriptive linguistics in this century, that the sentence has been, for the vast majority of linguists, the upper limit of investigation, and that a sociolinguistic description would need to go further and attempt to find linguistic structures in which sentences – or perhaps, better, 'utterances' – would themselves form component parts.

In the description of discourse – language above the level of the sentence – three approaches stand out in contrast with each other (Widdowson, 1971); analysis in terms of *code, text* and *discourse.* We shall take each of these in turn below.

8.2.1 Code Analysis

Code analysis, termed *microlinguistics* by Hill (1958), has been the traditional approach to the description of language during this century. Structuralist methods entailed the taking of stretches of language longer than the sentence – 'texts', spoken or written – but the analytical technique focussed on the sentence as its largest unit and sought to demonstrate (1) how individual sentences were constructed of 'immediate constituents'; units of smaller size and (2) how sentences containing different lexical items could be regarded as being representatives of the same 'pattern'. Transformational generative linguistics, too, has sought to demonstrate essentially the same kinds of relationship, though by radically different methods. Both approaches limit themselves to the statement of intrasentential relationships and processes – subject to predicate, NP to VP etc. – and neither has been concerned with intrasentential connections which link sentence to sentence within a cohesive text.

8.2.2 Text Analysis

Even before Hill's distinction between *micro-* and *macro*-linguistics had been proposed, a number of descriptive linguists, dissatisfied with the obstacle presented by the sentence as the upper limit of description, had turned their attention to what they called 'discourse analysis' but which, for reasons which will become clear below, we shall term 'text analysis'. Chief among these was Harris who, in two pioneering papers (1952, a, and 1952, b) attempted to demonstrate the syntactic and semantic mechanisms by which sentences are connected to create a coherent text. There is little need to describe Harris's technique in detail here, although it might be fairly said that in many ways it represented an attempt to apply the tried methods of phonology – the notions of phonemes with free and conditioned allophonic variants – to connected textual data. Harris's main contributions were (1) to reaffirm the need to integrate semantic considerations into what was commonly felt to be syntactic analysis – an issue still hotly debated even now – and (2) to provide a basis for further work on stylistic variation which led to the fruitful notion of 'register' commented on earlier in this book (1.4.3.1).

Work on register (Halliday *et al.*, 1964, Gregory, 1967 – see 3.3.1.2 above – and Crystal and Davy, 1969 – see 3.3.1.3 above) shared a common assumption; linguistic forms were to be taken as primary and the 'situational constraints' with which they co-occurred as secondary, i.e. the technique required that form should be correlated with function but that function should be viewed as the dependent variable. Such an approach, while clearly macrolinguistic, in Hill's sense, was not sociolinguistic, since its emphasis was still on the text and the relationships between elements of the text, and only secondarily on the functions of the text in its use as a part of human communication.

Even more closely linguistic has been the work of Hasán (1968), focussed on cohesion between sentences and exemplified by analyses of such features as pronominalization, anaphoric and exophoric reference and the like.

All of these approaches can be conveniently labelled 'text analysis' in view of their concentration on the correlation of linguistic form with linguistic form as an indicator of textual cohesion, and can be seen, because of the strongly formal orientation, to contrast with the more functional and sociolinguistic techniques of discourse analysis which we shall consider below.

8.2.3   *Discourse Analysis*

Beyond text analysis we find a number of approaches which have been termed discourse analysis (by Widdowson, op. cit.) which we have already touched upon, at least in the case of Hymes (1972, see 3.3.2.1 above) and his taxonomy of SPEAKING.

Two contrasting lines of investigation can be seen in discourse analysis: the work of stylisticians in their attempts at the discovery of the structure of *narrative* (Chatman, 1969, Todorov, 1966, Barthes, 1966 and, though from a somewhat different perspective, that of Levi-Strauss, 1972) postulating narrative units such as episodes, events and the like, and that of socially oriented linguists and linguistically oriented social scientists (e.g. the ethnomethodologists on whom we shall comment later, see 8.4.3 below).

We shall confine ourselves here to a brief outline of one strand of current research which has implications not only for descriptive sociolinguistics but also for the application of sociolinguistic information in applied linguistics (a point taken up again below under 8.4.5): the analysis of discourse in the classroom (Sinclair and Coulthard, 1975).

Drawing on the theoretical position of Halliday (1961), interestingly, a linguist who regards himself as a neo-Firthian, Sinclair and Coulthard have evolved a system of analysis for the description of the language used by teachers and pupils which depends on the concept of *rank;* a hierarchy of units extending from the largest — *lesson* — through successively smaller units — *transaction, exchange, move* — to the smallest : *act.* Each unit is made manifest by the occurrence of at least one unit from the lower rank and, it is suggested, classroom interaction, or at least the linguistic components of it, can be shown to be an ordered progression of transactions, normally with clearly marked boundaries initially and finally, made up of exchanges which are themselves made up of moves which are in turn made up of acts. They have found some correlation, as one would hope, between the non-linguistic organizational hierarchy — course, period and topic — and their own levels within the discourse scale, and between that and the syntactic rank scale: *sentence, clause, group, word, morpheme.* The correlation is, of course, by no means perfect but, for example, topics tend to co-occur with transactions, moves with sentences and acts with clauses.

Much work remains to be done and many theoretical issues, most with important practical consequences, still remain to be resolved; e.g. it is probably true that most adult language is multifunctional, i.e. ambiguous, but it is equally true that there seems, in a particular situation, to be a 'preferred reading' for any utterance. Consider the motorist who interprets the police utterance 'Would you accompany me to the station?' in terms of its syntactic structure — a question requiring a 'yes/no' answer — rather than its function — an order! However, the system, crude though it still is, offers considerable hope for the analysis of discourse, and is currently being extended into other areas of interaction, e.g. committee meetings (Bell, 1975), TV interviews (Pearce, forthcoming) etc.

8.2.4 *Summary*

Recent work on linguistic structures larger than the sentence has begun to move linguistics into the area of macrolinguistics and towards the traditional approaches to language adopted by students of rhetoric. Some linguists are continuing to work towards the discovery of the devices through which lexical coherence is manifested in a text by the use of sentence-linking devices. Such research has been termed *text analysis,* and is represented by non-literary stylistics in particular, often under the informal label of *register.* In addition, work in *discourse* is progressing in which the emphasis is on the rhetorical coherence of a piece of discourse that makes it hold

together as appropriate interaction in language. Rather than merely indicating how form coheres with form, such studies centre on function and
the linguistic means at the disposal of the user as he attempts to take
part in human communication. Yet another approach to the description
of longer pieces of language can be seen in the work of literary stylisticians
and anthropologists seeking to find structure in narrative and myth by
suggesting hierarchies of units of narrative.

Work in discourse, in the most general sense of the term, can then be
seen to link several disciplines and approaches in a similar if not actually
common endeavour: yet another happy omen for those who wish to see
linguistics again recognized as a social and human science.

8.3   COMMUNICATIVE COMPETENCE

Throughout this book, we have been referring, either directly (1.3.1.1.,
1.5.1.2 and 3.2.1) or indirectly (1.4.2, 3.1 and 4.3.2) to the notion of
communicative competence; the knowledge possessed by the language
user, not only of the formal code, but of the social implications of
linguistic choices which are available to him as he uses his language in the
course of his life as a participant in the speech events which are so much a
major constituent of human society. We shall therefore, in this section,
address ourselves to considering three key topics: the relationship between
linguistic and communicative competence, the functions of communicative
competence as a kind of mixing device which relates available linguistic
forms to social functions, and the relationship between 'ideal' and 'actual'
in a theory of communicative competence exemplified by the views of
two scholars, Hymes and Habermas.

8.3.1   *Linguistic and Communicative Competence*

The notion of linguistic competence proposed by Chomsky (1957, etc.)
and accepted by most orthodox linguists requires no extended discussion
here, but a contrast between it and communicative competence is clearly
appropriate.

Linguistic competence is seen as the innate knowledge of the ideal
speaker-hearer which permits him to create and recognize the grammatical
sentences of his language. It is, in keeping with the view of language as a
closed system (see 2.3.1 on the distinction between open and closed
systems), concerned with the knowledge of the code implied by the ability
of the ideal speaker-hearer to judge, out of context, the grammaticalness
or ungrammaticalness of sentences. In semiotic terms (Morris, 1946),
competence relates to knowledge of syntax, and it is on this carefully

delimited base that the substantial advances in linguistics which have been achieved in the last two decades have been made. However we noted earlier (1.5.1.2), in our discussion of the strong claim of sociolinguistics made by Searle, that there were important reasons why this base should now be extended to include social aspects of language use, and it is to efforts in this direction that we now turn.

Communicative competence, building on the concept of linguistic competence, can be seen as the innate knowledge which permits the user of a language to create and comprehend utterances, to issue the communicative tokens of speech acts, in context. Such knowledge is, clearly, concerned with the level of discourse in which language operates as an open system in constant interaction with its environment, and is therefore an instance of pragmatic knowledge of which syntactic and semantic knowledge are a part. A specification of communicative competence can be recognized as an attempt to define not only how a user is able to judge grammaticality but also how he is able to recognize what is acceptable as a speech act in a social situation.

Such a view of competence implies a correlation of both linguistic and social skills and knowledge, and requires that the sociolinguist create a satisfactory model which specifies the 'rules of speaking' in a way which describes and explains the use of situated language. We shall return to this issue below (8.3.2), but first of all wish to consider what is meant by the idea of 'knowing' a language.

Searle (1969, pp. 14 f.) distinguishes knowing *how* from knowing *that*, during a brief discussion of the relationship between innate knowledge and the access to that knowledge available to its possessor. The distinction is one of some importance, since a major problem with the communication of knowledge lies in its formulation in some readily acceptable and shared codification. The ideal speaker-hearer may well have a tacit knowledge of the structure and the potentialities of his language, but bringing such knowledge out and making it accessible to others is a key methodological, and indeed philosophical, problem. We need to distinguish between characterizing talk on the one hand and explaining it on the other, and to recognize that the ability to talk at all implies and makes possible its characterization and explanation. Searle, begining with such assumptions, sets out his intentions in the following way: 'I wish to offer certain characterizations and explanations of my use of elements of . . . language. The hypothesis on which I am proceeding is that my use of linguistic elements is underlain by certain rules. I shall therefore offer linguistic characterizations and then explain the data in those characterizations by formulating the underlying rules' (ibid.). This, in essence, is the programme which a describer of communicative competence must also follow: general-

ization, whether based on inductive or deductive techniques, leading to the
formulation of rules which explain the generalized behaviour.

8.3.2   *The Nature of Communicative Competence*

Much of the body of this book (especially chapters 3-5) has been taken up
with the attempt to describe and explain the complex phenomenon of
human communication in language. In the course of this, we have touched
upon many of the elements which need to be incorporated in a model of
communicative competence – the wide range of communication channels
and content available to the user of language, and his ability to choose, on
the basis of that content and his intentions, the appropriate means for
transmitting his meanings from his repertoire of linguistic and social
skills. To specify communicative competence would be no more and no
less than to explain, by postulating an underlying rule-system, how it is
that all these elements can be manipulated by the user to make him
capable of producing speech acts appropriate to the speech events he is
involved in, i.e. to propose the rules of speaking by means of which man
participates in social life as an active member of a human community.
The task is an enormous one and so far only hints at a solution can be
made. We have ample evidence that all normal human beings, even at a
very early age, play large numbers of roles which function within sets of
role-relations with other role-players, and that attached to these interactions
are appropriate behaviours, some of them linguistic. All, then, command
extensive repertoires of codes on which they draw. More; the 'real-time'
nature of spoken communication makes rapid revision and actual code-
switching on the basis of feedback inevitable and frequent, not merely
within languages in the form of changes of 'style' but, as we saw earlier
(5.5), between languages where the speech community contains numbers
of bilinguals. So, not only are we faced by the problem of showing how
communicative competence acts as a device for correlating linguistic
choices with social functions, but how such correlations are reassessed
in the course of speech events by the fluent user of language.

Hymes (1971) provides a starting point. We made use earlier (3.3.2) of
his acronym SPEAKING as a handy mnemonic for the components of the
communicative situation. We can now take a further suggestion of his
concerned with the issue of judging utterances as the basis of a skeletal
framework for a model of communicative competence.

Rejecting the sharp competence-performance distinction proposed by
Chomsky, in which judgments of grammaticality were made in respect
of competence and acceptability in respect of performance, Hymes (ibid.)
suggests that an adequate theory of language use must take account of

four different kinds of judgment, only one of which is grammatical, in the Chomskian sense. Judgments of socially situated language depend on:

1) Whether and to what extent something is *formally* possible. In linguistic terms, 'formally possible' clearly means 'grammatical', but it is equally feasible to apply the distinction to the cultural level and consider whether an act is formally possible within the framework of the norms of a particular culture.

2) Whether and to what extent something is *feasible*. This represents one aspect of language contained within the notion of 'acceptable' (Chomsky, 1965, pp. 10-15) and classified as belonging to the study of performance. Utterances which are not, or to some degree not, feasible are exemplified by such features as nesting, self-embedding, multiple-branching constructions, in which psycholinguistic factors related to memory limitations, perception and the like come into play to make such sentences 'bizarre and outlandish' and not 'immediately comprehensible without paper-and-pencil analysis' (ibid.).

3) Whether and to what extent something is *appropriate*. Once again, this aspect is touched upon in Chomsky (ibid.) and related to, for example, 'intonational and stylistic factors', i.e. though included within 'performance', such factors clearly imply 'rules of speaking' and judgments of appropriateness that must be related to interconnections between scenes, participants, channels and linguistic forms.

4) Whether and to what extent something is *done*. In transformational-generative theory, this aspect has been consistently disregarded since the frequency of occurrence is not of interest to the grammarian, who is primarily concerned with the question of possibility in the formal sense used above.

We shall, below, also subsume this element of the judgment of acceptability under the other three heads, since their formulation implies that the degree to which something is done is, in any case, part of its possibility, feasibility and appropriateness.

In a general sense, communicative competence can be thought of as covering the overall speaking and comprehending abilities of the language user in making use of language in communicative situations. How idealized this user or these situations should be considered to be is a question we shall discuss below (8.3.3) after more thought about the nature of communicative competence.

Hymes further suggests that communicative competence depends on the recognition of two aspects previously not clearly distinguished: tacit knowledge and ability for use. The point is that it is one thing to *know* and quite another to *do*. This is, however, not a reassertion of the competence-performance distinction, but an absorption into the notion of communicative competence of part of what had previously been labelled 'performance', since performance, in the Chomskian sense, represented not only ability for use but also actual use, i.e. performance was, at one and the same time, some of the 'grammatically irrelevant conditions [involved] in applying... knowledge of the language ...' in actual use (Chomsky, op. cit. p. 3), and 'the actual use of language in concrete situations' (Chomsky, op. cit. p. 4); part of the reason for the existence of the data and the data itself.

There are important implications in this for linguistic theory as a whole. Of major interest is the need to recognize that the attempt to explain the feature of 'creativity' which is so typical of human language — 'the means for expressing indefinitely many thoughts and for reacting appropriately in an indefinite range of new situations' (Chomsky, op. cit. p. 6) — implies a socio-cultural orientation to the data. Whereas orthodox linguistic theory has begun with the formal properties of the code and worked outwards from there to social function, the new sociolinguistic orientation, or more properly, that of the sociology of language, must begin with function and work back towards form. Instead of language being seen as a code which correlates, in some way, with social life (the closed system view), a linguistic theory which is not, as de Saussure put it 'hors de sa realité sociale' — divorced from its social reality — must be based in the socio-cultural system within which it operates and of which it forms a part. It must, therefore, approach its data as representing patternings of communicative acts and purposes. Such a theory rests on three primary assumptions: (1) that each social relationship entails and, indeed crucially consists of selecting or creating communicative means which are considered appropriate to it by the participants; (2) that the organization of these means implies a structure which is not revealed by the analysis of the means alone; and (3) that the means available in any relationship condition both its nature and its outcome. If we accept this view of linguistic theory, we necessarily accept Searle's 'strong claim' for sociolinguistics, i.e. that the goal of linguistics is, and this is not disputed by more orthodox linguists, the study of *langue* or *competence* but that an adequate study of *langue* consists of a study of *speech acts* (see 1.5.1.2 above).

How then are we to specify the nature of communicative competence and the rules which make it operative? We suggested earlier (3.2.1) that communicative competence might be thought of as a kind of 'mixer' which performed the function of balancing available linguistic forms chosen by drawing on the linguistic competence of the user, against available social functions housed in some kind of social competence. We shall take up this suggestion now and expand our earlier notions, redesigning part of figure 3.4 as we do so and representing our model by figure 8.1 below.

FIGURE 8.1 *Communicative Competence*

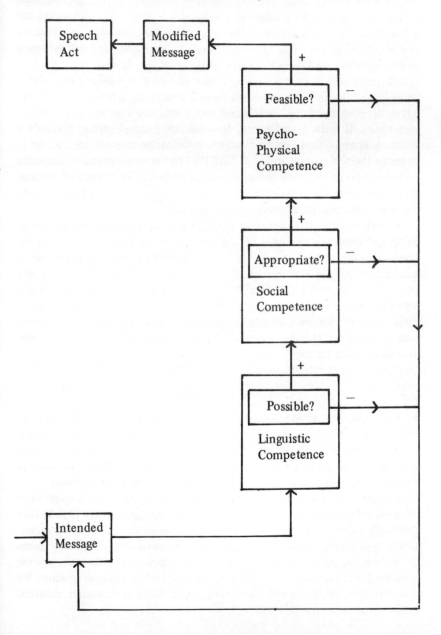

This model suggests that a message needs to be processed three times in terms of its possibility, appropriateness and feasibility, that this processing is by reference to the three related competences, and that each question may need to be asked more than once for each message. A message needs to be possible not only in terms of its form but also its content and instrumentalities. Similarly, its appropriateness depends on the social constraints acting upon it, and its feasibility on the extent to which the user can create the form of the message. We see the communicative competence of the language user as being the ability to weigh a series of factors against each other in such a way as to produce a message which satisfies the three criteria and hence can function as an acceptable speech act. It must be admitted, however, that the model as it stands is still very crude. Future research on communicative competence must seek to assign Hymes' parameters of SPEAKING to the appropriate competence without overlap, indicate the connections between each and, if possible, demonstrate whether or not there is some hierarchical relationship between them, i.e. are some parameters more important than others?

By introducing the notion of a psycho-physical competence, we have, in fact, disposed of the issue of communicative performance as a separate level of description, but are left with a related problem, that of level of abstraction of the description. We have been outlining communicative competence in terms of 'users', 'situations' and so forth without stating whether and to what extent we envisage these elements as idealized. Two clear views of this are found in discussions of communicative competence, one typified by Hymes, the other by Habermas. We shall discuss these two approaches below.

8.3.3   *Two Views of Communicative Competence*

In his statement of the primary concern of linguistic theory, Chomsky (1965, p. 3) highlights three aspects of variation and declares the extent to which he sees them as idealized: the speaker-listener, the speech community, and the situation of actual performance. For him, the first two are idealized while performance, viewed as no more than the outcome of competence, is not. It might seem that all the sociolinguist needs to do in attempting to define the concerns of sociolinguistic theory is to replace Chomsky's terms 'ideal' and 'homogeneous' with the term 'actual'. Such is not, however, the case, since description on so narrow a base would lead to statements of the communicative competence of individuals – the sociolinguistic equivalent of the *idiolect* – rather than of groups and communities. Some idealization is required if generalizations are to be made with confidence.

Hymes adopts a position consistent with his anthropological training; he seeks to '. . . show the ways in which the systematically possible, the feasible and the appropriate are linked to produce and interpret actually occurring cultural behaviour' (Hymes, 1971a, p.23) i.e. 'the study of language within the context of anthropology' (Hymes, 1964, p.xxiii). His approach is, then, to take actual speaker-listeners in an actual speech community whose language use he observes in actual situated performance. This data, ultimately, will be codified into a model of speaking and its rules constitute a theory of communicative competence.

Habermas (1970) takes a more sociological view of the matter, arguing that '. . . in order to participate in normal discourse, the speaker must have − in addition to his linguistic competence − basic qualifications of speech and symbolic interaction (role-behaviour) at his disposal, which we may call communicative competence. Thus, communicative competence means the mastery of an ideal speech situation' (op. cit. p. 138). He specifically proposes to use the term in the sense that Chomsky uses linguistic competence, i.e. communicative competence relates to a system of rules which generate an ideal speech situation. He takes issue with Hymes' view which he considers to be limited and essentially correlational: the 'linguistic codes which link language and universal pragmatics with actual role systems' (op.cit. p. 147, note 19).

Contrasting though these two approaches to the concept of communicative competence are, both may be seen as attempts to expand in a functional direction the '. . . system of rules we have mastered [that] enables us to understand new sentences and produce a new sentence *on an appropriate occasion* . . .' (Chomsky, emphasis added), by shifting the focus of attention from the sentence to its context of use. Ultimately, both Hymes and Habermas share a common goal; the difference between their present stances is primarily one of degree of abstraction, and given the lack of evaluate procedures (referred to above in 8.1.3.1) there is no way at present of choosing in a principled manner between them.

8.3.4 *Summary*

The shift of emphasis from contextless form to contextualized function implies a changed view of the nature of language, from a closed to an open system and hence an expansion of what needs to be described and explained and of the methods necessary for such description and explanation. Linguistic theory, it is argued, needs to concern itself not merely with the 'brute facts' of the code but with the 'institutional facts' of its use (the terms are from Searle, op. cit. p.50); in order to achieve this goal, linguistics must aim at a theory which explains communicative competence by drawing up 'rules of speaking' on which human interaction is crucially based. Such rules must take into account the degree to which speech acts are formally, practically and socially possible and appropriate as elements in human communication. We have suggested that a fruitful approach might be to consider communicative competence as a kind of 'mixer' which weighs linguistic, psycho-physical and social constraints against each other and achieves through balancing these speech acts which are acceptable at all three levels.

8.4   THE RELATIONSHIP BETWEEN SOCIOLINGUISTICS AND OTHER DISCIPLINES

In this final section, we shall take up again, in a little more detail, some of the 'relationships between sociolinguistics and other disciplines, both theoretical and applied, at which we have earlier hinted.

Initially, we shall concentrate on the relationships which exist, or can be made to exist by future interdisciplinary effort, between sociolinguistics and what may be informally termed the 'human sciences'. Next we shall consider how insights derived from sociolinguistic research might be drawn upon in the applied aspects of these sciences, as an attempt to '. . . assist in the solution of societal problems' (Fishman, 1970, p.103).

One important point should be made before we begin such a survey. The social sciences may be typified as lacking precise boundaries between themselves. They are 'a continuum, with peaks' (Kjolseth, 1974), the peaks being labelled but the extremities of each discipline merging imperceptibly into the next. It is possible to see one axis of this continuum as extending from the most specific and individual to the most general and, ultimately, universal in subject matter, i.e. from neurology through psychology, social psychology, microsociology and macrosociology to anthropology. With each of these, linguistics has, actually or potentially, connections and overlaps which we shall consider below.

8.4.1   *Sociolinguistics and Linguistics*

Running through this book has been a concern with the relationships between sociolinguistics, the sociology of language, and orthodox descriptive and theoretical linguistics. What remains to be attempted here is some kind of integrative summary which will, in addition, point the way ahead for sociolinguistics and its parent disciplines.

We commented earlier (1.3.1) on the way in which linguistics, in the earlier years of this century, turned away from the traditional historical orientation which had been prevalent in the nineteenth century and earlier

and, at the same time, excluded from its field of interest the social correlates
and motivations of language use and change, in an attempt to describe
language as a logical and closed system. During the course of the century,
however, dissatisfaction with such asocial linguistics has steadily increased
and led to the emergence of a socially oriented linguistics – sociolinguistics,
if the weak claim for the endeavour is accepted, the sociology of language
if the stronger claim is preferred (see 1.5.1 on this) – the goals, approaches
and problems of which have been the subject of this book. Two theoretical
aims in particular can be isolated (Shuy and Fasold, 1972, p.2): the desire
to create a sounder empirical base for linguistic theory and the belief that
the social factors involved in the actual use of language are legitimate
topics for linguistic investigation. Both of these aims imply an interest in
issues previously ignored or, at best, treated in a cursory manner by orthodox
linguistics: variation, the artificial barrier of the sentence, and the problem
of linguistic change.

The fact of variation and the problems this creates in the description
and explanation of language has been a major topic of this book (particularly in chapter 2) and therefore needs no extra discussion here. An
important point may, however, be made. Many linguists, who would not
consider themselves as sociolinguists but as grammarians, are increasingly
accepting that variation is far from being of peripheral importance, describable at a secondary level of analysis under the head of 'performance',
and that '. . . we must confront squarely . . . the fact that variation is
central' (Ross, 1973, p.129), and hence that linguists must take into account
not only questions of 'grammaticality' in relation to attested linguistic
data but also the more complex and socially dominated aspects of
'acceptability' of usage. How such judgments are to be arrived at, and how
systematized within a comprehensive linguistic description, are questions
of major theoretical and practical importance which now face the discipline
and on which sociolinguistics, whether narrowly or broadly conceived,
must necessarily take the lead.

The sentence barrier, so long the upper limit of investigation, now
shows signs of weakening as the social interaction aspect of language is
restated. This restatement is coming particularly from those working in
the field of discourse (see 8.3 above) who either explicitly or implicitly
deny the Chomskian assumption of a monologic model of language in
which the ideal speaker-hearer does not interact by participating in dialogue,
alternating the rule-governed roles of speaker and listener (Habermas, op.
cit. p. 131). Once the sentence is passed as the largest unit which the
linguist can describe, we shall have again reasserted the ancient dichotomy
between grammar and rhetoric (on which we commented earlier; see
1.4.2) and will again begin to offer practical assistance to the language

teacher, whether of the L1 or the L2, a point we intend to take up again below.

Linguistic change, too, can now be seen in a different light, most clearly when the techniques of implicational scaling are applied to seemingly chaotic data (see 2.4.3 and 5.4 above); indeed some investigators (particularly C.J. Bailey, 1969) now contend that there is, in fact, no real difference between synchronic and diachronic linguistics; that the waves of linguistic change which passed through speech communities in times past are essentially comparable to those which are on the move at the present time. We have already drawn attention to this above (8.1.1) in our discussion of Labov's Uniformation Principle, which we suggested might be seen as one of the axioms of sociolinguistics.

These three implications of the attempt to create a more empirically bound base for linguistic theory have the interesting additional effect of beginning to blur the distinction between linguistics on the one hand and the previously distinct but related fields of dialectology, rhetoric and historical linguistics on the other, and lead us to hope that a rapprochment may soon be reached to the mutual enrichment of all (see comments above under 1.4.1 and 1.4.2).

The attempt to include social factors in the mechanisms of linguistic choice has also thrown up three key issues: the means available for the correlation of linguistic and, what had previously been termed 'extra-linguistic' phenomena, the problem of relating linguistic form to social function, and the degree to which the attitudes of users are seen to be important factors in their linguistic behaviour.

At first, sociolinguistics was frankly correlational, seeking to take linguistic facts and work out statistically significant correlations between them and social facts (see Bright's 1966 definition, 1.5 above); but as Labov was quick to point out (1971, p.463) '. . . there is no limit to the number of correlations between linguistic and social factors which might be described'; hence sociolinguistics has had to develop from a merely descriptive science, making use of correlational techniques in the handling of its data, towards becoming an interdisciplinary science involved in the '. . . theoretical problems of linguistics, anthropology and sociology. . . likely to make significant contributions to our knowledge of language. . . [and] . . . social behaviour' (ibid.).

The attempt to relate form to function has already been discussed at some length in our outline of functional models of language (chapters 3 and 4) but two points still remain to be emphasized here. The correlation of form and function is far from simple, in part because there is rarely a sentence that cannot be made — by changes in intonation, by gesture, by the rest of its context of use, including the shared presuppositions of the speakers and hearers — to mean virtually anything, and, in part, by the fact that in adult language use most speech acts are multifunctional, e.g. a common committee meeting strategy is for the chairman to introduce what are intended and accepted as directives in the form of a question — 'Shall we move on now to discuss the next item on the agenda?' — a technique which also permits other participants to treat the utterance as a 'yes-no' question without causing the chairman to lose face. That adult language is so clearly multiply ambiguous but that one meaning is usually accepted as dominant within a particular set of conventions is the major stumbling block for those in search of the rules which certainly appear to govern human interaction in language and which constitute such a typical part of social life. At present, though, we appear to be faced by a task as intractable as that suggested, in a different context, by Geach (1969, p.25) in '. . . devising a mathematical formula which would yield the present coastline of England and its border with Scotland'! But the increased interest of theoretical linguists not only in semantics but equally in some aspects of pragmatics, and the work of many philosophers on speech acts and their relationship with linguistic form and social use, do tend to a rather more optimistic view, at least in the long term.

A crucial change in interest can be seen in the re-evaluation of attitude in relation to language. Linguistics has attempted, most noticeably in this century, to be 'objective' in its judgements, avoiding value judgements deriving from the subjective assessments of language made by individual users. As work both in theoretical and sociolinguistics has progressed, it has become more and more clear that attitudes are often extraordinarily clear and consistent factors on which the linguist can lean in his attempts to explain the complex and extensive phenomena of human language. Apart from substantial evidence that users of a language are very well able to judge social and psychological characteristics of others on the basis of speech samples alone (Harms, 1961, and wide ranging surveys by Agheyisi and Fishman, 1970, and Williams, 1973) — an interesting fact even from the simple correlational point of view — it is rapidly becoming clear that the most useful definition of the speech community itself depends not on such difficult measures as mutual intelligibility (see Hockett's attempt in this direction discussed earlier in 2.4.1.1) but on the attitudes of its members to language and its functions. Crudely, a speech community can now be seen not as a group of individuals who share a common language, membership being discoverable by some objective measure of similarity of linguistic form, but a group of individuals who *believe* themselves to belong to such a community (see, among others, Blom and Gumperz, 1972).

8.4.2   *Sociolinguistics and Anthropology*

The mention of the speech community leads very naturally to a consideration of the relationships between sociolinguistics and anthropology. We touched upon this topic earlier in the book (3.1.2) and shall therefore expand here on the, at first, surprising similarities between the goals of cultural anthropology and sociolinguistics.

Cultural anthropology has, in its theoretical orientations, changed direction and focus in ways which parallel, to a remarkable degree and over much the same time-scale, the development of linguistics during this century. At first, just as in lingusitics, the emphasis was on change and development with both evolutionists and diffusionists seeking patterns of change in the cultures they were studying. Soon a new approach stressing static description appeared, led by functionalists who sought to describe the internal organization of cultures, to compare one culture with another and, ultimately, to arrive at universally applicable laws of society. The similarity between the diachronic approach of the earlier theory to that of historical linguistics and dialectology, and the synchronic approach of the functionalists to structural and contrastive linguistics is irresistible. Indeed similarity goes even deeper. Both the evolutionists and the functionalists attempted '. . . to construct monolithic, unitary systems which purported to either explain cultures or their development' (Tyler, 1969, p.3) just as, until very recently, linguistics has; and, as a necessary result of such an orientation, variation was '. . . either simply dismissed or artificially worked into the scheme as indices of change, diffusion, survival, innovation, dysfunction, abnormality, cultural disintegration, opportunities for the exercise of social control and the like. The only important variations were variations between cultures' (ibid.).

Recently, the intellectual reappraisal of the mechanistic philosophical basis of structural linguistics and of the kind of structural anthropology outlined above has given way to a more mentalist view which has created both a cognitive linguistics – that of the transformationalists – and a cognitive anthropology whose stated aim is the attempt '. . . to understand the *organizing principles underlying* behavior' (ibid., original emphasis). Such a view clearly comes close both to the aims of orthodox and sociolinguistics but is, particularly in its fresh attitude to variation, much closer to sociolinguistics. Most striking is the definition of the goals of anthropology accepted by many scholars, a definition which is extraordinarily similar to that which we have been using above for sociolinguistics, particularly in our discussion of the nature of communicative competence (8.3). Goodenough (1957, p.167) suggests that '. . . a society's culture consists of whatever it is one has to know or believe in order to operate in a manner acceptable to its members, and do so in any role that they accept for any one of themselves', and goes on to define language in precisely the same terms and in a way which is quite acceptable as a definition of communicative competence: '... whatever it is one has to know in order to communicate with its speakers as adequately as they do with each other and in a manner which they will accept as corresponding to their own' (op. cit. p.168).

More recently, an even more direct comparison between descriptive linguistics and cognitive anthropology has been drawn: '. . . descriptive linguistics is but a special case of ethnography since its domain of study, speech messages, is an integral part of a larger domain of socially interpretable acts and artifacts' (Frake, 1969, p.123); indeed, the aims, interests and methods of those involved in the ethnography of speaking, anthropological linguistics, the sociology of language − the interdisciplinary fields which take as their starting point the 'strong claim' made by Searle (*q.v.* 1.5.1 and 8.3 above) − all involve the attempt to harmonize the approaches of several 'parent' disciplines in the direction of achievement of a common goal: the description of '. . . an infinite set of variable messages as manifestations of a finite shared code, the code being a set of rules for the socially appropriate construction and interpretation of messages' (Frake, ibid.) which would lead to a theory of codes and a theory of culture. It is, then, quite possible to follow Frake in seeing sociolinguistics as a part of a cognitive anthropology, just as (as we shall see below in 8.4.4) Chomsky has suggested that linguistics forms part of cognitive psychology, and by the same argument: 'Since the code is construed as knowledge in people's heads, such a theory should say something of general relevance about cognition and behavior' (ibid.).

8.4.3   Sociolinguistics and Sociology

The relationship of sociolinguistics to sociology, like that to anthropology, has already been noted in brief earlier in this book (see 3.1.3). The function of this section is, therefore, to expand a little on what was said there, but more particularly to show how many of the orientations of present-day sociology correspond closely to those of sociolinguistics, to indicate how similar a line of development both demonstrate in relation to their approaches to their subject matter, and to point out one or two assumptions and concepts of sociolinguistics which appear to have substantial relevance for sociology.

Like anthropology, sociology has changed its orientation towards its data and its conception of its goals several times during this century. Common to anthropology, linguistics and sociology in the early years of

this century were views of their data from either a historical or a comparative perspective. In sociology and, indirectly, in linguistics as well, the
theories of Durkheim (died 1917) mark an important new departure in
their emphasis on the study of 'social facts', a notion easily transferable
into linguistics as the 'linguistic facts' of de Saussure. Equally, Durkheim's
distinction between the *individual* and the *social* closely parallels de
Saussure's contrast between the individuality of *parole* and the general and
social nature of *langue* (we first commented on this in 1.3.1.1 above). It is
possible to argue, as some anthropologists would (e.g. Ardener, 1971, p.
xxxii), that by accepting such a dichotomy de Saussure's linguistics was,
in essence, sociolinguistic rather than purely linguistic. However, later
linguists chose, as we have seen, to emphasize the nonsocial aspects of
form rather than function and, essentially sociolinguistic or not, de
Saussure's influence has been away from, rather than towards, the social
aspects of language use.

   In addition to the historical and comparative views of sociology, the
first quarter of the century presented a functionalist approach to the
description of society, most closely associated with the name of the social
anthropologist Malinowski, whose emphasis on the detailed and meticulous
description of actual behaviour in particular societies had (as we saw above
under 3.3.1.1) a crucial impact on the thought of Firth and, through him,
on many British and Commonwealth linguists up to the present. Firth,
under the influence of Malinowski, defined linguistics as a social science
and stressed its strongly empirical nature: 'In linguistics, as in other social
sciences, we start with man's active participation in the world we are
theorizing about . . . linguistics accepts speech and language texts as related
to the living of, and therefore to the "meaning" of life. . . ' (Firth, 1957,
p.2).

   Finally, the formal or systematic sociology of Simmel – a contemporary
of Durkheim – though not widely taken up until recently (see Bottomore,
1962, p.53) has, by seeking to build up a typology of social relations
rather than universalistic explanations of the whole cultural life of Man,
laid the foundations of the work of the ethnomethodologists (*q.v.* below)
and has the most obvious implications for microsociolinguistics.

   Running through sociology there appear to be two levels of description
or focuses of interest which can be traced back to Comte during the first
half of the last century (Inkeles, 1964, pp.3f.): *social statics*, concerned
with micro-analyses of the institutions and relationships between the
institutions of particular societies; and *social dynamics*, concerned with
the description of whole societies and the interactions between them.
The distinction can be restated in several ways, all of them relevant to
sociolinguistics: the distinction between static and dynamic models, (see

chapters 3 and 4 above), synchronic and diachronic (see 1.3.1.2), and micro- and macro- description (see 1.4.3).

However, common to virtually all sociology are four major assumptions: *institutions*, ranging from the family to the state, are a key topic of investigation; the *interrelations between institutions* need to be stated; *society* is the basic unit of analysis and the comparison of societies an important corollary of this; and, finally, *social acts* and *social relations* require description and explanation. Even a bald list of the subject matter of sociology (e.g. Inkeles, op. cit., table 1 p.12) treated as one set of factors to be correlated with language, gives a comprehensive programme for research into the sociology of language. However, recent developments in the direction of a cognitive sociology (cf. cognitive anthropology in 8.4.2 above) suggest a level of explanation more abstract and closer to the present 'mainstream' of linguistics than would, even ten years ago, have been thought possible.

Ethnomethodology (typified by Garfinkel, 1972) has been equated with microsociolinguistics (Fishman, 1970, p.44), for it is concerned with the interpretive processes which underlie communicative acts, whether verbal or nonverbal; an aim virtually identical with the sociolinguistic attempt to specify communicative competence (see 8.3.2 above). This concern has led to a view of 'meaning' far closer to Firth's than to that of more recent linguists, i.e. for the ethnomethodologist, just as for Firth, meaning is crucially 'situated meaning', 'constructed in specific contexts by actors who must actively interpret what they hear for it to make sense' (Garfinkel, op. cit. p.302). Such a view of meaning as interpretative abilities which unite competence and performance (Cicourel, 1973, p.100) clearly corresponds more closely to the sociolinguistic concept of communicative competence than to the syntactically dominated linguistic competence of transformational-generative linguistics.

In his view of culture, the ethnomethodologist adopts a position reminiscent of the sociolinguistic conception of a speech community as a group with shared attitudes to language and language use; culture is seen as shared rules of interpretation, not shared knowledge, i.e. 'commonsense' knowledge of what can count as reasonable, factual, related etc. How far such an approach leads to universal rules is, as yet, unclear, since ethnomethodology is still strongly empirical in its orientation, although Garfinkel suggests (op. cit., p.306) that there certainly appears to be '. . . some highly general and most probably universal processes through which meaning is conveyed in natural conversation', a point on which we have already touched earlier in our discussion of discourse (see 8.3 above).

An even closer similarity between the attitudes of ethnomethodology and sociolinguistics can be seen in their view of what constitutes data:

'What, for grammarians, may be data not worth saving — clipped, elliptical, incomplete sentences — may be. . . the precise way of accomplishing some particular thing that is being said' (Garfinkel, ibid.). In short, the closeness of interest which links ethnomethodology and sociolinguistics suggests fruitful areas of combined research on situated language, the more so since ethnomethodologists tend in their initial training to be social scientists who have become interested in language, while sociolinguists, by and large, have had the converse training and development of intellectual approach.

8.4.4 Sociolinguistics and Psychology

We commented earlier (3.1.4) on psychological, or more properly, social-psychological models of language, and intend here to indicate the relationship between orthodox linguistics, typified by transformational linguists and psychology on the one hand, and psycholinguistics and sociolinguistics on the other.

Psychology, in common with the other 'human sciences', has in the past 100 years moved several times in its methodology and theory between the introspection-based approaches of a mentalist philosophy and the empiricism of mechanical views of the structure and function of its subject matter. In simple terms, the introspection of the late nineteenth century (Wundt, died 1920) gave way to the empiricism of Watson (1913), creating the behaviourist theories which were to dominate the subject until recently. Then strongly argued objections resting on mentalist assumptions were voiced in favour of a return to an updated use of introspection (see Kendler and Kendler, 1968, for a brief and informative summary).

These changes in attitude and approach in psychology have had, in addition to their importance in that discipline, profound effects on linguistics; the theories of the behaviourists were incorporated into structuralist linguistics from the time of Bloomfield (1933), and those of anti-behaviourists being taken as the basis for the attack on structuralism which paved the way for the transformational-generative linguistics of the present day. The mainstream of linguistic thought would probably still accept Chomsky's assertion that linguistics is a '. . . branch of cognitive psychology . . .' (Chomsky, 1972, p.1), a '. . . subfield of psychology . . .' (op. cit. p.28). Most would postulate close connections between the structure and function of the human mind and the notion of linguistic competence, and take such connections to be axiomatic to their work.

However, theories of language *use*, whether defined in terms which retain the competence-performance dichotomy or in terms of a broader concept of communicative competence, need to take into account less idealized data, may require a more empirical methodology and necessarily lean heavily on social psychology in their attempts at explanation.

Psycholinguistics may be defined as a branch of psychology which attempts to answer the question: 'What knowledge and skill must a human being possess so as to produce sentences which are felt by the *native speaker* to be grammatical and acceptable?' (Hörmann, 1971, p.45, original emphasis). Such a task must involve the discovery of '. . . how the processes which lead to the production of sentences work and how they are acquired. . .' (ibid.), and, specifically, '. . . it is the task of the psycho-linguist to design performance models for the language user. . .' (op. cit., p.233). It will have been noted how the terms 'skill' and 'produce' have been used above, implying a functionalist approach to the description of language which fits well with the micro- end of work in sociolinguistics. Broadbent (1970, p.90) makes the position of the psycholinguist very plain when he argues that the 'utterances' generated by a transformational grammar '. . . are produced by some mechanism which may well have a quite different basis of operation', and insists that '. . . there is no necessary reason for supposing that a mathematically tidy description of the output will give one an insight into the deep underlying mechanism' (ibid.).

Considerable work has been carried out by psycholinguists on such features as, for example, hesitation phenomena (Goldman-Eisler, 1968), which are of great relevance to sociolinguistic research into the actual structure of unedited linguistic data and, as such, are leading to models of what we called above (8.3.2) the 'psycho-physical' competence of language users, one of the elements which we suggested combines to create overall communicative competence. In addition, our own outline of the mechanisms of bilinguial code-switching (5.5) is, in fact, rather more psycho- than socio-linguistic in its orientation by its emphasis on data produced by psychological and physiological factors in the individual mind.

8.4.5 *Sociolinguistics and Education*

In the four sections above we have been outlining ways in which the goals and techniques of sociolinguistics co-occur with or are complementary to those of the descriptive sciences which have, in whole or in part, an interest in the explanation of language. Our focus moved from the broad field of anthropology to the narrower and more personal field of psychology, and we were able to show interesting interconnections between these disciplines and sociolinguistics. But, in addition to connections at the descriptive and theoretical level, several can be suggested where these disciplines are applied as part of the processes of planned change in a society. In particular, we can see 'the growing feeling that . . . sociolinguistic knowledge should be applied, if possible, to urgent educational problems' (Shuy and Fasold, op. cit., p.2), the relationship between differing socio-linguistic codes and the ability to take full advantage of formal educational facilities, the relevance of sociolinguistic factors to L2 learning and teaching, sociolinguistic parameters involved in language planning . . .We can, initially at least, feel hopeful that a more strongly social orientation to the description of language such as is exemplified by sociolinguistics should be of more use to education than the asocial linguistics out of which and in reaction against which the field has developed. Indeed, on the issue of the utility of linguistic theory to the language teacher, Chomsky and many others are '. . . frankly, rather sceptical about the significance, for the teaching of languages, of such insights and understanding as have been attained in linguistics. . . ' (Chomsky, 1966, p.43). The question is whether sociolinguists too ought not to be as sceptical.

If we take the question of the teaching of the mother tongue, not solely to 'disadvantaged' children, it is clear that a major goal should be to increase the child's awareness of the range and functions of his language, and to build greater skill in its use onto the existing base the child already has even before beginning formal education. As Shuy argues, the develop-ments in sociolinguistics are of a kind which bring descriptive work in the discipline closer to the concerns of the schools; in particular, the focus on variation puts the insights of sociolinguistics into a position in which a far better match can be made between the academic concerns of the linguist and the setting in which the child operates. 'The child is surrounded by people who speak with variation based on social status, sex, age and style. He is faced with conflicting pressures to conform to the norms of his peers, his parents, his school and his region. . :' (Shuy, 1974, p.156); sociolinguistics, by dealing with realistic rather than abstract language situations, accepting the fact of variation and evolving principled methods of describing and explaining the phenomenon, '. . . gets right to the heart of many school problems involving writing, reading and talking' (op. cit. p.157). Shuy further suggests that native language teaching has until now lacked the tools to cope with many of its problems, and that '. . . socio-linguistic information may be used to help rethink the education of teachers, the development of instructional materials and techniques and the building of educational programs of various sorts' (ibid.).

L1 teaching can, then, benefit in three clear ways from sociolinguistic research: by increasing the awareness and knowledge of teacher and taught, by improving teaching materials and learning aids, and by intro-ducing a sociolinguistic parameter into the decision-making processes adopted by educational planners and administrators.

L2 teaching has for many years been influenced by the theories of linguistics and psychology. Indeed, it has been suggested that language teaching has been and will continue to be 'a child of fashion in linguistics and psychology until the time it becomes an autonomous discipline which uses these related sciences instead of being used by them' (Mackey, 1966, p.206). One can see the force of this argument but still offer some support from sociolinguistics to the language teacher. At a trivial level, it follows from the concern of sociolinguistics with situated language and the relationships between code choice and social purpose that a clear description of such topics and the formulation of rules governing such relationships must be of value to the language teacher. For example, the work in discourse, whether in the classroom, the hospital or the industrial meeting, has clear relevance to the creation of realistic courses 'for special purposes' as have the recent pragmatic studies of, to cite a single example, interaction in the restaurant (Ehlich and Rehbein, 1974). Practical applications can be found in the 'situational' and 'notional' syllabuses created or in preparation for a range of languages and needs (see Wilkins, 1974, for a concise survey up to that date).

More important, at least from a theoretical point of view, is the need to reaffirm the usefulness of contrastive analysis, not purely at the level of form (the approach developed by Lado, 1957) but at the level of function. Studies are urgently needed which compare and contrast such socially relevant systems as the range and meaningful distinctions carried by the address techniques employed by different languages and speech communities (we discussed address in English earlier under the heading 'Social Rules', 4.2.3 above). It has often been pointed out (e.g. Clyne, 1974, p.23) that much of the 'foreignness' of the L2 user of a language arises directly from an inability to comprehend and use social rules of this kind; clearly, a major aim of the language teacher should be to reduce the non-native behaviour of his learners. We can, therefore, see in the application of a sociolinguistic dimension to contrastive analysis a new and fruitful way of making use of a technique already established as part of the applied linguist's stock in trade.

8.4.6 *Summary*

We have ranged rather widely in this section over the contributions which sociolinguistics might make to the descriptive and theoretical disciplines of linguistics, anthropology, sociology and psychology, and also over the ways in which information gained by sociolinguistic research might be applied, particularly in education and, within education, to the area of language learning, L1 and L2. It seems fair to conclude that there is a growing awareness in all these disciplines of an increasing communality of goals and methods which augurs well for the growth of an interdisciplinary sociology of language which will make useful contributions to the solution of common theoretical and methodological problems, and equally may be able to provide information which will be, through its applications in education, of benefit to the whole of society.

8.5 CONCLUSION

A book such as this is very difficult to bring to any kind of conclusion. Research is still going on which not only adds to the stock of knowledge in sociolinguistics itself, but, as we have seen above, has implications for related disciplines, both pure and applied. Orthodox linguistics can gain or lose much from its acceptance or rejection of a more social approach to the description and explanation of language. Linguistics can either shift its focus away from an exclusive interest in the code towards an acceptance of the legitimacy of a linguistic description which combines form and function − code with use − or turn back on its traditionally narrower field of study − the code alone − leaving the social aspects of language use to a semi-autonomous Sociology of Language. Even if sociolinguistics, in the strict sense of the term proposed by Fishman (1.5), fails in its bid to make all linguistics sociolinguistic, the linguistic discipline can never be the same again; the attempt to include meaning in a description involves some social features, an uncomfortable position for those who would prefer to leave such issues to more clearly labelled social scientists!

Rather than attempt to produce here a conclusion based on a summary of the chapter conclusions found in the rest of the book, let us return to the man to whose memory this book is dedicated − part in jest but partly with serious intent − Jephthah the Gileadite, since it is in his actions that we can see the hope for the future of the discipline and the dangers which may beset it. On the question of methodology, Jephthah clearly approved of the straightforward correlational approach on which early work in sociolinguistics was based. Given a powerful *indicator,* the strong correlation between the ability to articulate the consonant [ʃ] and membership of the Gileadite tribe, and, conversely, and equally strong correlation between inability and membership of the Ephraimite tribe, Jephthah was able to conduct, by a simple field-method technique, an apparently successful piece of sociolinguistic research. Each soldier, as he came to the fords of the river Jordan, which had been fortified by the Gileadites, was asked the direct question, 'Say Shibboleth', a not unreasonable item to include in a conversation at a river's edge, since it meant, and still means in Modern Hebrew, 'a stream'. Results presumably varied from total success to total failure, but Jephthah appears to have taken the 'all-or-none' approach to his data and recorded plain '+' or '-' scores for his informants. Clearly there was a danger in this, there being the perennial problem of the social sciences: how do you cut a continuum into discrete units without recourse to methods which are, in the end, arbitrary? However, Jephthah, as we recognized in our dedication, may well have been the first *descriptive* sociolinguist, making use it is true of a rather simplistic model of the relationship between linguistic and social variation, and a somewhat crude research design and fieldwork technique; but he was also an *applied* sociolinguist, attempting to apply his sociolinguistic expertise to the solution of a grave social problem, the infiltration of his armed forces by a 'fifth column' of the enemy. His application of rather rough techniques can presumably be justified in the light of the state of emergency in which he was forced to operate. We see yet another lesson for ourselves here. If the sociolinguist wishes to assist in social planning and change, he may well need to come up with results long before he is ready; but if we wish to be applied linguists at all, we cannot keep asking those who have come to us for help to wait until our models, methods and theories are perfect — they never will be. Finally, Jephthah has another message for us. On the basis of the analysis of the data he obtained, he took social action on a large scale; anyone who was unable to pronounce Shibboleth in the Gileadite manner '. . . they took and slew. . . and there fell at that time of the Ephraimites forty and two thousand' (Judges, 12.6). The moral is plain; be circumspect in making drastic language-planning decisions on the basis of possibly inadequate data and methodology — the results could be disastrous in the long term, if not as in the Ephraimites' case the short term as well!

Bibliography

ABERCROMBIE, D. (1967) *Elements of General Phonetics,* Edinburgh: University Press.
—— 'Paralanguage' in *British Journal of Disorders of Communication,* 3, 1968, pp.55-9. Reproduced in Laver, J. and Hutcheson, S. (eds) (1972) pp.64-70.
ACKOFF, R.L. (1962) *Scientific Method: Optimizing Applied Research Decisions,* New York: Wiley.
AGHEYISI, R. and FISHMAN, J. (1970) 'Language Attitude Studies: a brief survey of methodological approaches' in *Anthropological Linguistics* XII (1970), pp.135-57.
AILA-BAAL, (1973) *The Communicative Teaching of English,* Seminar, Lancaster.
ARDENER, E. (ed.) (1971) *Social Anthropology and Language,* London: Tavistock.
ARGYLE, M. (1967) *The Psychology of Interpersonal Behaviour,* Harmondsworth: Penguin.
—— (1969) *Social Interaction,* London: Tavistock and Methuen.
ASHBY, W. R. (1952, 1960) *Design for a Brain,* London: Chapman & Hall.
AUSTIN, J. L. (1958) 'Performative-Constative'. Paper delivered in 1958; printed in Caton, C.E. (ed.) (1963) pp.22-54.
—— (1962) *How to Do Things with Words,* Oxford: OUP.
BACH, E. and HARMS, R. (eds) (1968) *Universals in Linguistic Theory,* New York: Holt Rinehart.
BAILEY, B. L. (1966) *Jamaican Creole Syntax,* London: Cambridge University.
BAILEY, C.-J. N. (1969) 'The integration of Linguistic theory: internal reconstruction and comparative method in descriptive linguistics', Working Papers in *Linguistics 2,* Honolulu: University of Hawaii.
—— and SHUY, R. W. (1973) *New Ways of Analyzing Variation in English,* Washington: Georgetown University.

BANJO, L. A. (1972) 'The Goals of University English Language Teaching in West African Universities'. Paper delivered to conference on the 'Implications of English for West African Universities', Sierra Leone.

BANSAL, R. K. (1969) The Intelligibility of Indian English, *Monograph No. 4*, Hyderabad: CIE. 1969.

BARATZ, S. S. and BARATZ, J. C. (1970) 'Early childhood intervention: the social science base of institutionalized racism' in *Harvard Education Review 40*, pp.29-50. Repr. in Cashdan, A. and Grugeon, E. (eds) (1972) pp.188-97.

BARKER, R. G. (ed.) (1963) *The Stream of Behavior*, New York: Appleton.

BARNES, J. A. (1963) 'Some Ethical Problems in Modern Fieldwork' in *British Journal of Sociology* XIV (1963) pp.118-34.

BARTHES, R. (1966) 'Introduction à l'Analyse Structural des Récits' in *Communications* VIII (1966).

BAUGH, A. C. (1951, 1965) *A History of the English Language*, London: Routledge.

BAUMAN, R. and SHERZER, J. (eds) (1974) *Explorations in the Ethnography of Speaking*, Cambridge University Press.

BAZELL, C. E. *et al.* (eds) (1966) *In Memory of J. R. Firth*, London: Longman.

BEALS, R. L. and HOIJER, H. (1953) *An Introduction to Anthropology*, (1965) 3rd edn, New York: Macmillan.

BEREITER, C. *et al.* (1966) 'An academically oriented pre-school for culturally deprived children' in Hechinger, F. M. (ed.) (1966) pp.105-37.

BELL, R.T. (1973) 'The English of an Indian Immigrant; an Essay in Error Analysis' in *ITL* XXII pp.11-61.

—— (1975) 'The Expanded EEC' in *Incorporated Linguist* (1975a).

—— (1975) *Interaction in Meetings: Feasibility Study*, mimeo. Lancaster (1975b).

—— (1975) 'On the use of the term "system" in Linguistics', *York Papers in Linguistics* (1975c).

BELL, D. C. and BELL, A. M. (1878) *Bell's Standard Elocutionist*, London: Mullen and Son.

BERNSTEIN, B. (1965) 'A Socio-linguistic Approach to Social Learning' in Gould J. (1965) pp.144-68.

—— (1966) 'Elaborated and Restricted Codes: an Outline' in *Sociological Inquiry*, 36, 2, pp.254-61.

BERTALANFFY, L. VON (1950) 'The theory of open systems in physics and biology', *Science* III (1950) pp. 23-9, reprinted in Emery, F. E. (ed.) 1969, pp.70-85.

BICKERTON, D. (1972) 'The Structure of Polylectal Grammars'. Paper delivered at 23rd Annual Meeting of Georgetown Round Table.

—— (1972) in *Georgetown University Monograph Series on Language and Linguistics no. XXV.*

BIRDWHISTELL, R. L. (1952) *Introduction to Kinesies: an annotation system for analysis of body motion and gesture,* Louisville.

BLACK, M. (ed.) (1965) *Philosophy in America,* Allen and Unwin and Cornell University.

BLOCH, B. (1948) 'A set of postulates for phonemic analysis' in *Language,* 24.

BLOM, J. P. and GUMPERZ, J. J. (1972) 'Social Meaning in Linguistic Structures: Code-Switching in Norway' in Gumperz J. J. and Hymes D. (eds.) 1972, pp.407-34.

BLOOMFIELD, L. (1933, 1965) *Language,* London: Allen and Unwin.

BOAS, F. (1911) *Handbook of American Indian Languages,* Washington: Smithsonian Inst.

BOGARDUS, E. S. (1925) 'Measuring social distance', *Journal of Applied Sociology,* IX, pp.299-308.

BOTHA, R. P. (1971) 'The Phonological Component of a Generative Grammar'. Excerpts from Botha 1971 reprinted in Fudge, E. C. (ed.) (1973) pp.213-31.

BOTTOMORE, T. B. (1962) 'Sociology: a guide to problems and literature', *Unwin University Books No. 13,* London: Allen and Unwin.

BOULDING, K. E. (1967) 'Expecting the Unexpected: the Uncertain Future of Knowledge and Technology' in Morphet, E. L. and Ryan, C. O. (eds) (1967) pp.199-203.

BRAZZAVILLE (1964) *Symposium on Multilingualism,* London: CCTA/ CSA Publications Bureau.

BRIGHT, W. (ed.) (1966) *Sociolinguistics,* Hague: Mouton.

—— (1968) 'Language and Culture' in *International Encyclopedia of the Social Sciences,* New York: Crowell Collier Macmillan, pp. 18-22.

BROADBENT, D. E. (1970) 'In Defence of Empirical Psychology' in *Bull. Br. Psychol. Soc.* XXIII (1970) pp.87-96.

BURLING, R. (1970) *Man's Many Voices: Language in its Cultural Context,* New York: Holt Rinehart.

BURNS, D. G. (1965) *African Education: an Introductory Survey of Education in Commonwealth Countries,* London: OUP.

BÜHLER, K. (1934) *Sprachtheorie,* Jena: Fischer.

DE CAMP, D. (1968) 'The Field of Creole Language Studies' in *Latin American Research Review,* 3, pp.25-46.

—— (1971) 'Toward a generative analysis of a post-creole speech continuum' in Hymes, D. (1971) pp.349-70.

CATON, C. E. (ed.) (1963) *Philosophers and Ordinary Language,* Urbana:

University of Illinois.

CAVE, G. N. (1973) 'Some Communication Problems of Immigrant Children in Britain' in AILA-BAAL Seminar, 1973.

DE CECCO, J. P. (1967) 'The Psychology of Language, Thought and Instruction: Readings', New York: Holt Rinehart.

CHATMAN, S. (1969) 'Analysing Narrative Structure' in *Language and Style* II (1969), pp.3-36.

CHERRY, C. (1957) *On Human Communication,* New York: MIT/Wiley.

CHOMSKY, N. (1957) *Syntactic Structures,* The Hague: Mouton.

—— (1965) *Aspects of the Theory of Syntax,* Cambridge Mass: M.I.T. Press.

—— (1966) 'Linguistic Theory' in *Language Teaching: Broader Contexts.* Report of N.E. Conference on the Teaching of Foreign Languages, Menasha. Wis. pp.43-9.

—— (1972) *Language and Mind,* enlarged edn, New York: Harcourt, Brace, Jovanovich.

CHOMSKY, N. and HALLE, M. (1968) *The Sound Pattern of English,* New York: Harper Row.

CICOUREL, A. V. (1973) *Cognitive Sociology: Language and Meaning in Social Interaction,* Harmondsworth: Penguin.

CLYNE, M. G. (1967) *Transference and Triggering,* The Hague: Nijhoff.

—— (1974) 'The Role of Sociolinguistics in a University German Course (for non-native speakers)' in Verdoot (ed.) 1974, pp.18-25.

COCHRANE, G. R. (1959) 'The Australian English Vowels as a Diasystem' *Word* 15, pp.69-88.

COOK, W.A. (1969) *Introduction to Tagmemic Analysis*, New York: Holt Rinehart.

CORDER, S.P. (1967) 'The significance of learners' errors', *IRAL,* 4, pp.161-170.

—— (1971) 'Idiosyncratic Dialects and Error Analysis', *IRAL,* 9, pp. 147-60.

—— (1973) *Introducing Applied Linguistics,* Harmondsworth: Penguin.

COSER, L.A. and ROSENBURG, B.A. (1964) *Sociological Theory,* New York: Macmillan, revised edition.

CRYSTAL, D. and DAVY, D., (1969) *Investigating English Style,* London: Longman.

CRYSTAL, D. and QUIRK R., *Systems of Prosodic and Paralinguistic Features in English*, The Hague: Mouton.

DANCE, F.E.X. (ed.,) (1967) *Human Communication Theory: original essays.* New York: Holt Rinehart.

DAS GUPTA, J. (1970) *Language Conflict and National Development,* Berkeley: University of California.

DAVIS, K. (1957) *Human Society*, New York: Macmillan.

DECKER, T. (1965) 'Julius Caesar in Krio', *SLLR*, vol. 4, pp.64-79.

DREITZEL, H.P. (ed.) (1970) *Recent Sociology*, New York: Macmillan.

DREVER, J. (1952) *A Dictionary of Psychology*, Harmondsworth: Penguin.

EHLICH, K. and REHBEIN, J. (1974) 'On Pragmatic Units in an Institution: Restaurant' in Verdoot (ed.) 1974, pp.42-70.

ELLIS, J. (1969) 'On contextual meaning' in Bazell C.E. *et al.* (eds) (1966) pp.79-95.

EMERY, F.E. (ed.) (1969, 1972) *Systems Thinking – selected readings*, Penguin Modern Management, Harmondsworth: Penguin.

ERVIN, S.M. and OSGOOD, C.E. (1954) 'Second language learning and bilingualism' in Osgood, C.E. and Sebeok, T.A. (eds) (1954) pp.139-46.

ERVIN-TRIPP, S.M. (1967) 'An Issei Learns English' in *Journal of Social Issues*, 23, pp.78-90.

—— (1973) 'An analysis of the Interaction of Language, Topic and Listener', revised version in Ervin-Tripp, S. (1973) pp.239-61.

—— (1973) *Language Acquisition and Communicative Choice*, Stanford U.P.

EYSENCK, H.J. (1952) *The Scientific Study of Personality*, London: Routledge and Kegan Paul.

FEIBLEMAN, J. and FRIEND, J.W. (1945) 'The Structure and Function of Organization', *Philosophical Review* LIV (1945) pp.19-44, reprinted in Emery F.E. (ed.) (1969), pp.30-55.

FERGUSON, C.A. (1959) 'Diglossia' in *Word*, 15, pp.325-340 and in Hymes, D. (1964) pp.429-39.

—— (1966) 'National Sociolinguistic Profile Formulas' in Bright W. (ed.), *Sociolinguistics*, 1966, pp.309-24.

—— (1971) 'Absence of copula and the notion of simplicity: a study of normal speech, baby talk, foreigner talk, and pidgins' in Hymes, D. (ed.) (1971) pp.141-50.

FICHTER, J.H. (1957) *Sociology*, (1971) 2nd edn, Chicago: University of Chicago.

FIDELHOLTZ, J.L. (1973) 'The Methodology and Motivation of Transformational Grammar' in Shuy, R. (ed.) (1973) pp.82-94.

FILLMORE, C.J. (1968) 'The Case for Case' in Bach, E. and Harms, R. (eds) (1968).

FIRTH, J.R. (1957, 1964) *Papers in Linguistics*, 1934-1951, London: OUP.

FISHMAN, J. (1968) 'Nationality-nationalism and Nation-nationism' in Fishman J. *et al.* (eds) (1968) pp.39-51.

—— (1970) *Sociolinguistics: a brief introduction*, Rowley Mass: Newbury House.

—— (1971) 'National languages and languages of wider communication in the developing nations', in Whiteley, W.H. (1971) pp.27-56.

—— (ed.) (1968) *Readings in the Sociology of Language*, The Hague: Mouton.

—— (ed) (1971) *Advances in the Sociology of Language I*, The Hague: Mouton.

—— *et al.* (1966) *Language Loyalty in the United States: the maintenance and perpetuation of non-English mother tongues by American ethnic and religious groups*, The Hague: Mouton Co.

FISK, M. (1964) *A Modern Formal Logic*, Englewood Cliffs N.J. Prentice-Hall.

FRAKE, C.O. (1969) 'Notes on Queries in Ethnography' in Tyler, *S.A.* (1996) pp.123-36.

FRANCIS, W.N. (1958) *The Structure of American English*, New York: Ronald Press Co.

FRIES, C.C. and PIKE K.L. (1949) 'Coexistent Phonemic Systems', *Language*, 25, pp.29-50.

FROMKIN, V. (1968) 'Speculations on Performance Models', in *JL*, 4. 1968, pp.47-68.

FUDGE, E.C. (ed.) (1973) *Phonology*, Harmondsworth: Penguin.

GEACH, P. (1969) 'Should Traditional Grammar be Ended or Mended? II' in Wilkinson, A. (1969) pp.18-25.

GIGLIOLI, P.P. (1972) *Language and social context*, Harmondsworth: Penguin.

GIMSON, A.C. (1962) *An Introduction to the Pronunciation of English* (1970) 2nd rev. edn, London: Edward Arnold

GLEASON, H.A. (1955) *An Introduction to Descriptive Linguistics*, (1961) rev. edn, New York: Holt, Rinehart.

—— (1965) *Linguistics and English Grammar*, New York: Holt, Rinehart.

GOLDMAN-EISLER, F. (1968) *Psycholinguistics: Experiments in Spontaneous Speech*, London: Academic Press.

GOULD, J. (ed.) *Social Science Survey*, Harmondsworth: Penguin.

GREENBERG, J.H. (1957, 1963) *Essays in Linguistics*, Chicago: Phoenix Books.

—— (1966) *The Languages of Africa*, Bloomington: Indiana U.P. Also part II of *IJAL*, 29, 1, 1963, The Hague: Mouton

—— (1971) *Language, Culture and Communication*, Stanford University Press.

GREGORY, M. (1967) 'Aspects of varieties differentiation', *Journal of Linguistics*, 3, pp.177-98.

GROSS, L. (ed.) (1967) *Sociological Theories: Inquiries and Paradigms*, New York: Harper Row.

GUMPERZ, J.J. (1961) 'Speech variation and the study of Indian civilization', *American Anthropologist*, 63, pp.976-88.

—— (1964) 'The Social Group as a Primary Unit of Analysis in Dialect Study' in Shuy, R.W., (1964) pp.127-29.

—— (1966) 'On the Ethnology of Linguistic Change' in Bright W., (ed) (1966) pp.27-49.

—— and HYMES, D. (eds.) (1972) *Directions in Sociolinguistics: the ethnography of communication*, New York: Holt Rinehart, and Winston Inc.

GURNEY, R. (1973) *Language, Brain and Interactive Processes*, London: Edward Arnold.

GUTTMAN, L. (1944) 'A basis for scaling qualitative data' *American Sociological Review*, 9, pp.139-50.

HABERMAS, J. (1970) 'Toward a Theory of Communicative Competance in Dreitzel, H.P. (ed.) (1970) pp.114-48.

HALL, R.A. (1961) 'Categories of the Theory of Grammar' in *Word* XVII (1961) pp.241-92.

—— (1962) 'The Life Cycle of Pidgin Languages' *Lingua XI*, pp.151-57.

—— (1964) *Introductory Linguistics*, New York: Chilton.

HALLIDAY, M.A.K. (1967) *Intonation and Grammar in British English*, The Hague: Mouton

—— (1970) 'Language Structure and Language Function' in Lyons, J. (ed.) (1970) pp.140-65.

—— (1973) *Explorations in the Functions of Language*, London: Edward Arnold.

—— et al. (1964) *The Linguistic Sciences and Language Teaching*, London: Longman.

HARMS, L.S. 'Listener judgments of status cues in speech' *Quarterly Journal of Speech*, XLVII (1961) pp.164-8.

HARRIS, Z.S. (1951, 1963) *Structural Linguistics* Chicago: Phoenix Books.

—— (1952) 'Discourse Analysis: a sample text' in *Language* XXVIII (1952) a. pp.1-30, b. pp.474-94.

HASAN, R. (1968) *Grammatical cohesion in spoken and written English*. London: Longman.

HAUGEN, E. (1953) *The Norwegian Language in America*, Philadelphia: University of Pennysylvania.

—— (1956) *Bilingualism in the Americas*, University of Alabama.

—— (1961) 'The Bilingual Individual' in Saporta, S., 1961, pp.395-407.

HEALEY, A. (1964) 'Handling Unsophisticated Linguistic Informants',

Linguistic Circle of Canberra Publications, series A, Occasional Papers no. 2, Canberra: Australian National University.

HECHINGER, F.M. (ed.) (1966) *Pre-School Education Today*, New York: Doubleday.

HENSON, H. (1974) *British Social Anthropologists and Language: A History of Separate Development*, Oxford: OUP.

HILL, A.A. (1958) *Introduction to Linguistic Structures*, New York: Harcourt, Brace and World Inc.

HOCKETT, C.F. (1955) *Manual of Phonology*, Baltimore: Waverley Press.

—— (1958, 1965) *A Course in Modern Linguistics*, New York: Macmillan, New York. 1958. 1965.

HÖRMANN, H. (1971) *Psycholinguistics: An Introduction to Research and Theory*, Berlin: Springer.

HYMES, D. (1967) 'The Anthropology of Communication' in Dance, F., (1967) pp. 1-39.

—— (1967) 'The Anthropology of Communication' (a) and 'Why the Linguist needs the Sociologist' (b) *Social Research* XXXIV (1967) pp. 632-47.

—— (1971) 'On Communicative Competence', original paper. Excerpts in Pride, J.B. and Holmes J. (eds.) (1972) pp. 269-293.

—— (1972) 'Models of the Interaction of Language and Social Life' in Gumperz, J.J. and Hymes, D., (1972) pp. 35-71.

—— (1974) 'Ways of Speaking' in Bauman and Sherzer (eds.) (1974) pp. 433-52.

—— (ed.) (1964) *Language in Culture and Society: a Reader in linguistics and anthropology*, New York: Harper & Row.

—— (ed.) (1971) *Pidginization and Creolization of Languages*, London: Cambridge U.P.

INKELES, A. (1964) *What is Sociology: an Introduction to the Discipline and Profession.* Englewood Cliffs: Prentice-Hall.

JAKOBSON, R. (1960) 'Closing Statement: Linguistics and Poetics' in Sebeok, T.A. (ed.) (1960) pp.350-77.

JONES, D. (1962) *The Phoneme: its Nature and Use*, 2nd edn, Cambridge: Heffer.

—— (1918, 1964) *An Outline of English Phonetics*, Cambridge: Heffer, 1964.

JONES, L. (1972) *Deep-sea Container Ports – systems appraisal and simulation modelling*, Bletchley: Open University.

KENDLER, H.H. and KENDLER, T.S. (1968) 'Concept Formation' in *International Encyclopaedia of the Social Sciences*, New York: Crowell-Collier-Macmillan, pp.208-10.

KJOLSETH, R. (1972) 'The Development of the Sociology of Language and its Social Implications' in *Sociolinguistics Newsletter* III, no. 1 (1972) pp.7-10 and 24-9.

KLOSS, H. (1968) 'Notes concerning a Language-Nation Typology' in Fishman, J.A. *et al.* (1968) *Language Problems of Developing Nations*, pp.69-85.

KRECH, D. *et al.* (1962) *Individual in Society: a textbook of social psychology*, New York: McGraw-Hill.

KROEBER, A.L. (1963) *Anthropology: Cultural Patterns and Processes*, New York: Harcourt Brace.

KURATH, H. (1939) *Handbook of the Linguistic Geography of New England*, Providence, Rhode Island: Brown University.

LABOV, W. (1963) 'The Social Motivation of a Sound Change', *Word*, 19, pp.273-309.

—— (1966a) 'On the grammaticality of everyday speech'. New York: Paper delivered to *Linguistic Society of America.*

—— (1966b) *The Social Stratification of English in New York City*, Washington: C.A.L.

—— (1966c) 'Hypercorrection by the Lower Middle Class as a Factor in Linguistic Change' in Bright, W. (ed.), (1966).

—— (1969) 'The Logic of Nonstandard English', *Georgetown Monographs on Language and Linguistics 22.* Exerpts in Giglioli, P.P., (1972) pp.179-216.

—— (1970) 'The Study of Language in its Social Context' in *Studium Generale 23*, pp.30-87. Repr. in Fishman, J. (ed.), (1971) pp.152-216.

—— (1971) 'The notion of "system" in creole studies' in Hymes, D. (ed.) (1971) pp. 447-72.

LADO, R. (1957, 1964) *Linguistics across cultures; applied linguistics for language teachers*, Ann Arbor: University of Michigan, p.141.

LAMBERT, W. and JAKOBOVITS, L. (1961) 'Semantic Satiation among Bilinguals', *Journal of Experimental Psychology*, 62, pp.576-82.

LAVER, J. and HUTCHESON, S. (eds) (1972) *Communication in Face to Face Interaction*, Harmondsworth: Penguin.

LAWTON, D. (1968) *Social Class, Language and Education*, London: Routledge and Kegan Paul.

LEAVITT, H.J. (1951) 'Some effects of certain communication patterns on group performance', *Journal of abnormal social psychology*, 46, pp.38-50.

LEECH, G.N. (1969) *A Linguistic Guide to English Poetry*, London: Longman.

—— (1974) *Semantics*, Harmondsworth: Penguin.

LENNEBERG, E.H. (1964) 'A biological perspective of language', pp.65-88 of Lenneberg (1964) in Oldfield, R.C. and Marshall, J.C. (eds), (1968) pp.32-47.

—— (ed.) (1964) *New directions in the study of language,* Cambridge, Mass: M.I.T.

—— (1967) *Biological Foundations of Language,* New York: Wiley.

LERNER, D. and GORDEN, M. (1969) *Euratlantica: changing perspectives of the European Elites,* Cambridge Mass: M.I.T.

LEVI-STRAUSS, C. (1972) *Structural Anthropology,* Harmondsworth: Penguin.

LIEFRINK, F.M.P. (1973) *Semantico-Syntax,* London: Longman.

LOTZ, J. (1956) 'Linguistic: Symbols make Man' from White Jnr., L. (ed.) (1956) *Frontiers of Knowledge,* pp.207-31. Reprinted in Saporta, S. (ed.) (1961) p.1-15.

LYONS, J. (1966) 'Firth's theory of "meaning" in Bazell, C.E. *et al.* (eds) (1966) pp.288-302.

—— (1968) *Introduction to Theoretical Linguistics,* London: Cambridge U.P.

—— (ed.) (1970) *New Horizons in Linguistics,* Harmondsworth: Penguin.

MACKEY, W.F. (1966) 'Applied Linguistics: its Meaning and Use' in *English Language Teaching* XX, no. 1 (1966) pp.197-206.

MANDELBAUM, D.G. (ed.) (1966) *Edward Sapir: Culture, Language and Personality - selected essays,* Berkeley: University of California.

MARTINET, A. (1961) *A Functional View of Language,* Oxford: OUP.

—— (1968) 'Néutralisation et syncrétisme', *La Linguistique,* 1, pp.1-20. Excerpts in Fudge, E.C. (ed.), (1973) pp.74-80.

MILLER, G.A. (1967) *The Psychology of Communication,* Harmondsworth: Penguin.

MOORE, W.E. (1963) *Social Change,* Englewood Cliffs: Prentice-Hall.

MORPHET, E.L. and RYAN, C.O. (eds) (1967) *Designing Education for the Future No. 1 : Prospective Changes in Society by 1980,* New York: Citation Press.

MORRIS, C. (1946) *Signs, Language and Behavior,* Englewood Cliffs, N.J.: Prentice Hall.

MORTON, J. (1964) 'A Preliminary Functional Model for Language Behaviour' *International Audiology,* 3, pp.216-25. Repr. in Oldfield, R.C. and Marshall J.C. (eds) (1968) pp.147-58.

MOSER, C.A. and KALTON, G. (1958, 1971) *Survey Methods in Social Investigation,* London: Heinemann.

NAGEL, E. (1961) *The Structure of Science – problems in the Logic of Scientific Explanation,* London: Routledge and Kegan Paul.

NOSER, A.A. (1965) *Official Pidgin Texts of the Common Prayers and the Dialogue Mass.* Alexishafen: S.V.D. duplicated booklet.

NATIONAL COMPUTING CENTRE (1973) *Computer Appreciation for the Majority*, Newton Abbot: NCC Publications.

O'CONNOR, J.D. and ARNOLD, G.F. (1961) *The Intonation of Collo-quial English*, London: Longman.

OGDEN, C.K. (1934) *The System of Basic English*, New York: Harcourt Brace.

OLDFIELD, R.C. and MARSHALL, J.C. (eds) (1968) *Language: Selected Readings*, Harmondsworth: Penguin.

ORTON, H. (1962) *Survey of English Dialects*, Leeds: E.J. Arnold.

OSGOOD, C.E. and SEBEOK, T.A. (eds) (1954) 'Psycholinguistics', *Journal of abnormal social psychology supplement.*

OSGOOD, C.E. *et al.* (1957) *The Measurement of Meaning*, Urbana: University of Illinois.

PALMER, F. (1971) *Grammar*, Harmondsworth: Penguin.

PATTERSON, S. (1969) *Immigration and Race Relations in Britain*, 1960-1967, London: OUP/IRR.

PEAL, E. and LAMBERT, W.E. (1962) 'The Relation of Bilingualism to Intelligence', *Psychological Monographs*, 76, no. 27.

PEARCE, R. (1973) 'Some Structural Complexities of Talk in Meetings' in *Working Papers in Discourse Analysis V*, Birmingham.

PERREN, G.E. and HOLLOWAY, M.F. (1965) *Language and Communication in the Commonwealth.* London: C.E.L.C./H.M.S.O., 88-5354.

PERREN, G. (ed.) (1971) *Science and Technology in a Second Language*, CILT Reports and Papers VII, London.

PIKE, K.L. (1967) *Language in Relation to a Unified Theory of Human Behavior*, The Hague: Mouton.

PITTENGER, R.E. and SMITH H.L. Jnr (1957) 'A Basis for Some Contributions of Linguistics to Psychiatry', *Psychiatry*, 20, pp.61-78.

PRATOR, C.H. (1968) 'The British Heresy in TESL'. Paper in Fishman, J. *et al.* (eds.), (1968) pp.459-76.

PRIDE, J.B. (1971) *The Social Meaning of Language*, London: OUP.

PRIDE, J.B. and HOLMES, J. (eds) (1972) *Sociolinguistics: selected readings*, Harmondsworth: Penguin.

QUINE, W.V.O. (1953) *From a logical point of view*, Harvard U.P., (1961) rev. edn, New York: Harper & Row.

RAYFIELD, J.R. (1970) *Languages of a Bilingual Community*, The Hague: Mouton.

REINICKE, J. (1959) 'Trade Jargons and Creole Dialects as Marginal Languages' in Hymes, D. (ed.) (1964) pp.534-46.

REVZIN, I.I. (1966) *Models of Language*, London: Methuen & Co.

RICE, F.A. (ed.) (1962) *Study of the Role of Second Languages*, Washington: C.A.L., p.123.

RIGTER, B. and MOORE, H. (1973) 'Towards a controlled use of

variables in language teaching' in *AILA-BAAL* Seminar.
—— (1974) 'Towards a Performance Model of Language Behaviour', mimeo. Leyden.
ROBINS, R.H. (1964, 1965) *General Linguistics: an Introductory Survey*, London: Longman.
—— (1967) *A Short History of Linguistics*, London: Longman.
ROBINSON, W.R. (1972) *Language and Social Behaviour*, Harmondsworth: Penguin.
ROSE, E.J.B. *et al.* (1969) *Colour and Citizenship: A Report on British Race Relations*, London: IRR/OUP.
ROSS, J.R. (1973) 'A Fake NP Squish' in Bailey C.-J.N. and Shuy, R.W. (eds.) (1973) pp.96-140.
ROY, N.C. (1962) *Federalism and Linguistic States*, Calcutta: Mukhopadhyay.
RUBIN, J. (1962) 'Bilingualism in Paraguay', *Anthropoligical Linguistics*, 4, pp.52-8.
—— (1968) *National Bilingualism in Paraguay*, The Hague: Mouton.
RUSSELL, B. (1946) *A History of Western Philosophy*, London: Allen & Unwin.
RYAN, A. (1970) *The Philosophy of the Social Sciences*, London: Macmillan.
SAMARIN, W.J. (1967) *Field Linguistics*, New York: Holt Rinehart,
SAPIR, E. (1966) in Mandelbaum, D.G. (ed.) (1966) *Culture, Language and Personality*, Berkeley: University of California.
SAPORTA, S. (1961) *Psycholinguistics: a book of readings*, New York: Holt, Rinehart.
SARBIN, T.R. (1968) 'Role: psychological aspects' in *International Encyclopedia of the Social Sciences*, New York: Crowell Collier and Macmillan, pp.546-52.
de SAUSSURE, F. (1915, 1964) *Cours de Linguistique Générale*, Paris: Payot.
SCHEGLOFF, E.A. (1968) 'Sequencing in Conversational Openings', *American Anthropologist*, 70.
SEBEOK, T.A. (ed.) (1960) *Style in Language*, Cambridge, Mass.: MIT.
SEARLE, J. (1965) 'What is a Speech Act?' in Black, M. (ed.) (1965) pp.221-239. Repr. in Giglioli, P.P. (ed.) (1972) pp.136-54.
—— (1969) *Speech Acts: An Essay in the Philosophy of Language*, London: Cambridge U.P.
SETLUR, P.H. (1973) *Towards a theory of code-switching.* Unpublished MA thesis, Lancaster.
SEUREN, P. (1969) *Operators and Nucleus*, London: Cambridge U. Press.
SHANNON, C.E. and WEAVER, W. (1949) *The Mathematical Theory of*

Communication, Urbana: University Illinois.

SHAW, M.E. (1968) 'Communications networks', *Advances in Experimental Social Psychology,* I, pp.111-47.

SHILS, E. (1964) 'The Primary Group in Current Research' in Coser and Rosenburg (1964).

SHUY, R.W. (ed.) (1973) *Some New Directions in Linguistics,* Washington: Georgetown University Press.

——— (ed.), *Social Dialects and Language Learning.* Champaign Illinois, N.C.T.E.

——— (1974) 'Sociolinguistic Strategies for Teachers in a Southern School System' in *AILA Proceedings II. 1972,* in Verdoot, A. (ed.) (1974) pp.155-71.

SIMON, H.A. (1945, 1965) *Administrative Behaviour: a Study of Decision-Making Processes in Administration Organization,* Toronto: Collier-Macmillan.

SINCLAIR, J.M. *et al.* (1972) *The English used by Teachers and Pupils,* Birmingham S.S.R.C. Report.

SINCLAIR, J.McH. and COULTHARD, R.M. (1975) *Towards an Analysis of Discourse: the English used by Teachers and Pupils,* Oxford: OUP.

SKINNER, B.F. (1957) *Verbal Behavior,* New York: Appleton-Century-Crofts Inc.

SOSKIN, W.F. and JOHN V. (1963) 'The study of spontaneous speech' in Barker, R.G. (ed.) (1963).

SOUTHWORTH, F.C. (1971) 'Detecting prior creolization' an analysis of the historical origins of Marathi' in Hymes, D. (ed.) (1971) pp.255-74.

SPENCER, J. (ed.) (1971) *The English Language in West Africa,* London: Longman.

STACEY, M. (1967) *Methods of Social Research,* Oxford: Pergamon.

STEWART, W.A. (1968) 'A sociolinguistic typology for describing national multilingualism' in Fishman, J. (1968) pp.531-45.

——— (1969) 'An Outline of Linguistic Typology for describing Multilingualism' in Rice, F.A. (ed.) (1962) *Study of the Role of Second Languages,* pp.15-25.

TAULI, V. (1968) *Introduction to a Theory of Language Planning,* Uppsala: University of Uppsala.

THORNE, J.P. (1965) 'Stylistics and generative grammars', *Journal of Linguistics,* I, 1, pp.49-59.

TIMASHEFF, N.S. (1975) *Sociolozine Theory: its nature and growth,* New York: Random House (revised edn).

TODOROV, K. (1966) 'Les Categories du Récit Litteraire' in *Communications* VIII (1966).

TORGERSON, W. (1957) *Theory and methods of scaling,* New York:

Wiley.

TRAGER, G.L. and SMITH, H.L. (1951) *An Outline of English Structure. Studies in Linguistics:* Occasional Papers 3, Norman Okl: Bettenburg Press.

TRUBETZKOY, N.S. (1973) 'Phonemes and How to Determine them' in Fudge, E.C. (ed.) (1973) pp.47-73.

TRUDGILL, P. (1974) *Sociolinguistics: an Introduction,* Harmondsworth: Penguin.

TURNER, G.W. (1969) *The English Language in Australia and New Zealand,* London: Longman.

TURNER, R. (ed.) (1974) *Ethnomethodology,* Harmondsworth, Middx: Penguin.

TYLER, S.A. (ed.) (1969) *Cognitive Anthropology,* New York: Holt, Rinehart.

UNESCO (1953) *The use of vernacular languages in education,* Monographs on Fundamental Education, No. 8, Paris.

—— (1953) *African languages and English in education,* Educational Studies and Documents, No. 2, Paris.

UNO. 1976 Report on the World Social Situation. New York: United Nations (1969).

VERDOOT, A. (ed.) (1974) *Association Internationale de Linguistique Appliquée: 3rd Congress Proceedings Vol. II: Applied Sociolinguistics,* Heidelberg: Groos.

VETTER, H.J. (1969) *Language Behaviour and Communication,* Itasca: Peacock Pubs. Inc.

VOEGELIN, C.F. and HARRIS, Z.S. (1947) 'The Scope of Linguistics' in *American Anthropologist,* 49, p.588-600.

WAKEFORD, J. (1968) *The Strategy of Social Inquiry,* London: Macmillan.

WAKELIN, M.F. (1972) *English Dialects: an Introduction,* London: Athlone Press.

WEBB, E.J. *et al.* (1966) *Unobtrusive Measures: Non-Reactive Research in the Social Sciences,* Chicago: Rand McNally.

WEINREICH, U. (1952) 'Is a Structural Dialectology Possible?', *Word,* 10, pp.388-400.

—— (1953) *Languages in Contact,* The Hague: Mouton.

WELLS, J.C. (1970) 'Local accents in English and Wales', *Journal of Linguistics,* pp.231-52.

WHITELEY, W.H. (1964) 'Swahili as a lingua franca in East Africa', *Brazzaville* (1964) pp. 183-88.

—— (ed.) (1971) *Language Use and Social Change: Problems of Multilingualism with Special Reference to Eastern Africa,* London: OUP.

WHORF, B.L. (1962) *Language, thought and reality.* Cambridge Mass:

M.I.T.
WIDDOWSON, H.G. (1971) 'The Teaching of Rhetoric to Students of Science and Technology' in Perren (ed.) (1971).
WILKINSON, A. (ed.) (1969) 'The state of Language' in *Educational Review* XXII, Birmingham.
WILLIAMS, F. (1973) 'Some recent studies of language attitudes' in Shuy R.W. (ed.) (1973) pp.121-49.
WURM, S.A. (1968) 'Papua-New Guinea Nationhood: The Problems of a National Language' in Fishman *et al.* (1968) pp.345-64.

Index

as data 50, 197
and Durkheim's individual facts 220
unsystematicness of 42
and weak claim of sociolinguistics 29
Performance *see also* 'Competence',
'Langue', 'Parole'
defined 197
and acceptability 208
and anthropology 63
and characteristic error 41
and communicative competence 210
as 'degenerate' competence 197-99
models of pscholinguistics 223
models of and 223
theory of 21
Philosophy
and cognitive function of language 83
of science 89
Phonetics *see* 'Phonology'
Phonology *see also* 'Variation'
assimilation and code-switching 143
and emic-etic contrast 81
and genetic explanations 17
interference in 124-27
interlingual identification in 124-27
in 19th century linguistics 23
and pattern systems 41
rules in 126
techniques applied to text analysis 203
units of; tone group, foot, syllable,
phoneme 70
and variation 35, 81
Pidgin Languages *see also* 'Languages'
and diglossia 135
European language based 157
linguistic characteristics of 161f
and planning policies 172
and process of pidginization 157-60
and sociolinguistic typologies 147
and transformational generative
linguistics 53
Planning *see also* 'Speech Communities',
'States'
language 28, 164-86
in endoglossic, exoglossic, mixed
states 170f
goals of 168-71
nationalism versus nationism 168
nationalism as macro-correlate
of solidarity 169
nationism as macro-correlate
of power 169
language status; national versus
official versus regional 169-78
policies: A, B and C 171-73
and prescriptivism 90
and sociolinguistics 224
in the Third World
choice of English in 135, 142
and urbanization 168
verbal 73, 141f
Pragmatics *see* 'Semiotics'

Prague School *see* 'Linguistics'
Psycholinguistics *see also* 'Psychology'
defined 223
and bilingual code-switching 223
and hesitation phenomena 70, 141, 223
and models of performance 223
Psychology
and affective function of language 83
behaviourist and structuralist
linguistics 222
and bilingualism 118
and evaluative function of
language 83
models in 66, 222
social- defined 66
and sociolinguistics 109, 222f
and sociology 66
and transformational linguistics 44, 222
Register *see also* 'Style', 'Variation'
as role-related code 114
-switching 143
and text analysis 204
as use-based variation 27
Repertoire
defined 62
bilingual 118
of child 111
in continua 136
as set of codes 105
Respondant *see* 'Informant'
Rhetoric
defined 69
descriptive 25
and discourse 205
in language switching 143
and sociolinguistics 23f, 216
in 20th century linguistics 18
Role
defined 110
and address forms 95f
and language 110
of pre-school child 111f
-switching 62, 73, 110
Rules *see also* 'Models', 'Scientific
Description', 'System', 'Theory'
defined 89f
types;
base 91
categorical 52, 91, 100
constative 93
context-free 137
context-sensitive 126
descriptive 90, 93
formation 91
inference 91
lexical insertion 52
phonological 52
prescriptive 90, 93
readjustment 52
regulative 93
transformation 52, 91
variable 53f, 91, 100

Index to Languages